90 0881856 4

D1757554

Contested Bodies of Childhood and Youth

Contested Bodies of Childhood and Youth

Edited by

Kathrin Hörschelmann
University of Durham, UK

and

Rachel Colls
University of Durham, UK

First published 2009 by
PALGRAVE MACMILLAN

Palgrave Macmillan in the UK is an imprint of Macmillan Publishers Limited,
registered in England, company number 785998, of Houndmills, Basingstoke,
Hampshire RG21 6XS.

Palgrave Macmillan in the US is a division of St Martin's Press LLC,
175 Fifth Avenue, New York, NY 10010.

Palgrave Macmillan is the global academic imprint of the above companies
and has companies and representatives throughout the world.

Palgrave® and Macmillan® are registered trademarks in the United States,
the United Kingdom, Europe and other countries.

ISBN: 978–0–230–20138–5 hardback

This book is printed on paper suitable for recycling and made from fully
managed and sustained forest sources. Logging, pulping and manufacturing
processes are expected to conform to the environmental regulations of the
country of origin.

A catalogue record for this book is available from the British Library.

A catalog record for this book is available from the Library of Congress.

10   9   8   7   6   5   4   3   2   1
19 18 17 16 15 14 13 12 11 10

Printed and bound in Great Britain by
CPI Antony Rowe, Chippenham and Eastbourne

This book is dedicated to our children, Karl and Edith

Contents

List of Figures

List of Tables

Notes on the Contributors

Catherine Alexander is a research associate in the Department of Geography, Durham University and is currently completing her PhD on youth geographies of fear in Newcastle upon Tyne, UK. She is a social geographer with research interests in participatory methodologies, well-being, social exclusion and social justice.

Natalie Beale, a social and cultural geographer with an interest in issues of health and well-being, identity and belonging, social justice, bodies, embodiment and performativity, participation, therapeutic landscapes and rural geographies, is a research student in the Department of Geography, Durham University, UK. Her PhD research explores young people's health beliefs and behaviours, and the spaces in which these are shaped and performed, in a rural area of north-east England. Her research has loosely focused around four key themes of children, young people and families, health and well-being, countryside, rurality and rural life and participatory research.

Lorraine van Blerk, a social geographer with research interests in social difference particularly with reference to the geographies of children and youth in east and southern Africa, is a lecturer in human geography at the University of Reading, UK. Her research includes studies of homeless young people, young sex workers and families affected by AIDS. She also has a particular interest in participatory research and methodology and is co-editor of *Doing Children's Geographies*.

Rachel Colls is a lecturer in human geography at Durham University, UK. Her research is broadly concerned with 'the body', and she has published work on childhood obesity, size acceptance and female clothing consumption.

Derek Colquhoun is Professor of Urban Learning in the Institute of Learning, Univerity of Hull, UK. His main research interest is in healthy school communities, including policy issues, curriculum development, professional practice and the health of children and adults in these school communities. He has published widely in these areas, including an edited collection entitled *The Health Promoting School: Policies, Programmes and Practice in Australia* (1997) with Karen Goltz and Margaret Sheehan. He has also managed major research projects and evaluations of projects in school communities in Australia and the UK. In 1993 he was awarded a World Health Organisation Overseas Research Fellowship (Health Promoting Schools in Denmark) (1993) and in 2000 was awarded an Education Trust Leadership Award for a study examining 'Models of School Governance and Community Connectedness'.

Pamela Dale is a researcher based in the Centre for Medical History at the University of Exeter, UK. She is currently working on a history of stress project funded by a Wellcome Trust Programme Grant. She has also researched and published on the history of learning disabilities, institutional care and special education, including the edited volume (with Jo Melling), *Mental Illness and Learning Disability since 1850: Finding a Place for Mental Disorder in the United Kingdom* (2006).

Myriam Denov obtained her PhD from the University of Cambridge, UK where she was a Commonwealth Scholar. She is presently an associate professor in the School of Social Work, McGill University, Canada. Her research and teaching interests lie in the area of children and youth at risk, with an emphasis on war and political violence and war-affected children. She has published widely in the realms of children and armed conflict, children's rights and gender-based violence, and has worked with vulnerable populations internationally, including former child soldiers, victims of sexual violence and people living with HIV/AIDS. Her current research, supported by the Social Science and Humanities Research Council of Canada, is exploring the militarisation and reintegration experiences of former child soldiers in Sierra Leone and Sri Lanka. She has presented expert evidence on child soldiers and has served as an adviser to government and NGOs on children and armed conflict, and girls in fighting forces. Her latest book, *The Making and Unmaking of Child Soldiers in Sierra Leone*, will be published by Cambridge University Press.

Elizabeth A. Gagen is a lecturer in the Department of Geography, University of Hull, UK. Her research interests are in children's geographies, feminist geographies and histories of mental and physical health. She has published on the role of psychology in disciplining children's bodies, the gendering of childhood play and the role of recreation in shaping military masculinities. Her most recent research looks at emotional literacy in contemporary British education.

Sarah Grogan is Professor of Health Psychology at Staffordshire University, UK. where she runs the Centre for Health Psychology. She is a Chartered Health Psychologist and has been involved in body image research since 1990. She is currently involved in research relating to the impact of body image on various health-related behaviours, including smoking, cosmetic surgery, exercise and anabolic steroid use. She has recently completed the second edition of *Body Image: Understanding Body Dissatisfaction in Men, Women and Children* (2008).

Malcolm Hill is Research Professor in the Glasgow School of Social Work, a joint School of the Universities of Strathclyde and Glasgow, UK. His main research interests include adoption and foster care, children's services, youth justice and young people's participation. In 2006, he co-authored (with Peter Hopkins) the Scottish Refugee Council report *'This is a Good Place to Live and Think about the Future': The Needs and Experiences of Unaccompanied Asylum-seeking Children and Young People in Scotland*. Recent co-edited publications include *Youth Justice and Child Protection* (2007) (with Andrew Lockyer and Frederick H. Stone) and *Children, Young People and Social Inclusion* (2006) (with Kay Tisdall, John Davis and Alan Prout).

Louise Holt is Lecturer in Human Geography at the University of Reading, UK. Her research interests broadly examine how embodied socio-spatial (in)equalities are reproduced and, more positively, can be transformed. Her specific research focus is children, youth and (dis)ability.

Peter Hopkins is a senior lecturer in social geography in the School of Geography, Politics and Sociology, Newcastle University, UK. His main research interests include critical perspectives on young people's geographies, urban geographies of race and ethnicity, geographies of religion and qualitative methods. In 2006, he co-authored (with Malcolm Hill) the Scottish Refugee Council report *'This is a Good Place to Live and Think about the Future': The Needs and Experiences of Unaccompanied Asylum-seeking Children and Young People in Scotland*. He is the author of *The Issue of Masculine Identities for British Muslims* and co-editor (with Cara Aitchison and Mei-Po Kwan) of *Geographies of Muslim Identities* and (with Richard Gale) *Muslims in Britain: Race, Place and Identities*.

John Horton is based in the Centre of Children and Youth at the University of Northampton, UK. He has worked on diverse research projects about children and young people's everyday issues and geographies, in different institutional and recreational contexts.

Kathrin Hörschelmann is a lecturer in human geography at the University of Durham, UK. Her research focuses on the cultural politics of post-socialist transformation, the geographies of gender, identity, youth culture and globalisation. She is the author of The City, *Children and Youth, Public Spheres after Socialism,* and *Spaces of Masculinities.*

Peter Kraftl is a lecturer in human geography at Leicester University, UK. He has published over twenty articles and book chapters on children's geographies, utopia and geographies of architecture. He has worked on numerous research projects exploring children's health, schooling, participation and play. With John Horton, he is currently preparing a book about cultural geographies.

Ruth Panelli, a social geographer with research interests in social difference and action, is Reader in Human Geography at University College London, UK. Her research includes studies of young people's experiences in rural and urban communities and contrasting environments Her publications include *Social Geographies: From Difference to Action,* and she is co-editor of *Global Perspectives on Rural Childhood and Youth: Young Rural Lives.*

Jo Pike is a researcher in the Food Health and Education Research group in the Institute for Learning, University of Hull, UK. She has an academic background in the social sciences and a professional background in public health and community engagement. She has managed several research projects, including the educational strand of the 'Eat Well Do Well' evaluation in Hull and the evaluation of the 'Shape Up Europe' project. An experienced researcher, she has developed and led international workshops and seminars on researching with children, the training and development of lunchtime staff in schools, and school canteens. Her current research interests are children, food and space, and she is currently completing her PhD exploring the construction of child–adult relations in primary school dining rooms.

Elspeth Probyn is a Research SA Chair and Professor of Gender and Cultural Studies Co-Director at the Centre for Postcolonial and

Globalisation Studies of The Hawke Institute, University of South Australia. She has published several books, including *Sexing the Self: Gendered Positions in Cultural Studies* (1993), *Outside Belongings* (1996), *Carnal Appetites: FoodSexIdentities* (2000) and *Blush: Faces of Shame* (2005).

Elsbeth Robson completed her undergraduate and postgraduate studies in geography at the Universities of Durham, UK, Tübingen, Germany, Ahmadu Bello, Nigeria, and Oxford, UK. She is a research fellow at the Centre for Social Research, University of Malawi and an honorary research associate of the Department of Anthropology, Durham University, UK. Her research work currently encompasses children and young people's livelihoods, transport and mobilities in sub-Saharan Africa. Her recent publications include *Global Perspectives on Rural Childhood and Youth* (2007) and *West African Worlds* (2005). She is a founding associate editor of the international journal *Children's Geographies*.

Sue Ruddick is an associate professor in geography and planning, University of Toronto, Canada. She has published extensively on the construction and contestation of youth, and contemporary departures from modern ideals of childhood. Her book *Young and Homeless in Hollywood* explores the changing constructs of at-risk youth in the United States. More recently, her work has focused on the writing of Baruch Spinoza, Gilles Deleuze and Antonio Negri and its implications for thinking a politics of ontology.

Inbal Solomon has recently completed her MA at the University of Ottawa, Canada. Her research interests include children and armed conflict, the implications of the ongoing conflict in the Middle East on civil society, the prevalence and attributes of militarisation in civil society, and children's rights.

Gill Valentine is Professor of Human Geography and Director of the Leeds Social Science Institute, University of Leeds, UK. Her research interests include social identities (with a specific focus on equality and diversity), consumption cultures and social studies of childhood, parenting and family life. Her research has been supported by the award of fourteen academic grants and she has (co)authored and co-edited fourteen books and over 100 journal articles and policy reports. She was one of the founding editors of the journal *Social and Cultural Geography* and is a former editor of *Gender, Place and Culture*. She is currently on the editorial board of five journals. Her research has been recognised by a Philip Trust Prize and a Royal Geographical Society award.

Karen Wells is Programme Director of International Childhood Studies at Birkbeck College, UK, where she teaches the political economy of childhood and material and visual cultures of development. She is the author of *Childhood in a Global Perspective* (2009). Her research interests are the impact of globalisation on childhood and the material and visual cultures of childhood, with a particular interest in 'race'. She has published widely on these issues, including in *Journal of Visual Communication, Visual Studies and Journal of Children and Media*.

Acknowledgements

We would like to thank all the contributors to the book for their generosity of ideas and their encouragement and commitment to see the project through to completion. We would also like to express gratitude to all the participants at the 'Contested Bodies of Childhood and Youth Conference', Department of Geography, Durham University, July 2006, whose presentations and conversations provided the inspiration for the book. We are particularly grateful to Kathy Wood for her help in organising and running the conference.

We wish to acknowledge the work of particular scholars of 'the body', including Sarah Whatmore, Gillian Rose and Elisabeth Grosz, whose ideas helped to shape the project in many ways. Thanks are also due to many of our colleagues at the Department of Geography, Durham University, for inspiring us to think critically about questions of embodiment and materiality. We are also extremely appreciative of Hamzah Muzaini's work on compiling the index. We have further benefited greatly from the support of Olivia Middleton at Palgrave Macmillan and Ruth Willats and would like to thank them for their advice and patience.

Finally, thanks to James and Ben for their love and support.

1

Introduction: Contested Bodies of Childhood and Youth

Rachel Colls and Kathrin Hörschelmann

Imagining, disciplining and performing young people's bodies

Young people's bodies are in the news. They occupy centre stage in media reports and political debates. A quick glance at news headlines from around the world gives a vivid impression of the tone of these debates:

Child obesity [in UK] 'doubles in decade'
(BBC News, 21 April 2006)

Children's life expectancy [in the US] being cut short by obesity
(*New York Times*, 17 March 2005)

Child hunger in US rose by 50% in 2007
(*Huffington Post*, 18 November 2008)

Child malnutrition soaring in eastern Congo
(*World Vision*, 18 November 2008)

Child hunger takes a heavy toll [in Latin America]
(*Toronto Star*, 12 July 2007)

Sex infections [in UK] in young up again
(BBC News, 15 July 2008)

Teen birth rates, homicides [in US] on increase, report shows
(*Washington Post*, 11 July 2008)

Where babies are busy making babies [in South Africa]
(*Arusha Times*, 17 November 2008)

Pregnancy policy unfair to girl child [in Uganda]
(*New Vision*, 13 November 2008)

Lancet urges parents [in UK] to act on under-age drinking
(*Guardian*, 14 March 2008)

1,000 youths receive free HIV/Aids test in Abia [Nigeria]
(*Vanguard*, 14 November 2008)

Youth [in Tanzania] get tested for HIV
(*Arusha Times*, 11 November 2008)

Violence is common among the young [in US]
(*Washington Post*, 22 July 2008)

Fight against yobs to target children [in UK]
(*Guardian*, 11 December 2005)

Recruitment of child soldiers [in Congo] rising
(*IRIN*, 12 November 2008)

While many of these headlines are concerned with young people's welfare, they also categorise them as essentially problematic, risky and at risk. This book takes issue with this one-dimensional construction of young people's bodies. Instead, it takes as its focus the imagined, disciplined and performed bodies of childhood and youth in order to capture better the complexity and diversity of young people's embodiment. The book is divided into three conceptually inspired parts – Imagining, Disciplining and Performing Bodies – the content of which are thoroughly intertwined and overlapping. It will be obvious to the reader that many of the chapters speak beyond the part in which they are placed. For example, the disciplining and performativity of young bodies entails certain imaginings, whilst images of child and youth bodies are made intelligible through particular disciplinary regimes. The performativity of bodies likewise responds to and reproduces discursive matrices of power that prefigure what is imaginable and permissible at any one time. We also seek to map some of the ways in which the performed bodies of childhood and youth exceed the purely discursive and go beyond the reiteration of disciplinary regimes and power relations, thus acknowledging the fleshy materialities and affective capacities of bodies. Further, we highlight how and why young bodies are contested politically, discursively and in everyday practice, thus raising a number of critical questions in each conceptual part.

In Part I, we ask not only how dominant images of ethnic, gendered and classed bodies are constructed, but also how the bodies of children and youth can be imagined differently. We question how young people themselves imagine their bodies and in what kinds of places and spaces. Part II problematises how and why notions of 'normal' and 'deviant' bodies have arisen and become dominant, and how such constructions affect the lives of young people. This also involves considering what challenges can be made to such norms, as well as the costs of contesting or having to live within dominant body norms. Finally, Part III asks to what extent young bodies are performed in relation to particular discursive and social matrices of power and to what extent these are circumnavigated and transgressed in everyday lived practice.

We cannot hope to give more than partial answers to these questions in this book. Consequently, we see much scope for further interdisciplinary engagements with the subject of childhood and youth embodiment, especially at a time when children's bodies have yet again become the focal point of many policy debates. Research on children and youth needs to respond to public concerns about 'problematic' young bodies, not simply by looking for 'pragmatic solutions', as often demanded by policy-makers and the media, but by questioning critically why certain young bodies become vilified in public debate, who stands to benefit from such vilification and the associated solutions put forward, how such debates contribute to the discursive construction and disciplining of certain groups of children and youth, and to what extent they entrench further and create new forms of marginalisation. It also needs to remain sensitive to the historical and cultural variability of how young people's bodies are understood and lived such as to be able to critique effectively ethnocentric, normative constructions of childhood and youth and to be able to respond to young people's diverse circumstances and needs.

In this introduction, we consider first how young people's bodies have come to be understood as both risky and at risk by exploring the multiple ways in which bodies matter to popular and academic debates concerning development, morality and the categorisation of childhood. We then highlight the difference that an embodied perspective can make to understanding the plurality of childhood and youth by exploring three cross-cutting themes that run through the book and outline ways of broadening our understanding of young people's embodiment by focusing more closely on their own conceptions and experiences of the body, on the body as *becoming*, on relational understandings of embodiment and on temporal and spatial dimensions of embodiment.

Multiple bodies, multiple approaches

Seen as both *risky* and *at risk*, young people's bodies become markers of the state of the social body now and in the future. They become emblematic of a series of societal fears and concerns, calling up deep-seated fears about the loss of romantic childhood, that apparently natural stage of playful innocence, while new regulatory measures are called for through which the child's body can be made to conform better to indicators of 'typical' child development. Concern is focused not solely on the well-being of individual children, but equally on the health of the nation, creating a biopolitical complex that sees the reform of youthful bodies as crucial to society's future (Griffin 1993, James 2000, Aitken 2001, Qvortrup 2005). Ironically, for such a biopolitics, the individual young person matters little. The child's body becomes knowable and significant only in relation to average measures, judged in terms of whether or not it conforms to norms of correct size, weight, motor ability, cognitive development by age, etc. Such measurements begin as early as the embryonic stage, with a range of medicalised monitoring techniques and guidebooks for parents-to-be. While such medical supervision has been beneficial for identifying potential health problems that may be ameliorated by early intervention, it has created ethical dilemmas and concerns for parents who, quite understandably, worry from the early stages of pregnancy whether their child will develop 'normally'. Individual children's bodies thus become part of a wider normative matrix which ties them to the social body from the moment of conception.

Despite this, the kinds of youthful bodies that we encounter in public debates are highly selective and often tell us little about the cultural and historical variability of childhood and youth or about the manifold ways in which children and young people experience, live with/in/through, and understand their bodies. Recent research in sociology, anthropology and geography in particular has drawn attention to the diversity of young people's embodied lives, highlighting, among other things, young people's desiring, working and caring bodies (see Robson 2000, 2004, Aitken 2001, Punch 2001a, 2001b, Aldridge and Becker 2003, Ansell 2005, van Blerk and Ansell 2007). Such bodies transgress how childhood is predominantly imagined and challenge preconceived ideas about childhood, as well as sexuality, work and care. Images of suffering young bodies are likewise either seen as diversions from accepted norms of a romantic childhood or located in places far from 'the West'. The suffering young body becomes symbolic of the vulnerability of children and of the failings of 'other' societies to protect and promote the well-being of their future generations. While such images can help to draw attention to major issues of injustice and child maltreatment, they rarely portray the rich diversity of young people's embodied lives, the complexity of ways in which specific societal expectations, regulatory systems and cultural norms are formed in different spheres of social life and how they intersect with particular lived, embodied experiences that encompass a wide range of emotions and affects. They also do little to help us understand the power relations through which young bodies come to be differently positioned.

Recent social research on children and youth has focused particularly on demonstrating the social constructedness of the categories childhood and youth, critiquing the power structures embedded in them and the neglect of young people's agency (James et al. 2001, James and James 2004, Valentine 2004, Qvortrup 2005). There has been a fruitful exchange of ideas between sociologists, anthropologists, geographers, social psychologists, historians and others, which has led to greater awareness of the cultural specificity of age (e.g. Amit-Talai and Wulff 1995). Relatively little attention has been paid to date, however, to questions of embodiment. Edited collections by Prout (2000a) and Panter-Brick (1998) notwithstanding, the social constructionist bent of much research on childhood and youth has led to a rather disembodied perspective, which in many ways reproduces the legacy of the Cartesian mind/body dualism by emphasising how the 'biological' body is inscribed by 'the social', without interrogating how both interrelate and affect each other through a complex network of embodied, socio-material relations (Prout 2000b, Aitken 2001).

In this book, however, we seek to bring together new work that addresses the interconnections between the imagined, disciplined and performed bodies of young people from a range of disciplinary perspectives. We foreground young people's embodied experiences in order to explore what difference an explicit focus on the body makes to our analyses of childhood and youth. The contributors continue to engage with questions of the cultural and social construction of young people's bodies and with the ways in which their social and moral positionings in the world and their individual experiences are influenced by social practices and age-based institutions. Several contributors, however, also seek to bring into sharper relief affective and emotional characteristics of young people's embodiment, their phenomenological 'being in the world' as corporeal beings, whilst highlighting their connections with human and nonhuman object-subjects, materials and structures (Bingham et al. 1999). This latter approach thus responds to Prout's call for a 'sociology of translation' (2000b: 11) that sees 'children as hybrids of culture and nature':

> This approach would place childhoods and bodies in relation to not only symbolic but also material culture. What produces them is not simply biological events, not only the phenomenology of bodily experience, and not merely structures of symbolic and discursive meaning – although all of these are important – but also the patterns of material organization and their modes of ordering. Examining childhood bodies in this view becomes a matter of tracing through the means, the varied array of materials and practices involved in their construction and maintenance – and in some circumstances their unravelling and disintegration.
>
> (ibid.: 15)

In light of the breadth of approaches open to scholars of children and young people's embodiment, the book is consciously structured to demonstrate this multiplicity. We consider this important for developing a more complex and nuanced understanding of young people's embodiment in a global context of heightened political debate surrounding 'the body'. Despite this diversity of perspectives, however, there are a number of shared themes across the chapters which we explore next. We do this first by considering the methodological challenges of conveying the plurality of young people's embodied experiences, second, by exploring the difference that an understanding of the body as 'unfinished' makes to our conceptualisation of childhood and youth, and third by examining the relevance of temporality and space to experiences, categorisations and understandings of young people's bodies.

Methodological challenges

This book is concerned with the embodied experiences of children and youth, not only highlighting the great diversity of young people's embodied subjectivities and their own roles in shaping them (James 1993, 2000, 2005, Christensen 2000), but also foregrounding the contested nature of normative, chronologically defined and western-centred body schemes. It shifts the focus from measuring young people's conformity with preset norms and indicators to understanding the wider range of bodily states through which children and youth encounter and mark their place in the world. Approaching embodiment from this angle requires careful thinking about the methodologies which we use to research young lives. Emotional and embodied responses are, for instance, difficult to capture and convey verbally and are often 'lost in translation'. We can experiment more with the kinds of languages and prosaic repertoires that we use in research, but would also be well advised to think about the potential of different methods such as drawing, filming/photographing, dancing, theatre (e.g. Hart 1997, Barker and Weller 2003, Lancaster and Broadbent 2003, Burke 2005) to convey different aspects of young people's embodied lives. Some of the contributors have used methods such a participatory diagramming and photography, but there is scope for much greater variety, not just in research methods but also in the formats that we use for publishing. Moreover, Woodyer (2008), in her work on children's use of toys, draws attention to the role of our own bodies as researchers in the research process. By videoing her fieldwork as part of an ethnomethodologically inspired approach, she not only enabled participants to reflect critically on the research and the 'researcher's gaze', but was also able to discern more readily how the relations between her own body and those of the participants were significant in making sense of children and young people's everyday experiences: in short, drawing attention to how our bodies become our research tools. It is also important to be cautious about the limitations of our methodological practices. For example, Gallacher and Gallacher (2008) question the extent to which 'participatory' methods always involve active and empowering participation from children and young people, detailing equally important instances of when participants appropriate, resist or manipulate research for their own gain.

By collecting and collating accounts of the bodies of children and young people through a range of practical and theoretical methodologies, we do not intend to represent definitively 'the' account of all child and youth bodies. Conversely, we also argue that thinking 'through' the body from the perspective of children and youth themselves should not equate to an individualistic phenomenology. Just as Allison James (1993, 2000), in her work with primary school children, uncovered the salience of social constructions of body size and ability for children's own understandings of age and difference, contributors to this volume show clearly how relations of power come to bear on young people's subjectivities and how young people themselves contribute to the reiteration of socio-material, embodied power relations. Social inequalities and cultural hierarchies continue to be signified and justified through bodily markers that make individuals 'knowable' as particular subjects (Butler 1990, 1993), '*constituted* through matrices of power/discourse, matrices that are continually reproduced through processes of re-signification, or repetition of hegemonic gendered (racialized, sexualized) discourse' (Nelson 1999: 337, cited in Aitken 2001: 103). Young people's bodies *become* gendered, sexualised, racialised, classed or (dis)abled through discursive constructions, temporal-spatial practices and institutional structures. Yet, by raising attention to children's and youths' lived experiences and understandings of such bodily hierarchies, as discerned through a range of methodological practices, the contributors enable us to see both the high emotional and social costs that such hierarchical orderings have for their young subjects and the extent to which they can and do become contested, when the matrices of power simply do not fit young people's more complex lived subjectivities.

Relational bodies and the life-course perspective

A second theme which cuts across many of the chapters is a concern with understanding bodies as relational and 'unfinished' (Shilling 1993, Prout 2000b). Work on the life-course (Teather 1999, Hockey and James 2003, Närvänen and Näsman 2004) and on generation (Alanen 2000, 2001, Mayall and Zeiher 2003) has sought to outline how age is negotiated in particular contexts and always in relation to other-aged subjects (James 2000, 2005, Vanderbeck 2007, Hopkins and Pain 2008). Alanen adopts the concept of *generationing* in order to express 'the complexity of social processes through which people become (are constructed as) "children" while other people become... "adults"' (2001: 129). Närvänen and Näsman remain critical of her use of generational categories and the sole focus on children and adults, but similarly argue for a relational understanding of age. They argue that the concept of life phases is more appropriate than that of 'generation' for recognising how a person's sense of age shifts in relation to others, for instance, depending on positions in the family and in institutions such as school or the workplace. A simple example of this is the 20-year-old who is a child to her parents, an older sibling to her brother, a younger sibling to her sister, a granddaughter, niece and aunt, a school-leaver, apprentice/student, a partner and (possibly) a mother. Depending on her relations with specific others in different institutional and spatial contexts, her age position changes together with her sense of self. As Närvänen and Näsman argue:

> The life phase concept makes it clear that children and childhood are not only defined in relation to another category (adults), but rather

in relation to other, different life phases and those who are living in them, and that the whole of this interaction can be problematized from a life-course perspective ... Childhood as a life phase is also characterized by specific materialized children's institutions, separate from the institutions in which life in other phases is lived. Children live in the pre-school, school and organized recreational activities for children ... The institutional environments of childhood define their specific positions, e.g. that of elementary school pupil compared to a university student or employee ... Here as well, we can study the ongoing definition, questioning, reproduction and changing of the social position patterns of childhood in everyday interaction.

(2004: 87–8)

This perspective is useful also for conceptualising the body in relation to age. Both feminist (Butler 1990, 1993, Braidotti 1994, Grosz 1994, Duncan 1996, Orr et al. 1996) and phenomenological work (Merleau-Ponty 1962; also Weiss 1999, Hamington 2004, Hass 2008) is inspirational here, since it understands embodiment in thoroughly relational ways. The body is seen in such work not as an individual entity, but as thoroughly intertwined with, nestling in and depending on other bodies, textures, materials and objects. To speak of 'the body' is in fact incongruous with such an understanding, since 'it' cannot exist in singularity, but only through its relations with, through and to others. This includes the human bodies that create and give birth to it, nourish and care for it, and interact with it through touch, hearing, sight, smell and a whole range of other, more diffuse affective relations. It also includes non-human objects and materials which produce the body as always hybrid, connected, interdependent and leaky/unbounded (see Grosz 1994). Such a reconceptualisation of embodiment is crucial for challenging oppressive social relations that rely on a hierarchical mind/body split and on self/other binaries, since it shows how different bodies, objects and materials interrelate rather than being divided into discrete and/or dependent and independent entities. It emphasises, further, what child and youth bodies can *do* and how bodies *become*, rather than focusing on what they *are* (Horton and Kraftl 2006, Kraftl and Horton 2007). Research on bodies understood as hybrid and relational has to date focused primarily on adult bodies. Our efforts to rethink childhood and youth from the viewpoint of the body, therefore, can draw on such work productively in order to challenge the perception that adulthood is a point of arrival for children and youth, but it can also go further to conceptualise interrelations with other bodies, spaces and objects from the early stages of childhood (e.g. Gallacher 2005 on children's spatial interactions in a day care nursery). Central to this approach is a need to develop a language for speaking about the seemingly less concrete but multi-sensual flows of affect and emotion through which human and nonhuman bodies relate (Thrift 2004, Davidson et al. 2005, Anderson 2006) – flows that may entail not only affirmative, positively connoted interactions, but also those that are violent, oppressive and hurtful.

The notion of a body as 'unbounded' and 'becoming' does not sit easily with traditional conceptualisations of the body as moving through progressive and distinct stages from childhood via adolescence to adulthood. Conceptualising the body as unfinished challenges discursive constructions of age as fixed by biological development and forces us to rethink the bases of age-group categorisations that are read too easily from bodily markers. The notion of 'maturity' has been crucial to how the bodies of children and youth have been understood in western society since at least the early nineteenth century (Ariès 1962, Armstrong 1983, Steedman 1995). By separating adulthood from childhood through arbitrarily chosen bodily markers, however, attention has been diverted from bodily changes that occur *across* the life-course (Shilling 1993, Christensen 2000, Prout 2000b). A relational perspective that views the body as always in the process of becoming underlines instead how bodily change is negotiated by individuals of any age and how social positions and subjectivities shift with changes in the body's appearance and capacities *throughout* the life-course. For children and youth, this means considering the ways in which they learn to position themselves as embodied subjects *vis-à-vis* other young people, friends and early sexual partners (James 2000, 2005) and through interactions with parents, grandparents, teachers and popular media. This also feeds into recent work on intergenerationality that is focused beyond the child–parent coupling (Hopkins and Pain 2007, Vanderbeck 2007), whereby it is recognised that it is important to understand how young people develop a sense of themselves as ageing bodies, as well as how they come to perform their embodied selves along lines of social difference.

Bodies in time and space

A third theme explored by many of the contributors is the significance of the temporal and spatial dimensions of experiences, categorisations and understandings of young people's bodies. The 'temporal' relates, on the one hand, to young people's understandings of their body in relation to personal and social time (James 1993, 2000, 2005, Ennew

1994) and, on the other hand, to changing historical conceptions of the youthful body. Authors such as Armstrong (1983), Steedman (1995) and Aitken (2001) have shown how conceptions of the child's body changed dramatically with the emergence of the biomedical sciences, developmental psychology and psychoanalysis, which sought for the first time in western history to delineate universal stages of child development against which children's behaviour and physical development were measured. On the one hand, these scientific endeavours undoubtedly contributed to the improved health standards enjoyed by western children today. Measures to improve child health were introduced by social reformists who were concerned with alleviating some of the dramatic social inequalities that led to high rates of infant mortality and maternal ill health among the poor. On the other hand, however, these scientific developments and reform programmes were tied to a politics of nation-building and were targeted at disciplining those 'unruly' sections of Victorian and turn-of-the century society whose actions and politics were seen as threatening to the ruling classes and their morality. The bodies of children and youth became a key target for measures of control and surveillance (Foucault 1977, Gagen 2000), which, in creating the 'normal' body, also defined what was deviant and abnormal, thus contributing to the marginalisation and exclusion of certain groups of young people.

At this time, the child's body also became a political battleground. It was, not unlike today, seen as central to and emblematic of the nation's future. With increasing militarisation leading up to the first and second world wars, education and after-school activities were more and more directed towards producing physically strong and healthy youthful bodies, able to 'defend' or reproduce the nation. This type of body politic was evidently closely linked to the (re)production of a particular *gender regime*. Furthermore, the child-focused body politic of late nineteenth- to early twentieth-century society manifested itself spatially with the emergence of new institutional spaces, which included the extension of school programmes to the poor, the founding of sports clubs, the creation of supervised playgrounds in public parks (Hart 2002) and the establishment of dedicated children's hospitals (e.g. Gagen 2000). While some of these developments were aimed at providing universal facilities to all children, others, such as poor schools and orphanages, continued to segregate and marginalise children seen as troublesome and/or from poor backgrounds.

The ways in which young people's bodies are understood, performed and lived are thus closely tied to historical changes in conceptions of childhood and youth and to transformations in the spatial organisation of societies. Age was and still is both defined by spatial orderings and in turn affects how particular places are understood and used. This relates both to institutional spaces of childhood and youth, which are rarely transgressed by adults other than those with caretaking responsibilities, and to the ways in which urban, rural and home spaces are appropriated practically by different age groups. Geographers have contributed much insight into the spatial dynamics of childhood and youth (Holloway and Valentine 2000; Valentine 2004) and have critiqued the age-based inclusions and exclusions entailed in the ordering of public space. The recent introduction of curfews and Anti-Social Behaviour Orders (ASBOs) in the UK is a particularly troubling example of such exclusions that affect often already marginalised young people (Woolley 2006). Few geographical studies of childhood and youth have, however, focused on questions of embodiment (see Colls and Hörschelmann 2009 for a special issue on the geographies of the bodies of children and youth) despite otherwise lively debates in geography on body-space, embodied spatial practices, gender performativity, sexuality, race and (dis)ability. Questions of young people's embodied, spatial practices have been taken up more thoroughly by social researchers interested in youth subcultures such as skateboarding (Borden 2001) and graffiti (Phillips 1999, Macdonald 2001). Borden (2001), in particular, has highlighted the significance of embodied practices to the making and contestation of space, while Macdonald (2001) shows how the performance of masculinity through physically challenging, daring engagements with marginal urban spaces is crucial to graffiti subculture. Such work reminds us to consider young people's bodies as not simply disciplined and constrained by the ordering of space, but also as performing subjectivities through the body that align with some, yet breach the boundaries of other matrices of power. It also points towards the affective in seeking a language that describes bodily experiences and sensations in their plurality, where they seep through, leak out and yet also connect with discursive and institutionalised social (spatial) orders.

Structure of the book

The themes briefly sketched in this introduction are elaborated upon and discussed in more detail by Gill Valentine in chapter 2 and in the three main parts, which examine young people's bodies as imagined, disciplined and performed.

All three parts engage in a number of ways with the three themes outlined above. Part I, 'Imagining Bodies', focuses on the ways young people's bodies are differentiated by gender, race, class and body size in media representations, political discourse and practice, as well as in young people's own imaginations. Sarah Grogan considers how a narrow range of body types promoted in western media affects the body image of young girls and women. She argues that a 'culture of slenderness' dominates the body perceptions of girls as young as five, who tend to prefer thinner figures to their own size and are familiar with calorie counting and other ways of managing their weight and body shape. Drawing on psychological research, Grogan makes the case for building self-esteem and confidence in girls and young women, since negative images of their bodies can prevent, rather than motivate, health-improving behaviour. A question raised by Grogan and taken up by Karen Wells is how young people learn identities of gender and race, the case that Wells examines. Wells analyses the Disney animation film *Tarzan* to examine the performative effect of racial identification via mimesis and the construction of racial subjectivities in popular culture. Through a lucid and nuanced reading of racial codes in *Tarzan*, Wells demonstrates how whiteness is produced through constructing Tarzan's belonging to an 'African' family of gorillas as problematic and reproducing the civilisation story of British imperialism. Children may take up the narrativities and performativities of race depicted in animation films such as *Tarzan* but, Wells argues, we need to remain sensitive to the plural readings that such films allow, such as depicting race as learnt/acquired and lived in different guises rather than being essential and fixed. The relationship between representations and performed identities is also the focus of Catherine Alexander's chapter, which considers the pervasive harmful effects of local and national media reports on young women who have committed low-level crime in a deprived area of Newcastle upon Tyne in the north-east of England. The young women are trapped in a cycle of stigmatisation and exclusion. Their bodies are scripted by the media as risky and deviant, not only because of their history of involvement in crime, but also because of their class. The young women contest this stigmatisation by seeking to adopt appearances and dress codes that either allow them to 'blend in' and 'pass' unnoticed, or to portray a 'hard', 'don't mess with me' appearance that transgresses conventional gender boundaries, but does not reduce threats to their personal safety and stereotyping. Alexander worked with the young women as part of an intergenerational project and she points towards ways of tackling exclusion and challenging class-based stereotypes through social work that bridges the gaps between older and younger residents of a deprived urban area.

The disciplining effects of media discourse are an issue tackled by Elspeth Probyn in relation to youth obesity. She traces how 'taste' has become not only a signifier of class, but also a matter of public spectacle, producing shame and disgust. It is a source of anxiety, moral panic and guilt, which individualises the problem rather than addressing its relation to social inequalities. Probyn argues that food has become one of the contributing factors to the depoliticisation of class, as issues such as obesity and anorexia are presented as matters of self-discipline rather than social inequality. She presents three case studies of school gardening and farm-to-school projects in Australia, the US and France, which go beyond moralising about unhealthy eating habits to reconnecting children with the circuit of food production, preparation and consumption. Such schemes are less about converting children to healthier eating through providing better knowledge and producing individual guilt, and more about practical engagements with the food production cycle from which most western children have become almost completely divorced.

In drawing together the four chapters in Part I, Sue Ruddick orients her summary around the different ways in which subjects are constituted *through* their bodies. She identifies specific technologies and sites through which children's bodies are imagined, produced and governed, which include minute bodily practices, site-specific assemblages and dominant tropes. In particular, she focuses on the emergence of 'fat' as the latest and most pervasive means of governing children's bodies, the place of 'nature' and 'naturalness' in accounting for and managing children's behaviour, the place of the child's body as both an absent presence and a reservoir for 'site-ing' unpopular or oppressive discourses, and finally, considers children's bodies as assemblages of practices as a way to make sense of the multiple contestations and constrictions that constitute them.

Part II, 'Disciplining Bodies', is concerned particularly with political practices that discipline, survey and control young people's bodies through interventions that seek to reduce perceived and actual risks to children and youth, while at the same time reconfirming and creating new categories of 'normal' and 'abnormal' bodies. Part II also brings to the fore bodies of young people that transgress romantic notions of childhood and youth, and that are too often left out of focus. Jo Pike examines the implications of a trans-European programme for tackling obesity which takes an ecological rather than biomedical and lifestyle approach and, like the projects considered by Elspeth Probyn, goes beyond the logic of blaming individuals and their families. The 'Shape

Up' project focused on addressing structural determinants of obesity by engaging children in activities for environmental change. Pike argues, however, that the project's reach was limited to the local and thus inadvertently reinforced the victim-blaming approach by focusing on the behavioural change of individual bodies and regulating the local (family and school) spaces that bodies inhabit whilst bypassing the wider social and structural determinants of obesity.

An historical perspective on public schemes to measure and improve child health is taken by Pamela Dale, who critically reviews the class politics of health visiting in England, but also shows how this scheme, which was introduced at a time of high infant mortality, led to marked improvements in child welfare. Dale argues that an exclusive focus on the disciplinary and controlling aspects of health visiting risks overlooking the significant contribution that the scheme has made to improving children's health and well-being. Peter Hopkins and Malcolm Hill are similarly concerned with the effects of public intervention on young people's well-being. Their analysis of the practices of assessing unaccompanied asylum-seeking children and youths points to the high degree of classification involved in such assessments. Unaccompanied asylum-seeking children are marked out by their status as asylum-seekers, by their skin colour and by assumptions about their age that structure their access to resources, as well as their use and experience of them. Their bodies are read and categorised by those assessing them, yet they also perform embodiment in particular ways in order to express other identities.

The chapters by Elsbeth Robson and by Inbal Solomon and Myriam Denov that follow shift our attention to performances of embodiment that transgress and subvert romantic notions of childhood. Robson highlights how children in sub-Saharan Africa participate in social life through bodies that work and care. She argues not only for closer attention to the bodily details of children's lives, but also for a rebalancing of the largely western focus of literatures on embodiment. For the children whose everyday lives Robson has researched in Kenya, Zimbabwe and Malawi work is an accepted part of growing up and is influenced by gender and age divisions. It intersects with school life and makes an important contribution to social reproduction, including care for siblings and livestock, cooking and cleaning. The HIV/AIDS pandemic has further led to a major burden of care being placed on children, who look after sick parents, relatives or younger siblings, if one or both parents die. These responsibilities take a high toll on their own physical and mental health, as Robson demonstrates. Yet, political measures that

aim to abolish child labour are controversial since they ignore the significance of children's work to their communities, their families and their
own future prospects (e.g. being able to pay school fees) in the interest of complying with western notions of an ideal, care-free childhood.
How far children's realities in both the Majority and Minority worlds
depart from such an idealised conception is further demonstrated by
Solomon and Denov's chapter on the militarisation of children's bodies. They show how militarisation is part of many children's 'normal'
upbringing and of their inculcation into the nation through apparently
banal practices, such as playing with military toys, while in many countries around the world, children's bodies are an actual tool, as well as the
most impacted victims, of war. Children are manoeuvred from a young
age into positions that support military ideals. Solomon and Denov
examine how their bodies become militarised in different global contexts through seemingly diverse, yet related practices of inculcation into
the nation and the military.

The effects of the disciplining practices elaborated in Part II on parents' and children's sense of bodily competence and compliance with
normative measures of development are further contemplated by Elizabeth Gagen. Gagen argues that examining the disciplining effects of
contemporary and historical institutions of childhood does not mean
denying children's agency, but exploring how, through practices of self-
government, subjects are produced from as early as pregnancy and
infanthood.

Part III, 'Performing Bodies', engages more closely with questions of
transgression, contestation and the lived, hybrid body. Natalie Beale
explores the relation between space, stigmatisation and young people's embodied experiences of health. Beale focuses on young people's
own practices of stigmatisation and shows how both local peer cultures
and broader social and cultural influences impact on young people's
understandings of health and identity. Based on Butler's performative
approach to embodiment and Goffman's concept of enacted and felt
stigma, Beale considers the relations of power, place and peer group hierarchy that mark out some young people's bodies as different and have
a high emotional cost. Based on qualitative research with high school
students in the north-east of England, Beale outlines the effects of stigmatisation on young people's ontological security, their sense of being
in, or belonging to, the world. Louise Holt, writing on the embodiment
of childhood (dis)ability, likewise focuses on the construction and contestation of bodily difference by examining how children in integrated

schools experience and learn to negotiate different embodied abilities. Holt argues that difference need not always be presented as otherness. The examples she cites give a vivid impression of the myriad ways in which disability is transformed into just 'one other' aspect of identity in children's daily interactions, transforming 'otherness' into plural differences through relations of recognition and empathy. Holt seeks to draw out the 'the messy reality of the young people's complex embodied experience' and shows how materiality and signification intertwine in the performance of children's diverse bodies.

Peter Kraftl and John Horton are similarly concerned with the messier realities of living bodies in relation to disciplinary discourses and practices, focusing on the bodily rituals of going to sleep. They contrast the vast literature advising parents on how to establish sleep routines with the far more diverse and mediated realities of negotiating sleep between parents and children. Sleep has become one of the yardsticks for measuring parenting success by fitting children's daily rhythms around the needs and routines of adults. Yet, in practice, it is almost always a terrain for contestation and negotiation between parents and their children. Kraftl and Horton examine the latter with a particular interest in intergenerational bodily, practical and material relationships, showing that bedtimes are enacted, interactional, strongly influenced by sociocultural norms, as well as deeply emotional/affective. The authors raise questions not only about our understanding of apparently passive bodily states and ways of representing the plurality of affects, but also about the relevance of sleep for conceptualisations of childhood and about continuities between child- and adulthood.

Lorraine van Blerk shifts our focus from the UK back to the pluralities and complexities of young people's bodies in the Majority world. Her research with young female sex workers in Ethiopia sheds light not only on the socio-economic conditions and relations of power that lead the young women to deploy their bodies as sexual commodities, but also focuses attention on the ways in which they negotiate client–sex worker relations, including risks to their own and their clients' health. One of the strategies employed by sex workers to respond to changing conditions, including difficult relations with clients and disguising health problems, is migration. This option is not open, however, to most bar and red-light sex workers, whose mobility is restricted by the owners of bars and brothels. Van Blerk identifies a number of policy implications arising from both migration and restricted mobility, such as difficulties in accessing health services and protection against diseases, particularly

HIV/AIDS. She argues that service provision needs to become more flexible so that these young women can access projects that provide them with information and more choice in their work.

Part III concludes with a commentary by Ruth Panelli who highlights the plurality of bodily performances illustrated by the case studies in chapters 13–17. Panelli emphasises the importance of recognising young people's embodied senses of belonging. She argues for greater attention to be paid to the plurality of human–nonhuman relations that constitute the materiality of young people's bodies. Such a refocusing of our academic lenses demands re-examining how we conduct research. Panelli concludes with a number of suggestions for a politics of knowledge production that 'may herald a messier, more exciting, less colonisable 'multiverse' of childhood and youth and the performances therein'.

Such a politics of knowledge, the beginnings of which we seek to capture in this book, would also need to contribute to a re-examination of political interventions that regulate, discipline, as well as promote the well-being of young people's bodies. It is a politics that would seek to affirm rather than rein in the plurality of bodily becomings, reconsider the validity of normative developmental schemes and of generational divides, and foreground young people's own experiences of dwelling as embodied beings within hybrid, human–nonhuman worlds.

References

Aitken, S. (2001) *Geographies of Young People: The Morally Contested Spaces of Identity* (London: Routledge).

Alanen, L. (2000) 'Childhood as generational condition: towards a relational theory of childhood in research', in *Childhood: Sociology, Culture and History. A Collection of Papers* (Esbjerg: University of Southern Denmark).

Alanen, L. (2001) 'Explorations in generational analyses', in L. Alanen and B. Mayall (eds) *Conceptualizing Child-Adult Relations* (London: Routledge).

Aldridge, J. and Becker, S. (2003) *Children Caring for Parents with Mental Illness: Perspectives of Young Carers, Parents and Professionals* (Bristol: Policy Press).

Amit-Talai, V. and Wulff, H. (1995) *Youth Cultures: A Cross-Cultural Perspective* (London: Routledge).

Anderson, B. (2006) 'Becoming and being hopeful: towards a theory of affect', *Environment and Planning D: Society and Space* 24: 733–52.

Ansell, N. (2005) *Children, Youth and Development* (London: Routledge).

Ariès, P. (1962) *Centuries of Childhood: A Social History of Family Life* (London: Random House).

Armstrong, D. (1983) *Political Anatomy of the Body: Medical Knowledge in Britain in the Twentieth Century* (Cambridge: Cambridge University Press).

Barker, J. and Weller, S. (2003) '"Is it Fun?" Developing Child-Centred Methods', *International Journal of Sociology and Social Policy* 23(1): 33–58.

Bingham, N., Holloway, S. L. and Valentine, G. (1999) '"Where do you want to go tomorrow?" Connecting children and the internet', *Environment and Planning D: Society and Space* 17: 655–72.

Borden, I. (2001) *Skateboarding, Space and the City. Architecture and the City* (Oxford: Berg).

Braidotti, R. (1994) *Nomadic Subjects: Embodiment and Sexual Difference in Contemporary Feminist Theory* (New York: Columbia University Press).

Burke, C. (2005) ' "Play in focus": children researching their own spaces and places for play', *Children, Youth Environments* 15(1): 27–53.

Butler, J. (1990) *Gender Trouble: Feminism and the Subversion of Identity* (London: Routledge).

Butler, J. (1993) *Bodies That Matter: On the Discursive Limits of 'Sex'* (London: Routledge).

Christensen, P. H. (2000) 'Childhood and the cultural constitution of vulnerable bodies', in A. Prout (ed.) *The Body, Childhood and Society* (Basingstoke: Macmillan).

Colls, R. and Hörschelmann, K. (2009) 'The geographies of children's and young people's bodies: editorial', *Children's Geographies* 7(1): 1–6.

Davidson, J., Bondi, L. and Smith, M. (eds) (2005) *Emotional Geographies* (Aldershot: Ashgate).

Duncan, N. (ed.) (1996) *BodySpace: Destabilizing Geographies of Gender and Sexuality* (London: Routledge).

Ennew, J. (1994) 'Time for children or time for adults', in J. Qvortrup, M. Bardy, G. Spitta and H. Wintersberger (eds) *Childhood Matters: Social Theory, Practice and Politics* (Aldershot: Avebury).

Foucault, M. (1977) *Discipline and Punish* (London: Allen Lane).

Gagen, E. A. (2000) 'An example to us all: child development and identity construction in early 20th-century playgrounds', in *Environment and Planning A,* 32: 599–616.

Gallacher, L-A. (2005) '"The terrible twos": gaining control in the nursery', *Children's Geographies* 3(2): 243–64.

Gallacher, L-A. and Gallacher, M. (2008) 'Methodological immaturity in childhood research?: thinking through "participatory methods"', *Childhood* 15: 499–516.

Griffin, C. (1993) *Representations of Youth. The Study of Youth and Adolescence in Britain and America* (Cambridge: Polity Press).

Grosz, E. (1994) *Volatile Bodies: Towards a Corporeal Feminism* (Bloomington, IN: Indiana University Press).

Hamington, M. (2004) *Embodied Care: Jane Addams, Maurice Merleau-Ponty, and Feminist Ethics* (Chicago, IL: University of Illinois Press).

Hart, R. (1997) *Children's Participation: The Theory and Practice of Involving Young Citizens in Community Development and Environmental Care* (London: Earthscan).

Hart, R. (2002) 'Containing children: some lessons on planning for play in New York City', *Environment and Urbanization* 14(2): 135–48.

Hass, L. (2008) *Merleau-Ponty's Philosophy* (Bloomington and Indianapolis, IN: Indiana University Press).

Hockey, J. and James, A. (2003) *Social Identities across the Life Course* (New York: Palgrave Macmillan).

Holloway, S. and Valentine, G. (2000) *Children's Geographies: Playing, Living Learning* London: Routledge.

Hopkins, P. and Pain, R. (2007) 'Geographies of age: thinking relationally', *Area* 39: 287–94.

Horton, J. and Kraftl, P. (2006) 'What else? Some more ways of thinking about and doing children's geographies', *Children's Geographies* 4: 69–95.

James, A. (1993) *Childhood Identities: Self and Social Relationships in the Experience of the Child* (Edinburgh: Edinburgh University Press).

James, A. (2000) 'Embodied being(s): understanding the self and the body in childhood', in A. Prout (ed.) *The Body, Childhood and Society* (Basingstoke: Macmillan).

James, A (2005) 'Life times: children's perspectives on age, agency and memory across the life course', in J. Qvortrup (ed.) *Studies in Modern Childhood: Society, Agency, Culture* (Basingstoke: Macmillan).

James, A. and James, A. L. (2004) *Constructing Childhood. Theory, Policy and Social Practice* (London: Palgrave Macmillan).

James, A., Jenks, C. and Prout, A. (2001) *Theorizing Childhood* (Cambridge: Polity Press).

Kraftl, P. and Horton, J. (2007) ' "The health event": everyday, affective politics of participation', *Geoforum* 38: 1012–27.

Lancaster, Y. P. and Broadbent, V. (2003) *Listening to Young Children* (Maidenhead: Open University Press).

Macdonald, D. (2001) *The Graffiti Subculture. Youth, Masculinity and Identity in London and New York* (Basingstoke: Palgrave).

Mayall, B. and Zeiher, H. (eds) (2003) *Childhood in Generational Perspective*, (London: Institute of Education, University of London).

Merleau-Ponty, M. (1962) *Phenomenology of Perception*, trans. Colin Smith (London: Routledge & Kegan Paul).

Närvänen, A-L. and Näsman, E. (2004) 'Childhood as generation or life phase?', *Young. Nordic Journal of Youth Research* 12(1): 71–91.

Nelson, L. (1999) 'Bodies and spaces do matter', *Gender, Place and Culture* 6: 331–53.

Orr, D., Earle, K., Kahl, E. and Lopez McAlister, L. (1996) *Belief, Bodies, and Being: Feminist Reflections on Embodiment* (Lanham, MD: Rowman & Littlefield).

Panter-Brick, C. (ed.) (1998) *Biosocial Perspectives on Children*, Cambridge: Cambridge University Press.

Phillips, S. A. (1999) *Wallbangin'. Graffiti and Gangs in L.A.* (Chicago: University of Chicago Press).

Prout, A. (ed.) (2000a) *The Body, Childhood and Society* (Basingstoke: Macmillan).

Prout, A. (2000b) 'Childhood bodies: construction, agency and hybridity', in A. Prout (ed.) *The Body, Childhood and Society* (Basingstoke: Macmillan).

Punch, S. (2001a) 'Negotiating autonomy: childhoods in rural Bolivia', in L. Alanen and B. Mayall (eds) *Conceptualising Child–Adult Relations* (London: Routledge Falmer).

Punch, S. (2001b) 'Household division of labour: generation, gender, age, birth order and sibling composition', *Work, Employment & Society*, 15(4): 803–23.

Qvortrup, J. (2005) 'Varieties of childhood', in J. Qvortrup (ed.) *Studies in Modern Childhood: Society, Agency, Culture* (Basingstoke: Macmillan).

Robson, E. (2000) 'Invisible carers: young people in Zimbabwe's home-based healthcare', *Area* 32(1): 59–69.

Robson, E. (2004) 'Hidden child workers: young carers in Zimbabwe', *Antipode* 36(2): 227–48.

Shilling, C. (1993) *The Body and Social Theory* (London: Sage).

Steedman, C. (1995) *Strange Dislocations: Childhood and the Idea of Human Interiority 1780–1930* (London: Virago).

Teather, E. K. (1999) *Embodied Geographies: Spaces, Bodies and Rites of Passage* (London: Routledge).

Thrift, N. (2004) 'Intensities of feeling: towards a spatial politics of affect', *Geografiska Annaler* 86B: 57–78.

Valentine, G. (2004) *Public Space and the Culture of Childhood* (Aldershot: Ashgate).

Van Blerk, L. and Ansell, N. (2007) 'Alternative care giving in the context of HIV/AIDS in southern Africa: complex strategies for care', *Journal for International Development*, 19: 865–84.

Vanderbeck, R. M. (2007) 'Intergenerational geographies: age relations, segregation and re-engagements', *Geography Compass* 1(2): 200–21.

Weiss, G. (1999) *Body Images: Embodiment as Intercorporeality* (London and New York: Routledge).

Woodyer, T. (2008) 'The body as research tool: embodied practice and children's geographies'. *Children's Geographies* 6(4): 349–62.

Woolley, H. (2006) 'Freedom of the city: contemporary issues and policy influences on children and young people's use of public open space in England', *Children's Geographies* 4(1): 45–59.

2
Children's Bodies: An Absent Presence

Gill Valentine[1]

Introduction

Chris Shilling (1993) famously described the body as 'an absent presence' in sociology – a characterisation that has also been applied to the body in geography (see Longhurst 1995) and more recently to the sub-discipline of children's geographies. The body has been absent in the sense that it has rarely been acknowledged as a dominant theme within this area of geographical research; and yet the body is present precisely because children's identities and place in the world have fundamentally been constructed in modern times and, in western societies at least, through their bodies. This chapter, therefore, draws out the significance of children's bodies, using the sub-disciplinary context of children's geographies in order to demonstrate how children's bodies are 'present' in particular ways by considering how they have become a symbol of the meaning of childhood itself; how the process of making the transition from childhood to adulthood necessarily involves the disciplining of children's bodies, producing struggles and contestation between children and adults about how they move and where they can or cannot go; how the body has been central to the production and contestation of children's own identities within their peer group worlds; and the extent to which children and young people can occupy and take up public space. This chapter concludes by reflecting on how children's geographers have borrowed mainstream social science concepts to understand children's bodies and identities, and to question what contribution children's geographers might make to the discipline – and wider social sciences – in return.

The child's body: the embodiment of good and evil

Children's bodies have been imagined in western thought in two strikingly different ways: as the embodiment of both 'innocence' and 'evil' (Valentine 1996a, Holloway and Valentine 2000). In the Romantic images of poets and artists such as William Blake and William Wordsworth children were imagined as innately good. The eighteenth-century writer Jean-Jacques Rousseau in particular contributed to what Chris Jenks (1996) has termed the 'Appollonian' view of childhood in which children are imagined as 'pure' and 'innocent' in contrast to the ugliness and violence of the adult world from which they must be protected. The discourse of the 'innocent child' which emerged in the eighteenth and nineteenth centuries laid the foundations for child-centred education, concerns about children's safety and vulnerability, and the belief that children should be everyone's concern because they represent the future (James et al. 1998). James et al. (ibid.: 152) note that this imagining of childhood explains the horror and outrage child abuse engenders in adults. They write: 'Children's bodies are to be preserved at all costs, any violation signifying a transgressive act of almost unimaginable dimensions. To strike a child is to attack the repository of social sentiment and the very embodiment of "goodness".' It is important to remember, however, that the Appollonian view of childhood is an imagining of childhood rather than the reality experienced by most children. The experience of childhood has never been universal; rather, what it means to be a particular age intersects with other identities so that experiences of poverty, ill health, disability, having to care for a sick parent or being taken into care have all denied many children this idealised time of innocence and dependence (see e.g. Stables and Smith's 1999 account of the lives of young carers).

In contrast to the Appollonian view of childhood, the Dionysian (Jenks 1996) imagining of childhood originates from the notion of original sin, in which 'evil, corruption and baseness are primary elements in the constitution of "the child"' (James et al. 1998: 10). The evil child threatens the stability of the adult world and is in need of education and discipline to enable it to develop sufficient bodily control to be civilised into membership of the human race. It is an imagining of childhood evident in books such as the William Golding's *Lord of the Flies* and in contemporary constructions of teenagers as troublesome and dangerous (Valentine 1996a, 1996b). While both the Appollonian and Dionysian understandings of childhood are always present in children's complex and diverse experiences, at different historical moments one or the other of these binary conceptualisations has often dominated the popular imagination. At these times, other meanings of childhood can be overlooked or forgotten, before being periodically rediscovered (Stainton Rogers and Stainton Rogers 1992).

Both these symbolic understandings children's bodies – as the embodiment of 'good' or 'evil' – have been used to justify children's exclusion from public space: the Appollonian understanding because it constructs children as less knowledgeable, less competent and less able than adults and therefore as vulnerable and in need of protection from adults and the adult world (Valentine 1996a); the Dionysian understanding because it constructs children as dangerous, unruly and potentially out of control in adultist public space (Valentine 1996a, 1996b). The process through which children make the transition from childhood to adulthood has therefore been about the management and discipline of children's bodies both to protect them from harm until they are adult enough to be responsible for themselves and also to discipline them in order to ensure they learn to behave in controlled, what are perceived to be adult-like, ways.

Making adults: disciplining children's bodies

According to the German sociologist Norbert Elias (1978/1982), the importance of body management and the control of the emotions emerged in the sixteenth century as taboos developed around bodily functions such as spitting and defecating, culminating in the emergence of concepts such as self-restraint, embarrassment and shame. Elias documented the role of Renaissance court society in promoting 'civility'. He argued that an individual's survival at court depended not on their physical force or strength, but on their impression management and etiquette. Individuals' social identity or status could be read from their bodily deportment and manners. Those who regarded themselves as socially superior attempted to distinguish themselves from others through their superior bodily control, while those who wanted to climb the social ladder had to ape their superiors. These moral 'codes' eventually trickled down through society and became practised to different degrees by all citizens, becoming part of our taken-for-granted, everyday behaviour. This process of 'civilising' the body has become fundamental to the process through which children in contemporary western societies make the transition from childhood to adulthood. This process takes place both within families and also through the site of the school.

Schools are places where children are both cared for and also contained. The principle of universal education emerged in the UK during the nineteenth century. Industrial capitalism at that time was characterised by the brutal exploitation of child labour. This began to concern middle-class reformers and philanthropists. They regarded children's bodies as a natural resource to be nurtured and protected and were worried that their brutualisation was dehumanising and would lead to moral and social instability (Valentine 1996a). At the time, working-class children were likened to packs of 'ownerless dogs' (May 1973: 7) roaming the streets, stealing, behaving immorally and making a nuisance of themselves. Education was perceived by philanthropists as a way of instilling discipline, respect for order and punctuality in working-class children before they could assimilate the deviant ways of their parents. Schools were therefore conceived of as 'moral hospitals' (ibid.: 12). Not only were they intended to impose middle-class values on the population as a whole, but they also had the benefit of helping middle-class parents to control their own children.

During this same period the first statutory distinctions were made between adults and children in the form of legislation recognising juvenile delinquency, and reformatory schools were introduced as a way of remoralising delinquent youths (Ploszajska 1994). These institutions were developed on the principle that the social and physical environment could influence behaviour. Boys' reformatories were located in the countryside away from the corrupting environment of the city; whereas, because girls were expected to aspire to domesticity, female institutions were established in the suburbs. The design and layout of these schools were also intended to facilitate the discipline and surveillance of the children (Ploszajska 1994). Similar concerns about the need to educate working-class children in the normative regimes of polite society in order to protect the middle classes and their offspring were also evident in the United States in the nineteenth and early twentieth centuries. Alongside the development of education and reformatory schools, the Playground Association of America was established with the aim of keeping children off the streets and transforming 'street urchins' into respectable adults-to-be (Gagen 2000).

The compartmentalisation of children's bodies into the compulsory institutional setting of the school, where their use of both time and space is controlled by teachers, has contributed to the development of a contemporary understanding of children as in a process of 'becoming', as physically vulnerable and passive dependants in need of care by adults and protection from the adult world, and as differentiated from adults in a deferential and hierarchical way (Valentine 1996a, Smith and Barker 2000). This process has also been exacerbated by the fact that, as a result of the increase in the number of women in the paid labour market and the corresponding expansion of out-of-school childcare services, today's children are spending increasing amounts of time in institution alised settings, which can be both liberating and oppressive for them (Smith and Barker 2000).

Compulsory schooling is, or at different times has been, the basis for the surveillance of children's bodies and the delivery of welfare services such as inoculation against common illnesses or the provision of nutritionally balanced meals; and is a place where individual children can be monitored for signs of neglect or abuse (Valentine 2000). Beyond this social role and the academic goal of passing examinations, schools are also spaces where children's bodies are acculturated into adult norms and expectations about what it means to be a 'good' citizen. Children are expected to learn to conform to authority and in doing so to become compliant and productive workers of the future. This is a process through which gender, class and racialised roles and identities are also (re)produced (e.g. Willis 1977, McDowell 2000a, 2000b), but it is also one through which schools can challenge young people's racism and explore the meaning of whiteness in young people's lives through anti-racist education (Nayak 1999a, 1999b).

The body is embedded in a whole range of practices through which schools ensure children's integration into a dominant culture. For example, teachers 'civilise' children, promoting particular forms of bodily control and comportment (to dress properly, to sit still, to be quiet, to have table manners, to be polite, to be punctual, to respect traditions such as saluting the flag, etc.) to enable them eventually to be admitted into adult society. Educational institutions are therefore a 'hot-bed' of moral geographies – of moral codes about how and where children ought to learn and behave (Fielding 2000: 231). Fielding argues that teaching, learning and management in UK schools is constructed 'through the moral beliefs and practices of the governors, headteachers, teachers, learning support assistants, the Local Education Authority (LEA), the Office for Standards in Education (Ofsted) and central government'. Through this moral framework messages are sent out to school staff about what it means to be a 'good' teacher and to children about what behaviour is expected from them. However, these messages may be interpreted differently: by particular schools which each evolves its own specific educational ethos, by individual teachers through the exercise of their professional autonomy, and through the individual agency of children in responding to them. In particular, children are not passively moulded by uni-directional processes of socialisation, but actively contest and rework adult frameworks (although there are limits to this, hence the number of children who are suspended and expelled from schools).

Drawing on empirical work in primary schools, Shaun Fielding (2000) demonstrates how members of staff with contrasting teaching styles manage the space of their classrooms differently to create different geographies (in terms of the design of the classroom, the spacing of desks and the spatial freedoms allowed to the children) and, through the response of the children to them, different moral orders. In this way, although schools as institutions represent spaces or power structures which are designed to achieve particular ends, they are not fixed, uniform or stable entities. Rather, through the adoption of different teaching practices and styles, teachers can be active agents in forming pupils' relationships with the school. As such schools are, as Philo and Parr (2001) argue, best understood as dynamic and precarious achievements.

Bodies that matter: peer groups

The child's body has not just been understood in terms of the discursive constructions discussed above, it has also been the subject of ethnographic studies which have sought to understand the body as an entity experienced by children within the spaces of their own social worlds and cultures and as fundamental to children's relationships with each other (e.g. James et al. 1998, Holloway and Valentine 2000). It is within the context of peer group cultures that young people learn how to mark out their bodies as the same as or different from others' and to manage tensions between conformity and individuality (James 1993). To be socially competent is to be acknowledged as 'one of the crowd' rather than being the anonymous one among the crowd, yet also not to express inappropriate individuality and therefore be excluded as an outsider (James 1993). In this way, young people's bodies and identities are embedded in complex networks of relations in which the power to permit or withdraw friendship – to include or to exclude – is central to children's school cultures.

In a study of the body in children's everyday lives James (1993) points out that children's perceptions of their own and Other bodies constitute an important source of their identity and personhood'. She argues that a ruthlessly patterned hierarchy characterises children's cultures.

While there is no necessary relation between physical difference and marginality or outsiderhood, different bodily forms are given significance in terms of social identity by other children. James identifies five aspects of the body that have significance for children's identities: *height* (specifically, the importance of physical development, where size marks social independence and 'titch' is a form of abuse), *shape, appearance, gender* (all based on adult, heterosexual notions of desirability and issues of morality) and *performance* (including dynamic aspects such as gracefulness and sporting prowess or ability). Children who deviate from the 'norm' are immediately labelled as 'different' by their peers, though the consequences for their individual identities of the social meanings that are ascribed to this difference varies. While some differences may be temporary (a growth spurt can help shake off the nickname 'titch'), others produce more permanent stigmatised identities. James further explores how children have to negotiate their changing bodies within the context of changing institutional settings in which the meanings of their bodies change drastically. Summarising her work, she explains (James et al. 1998: 156):

> in the later stages of nursery school children came to think of themselves as 'big'; their apprehension of the difference between themselves and children just entering the nursery plus the significance of the impending transition to primary school signalled their identity. But once they had made the transition and were at the beginning of their career in primary school, they were catapulted back into being 'small' once again. This relativity produced a fluidity in their understanding of the relationship between size and status, generating what James identifies as a typical 'edginess' among children about body meanings. The body in childhood is a crucial resource for making and breaking identity precisely because of its unstable materiality.

While physical development or size/age is the most institutionalised principle for grouping children at school, among the children themselves gender is perhaps the most important basis for constituting social groups. Within schools there is often a strong sense of gender opposition (boys vs. girls) in which children mark out and ritualise gender boundaries (Thorne 1994). This is evident in the way pupils take up and contest different spaces within school grounds at break and lunchtime (Valentine 2000). Kris Krenichyn's (1999) study of a New York high school, for example, found that boys dominate the basketball court and that girls are made to feel unwelcome there. Instead, most of the girls take up spaces on the stairwells, fearful that if they gain access to alternative privileged spaces such as the games room the boys will overrun them. Studies of British schools have suggested that different girls' friendship groups cluster in different 'desired places' (toilets, behind outbuildings, etc.) and that these relationships and attachments are critical to girls' identity formation and sense of self-worth (Gilligan 1982).

Contemporary adult understandings of childhood as a time of 'innocence' and 'vulnerability' mean that schools are often imagined to be desexualised institutions (Epstein and Johnston 1994). Yet sex and sexuality are important in a whole repertoire of child–child and even pupil–teacher interactions, including name-calling, flirting, harassment, homophobic abuse, playground conversation, graffiti, dress codes, and so on (Haywood and Mac an Ghaill 1995). Adult heterosexual cultures are refracted through children's peer cultures. In particular, a number of studies have demonstrated that girls are under pressure to construct their material bodies into particular models of femininity, that they are judged more harshly on their bodies than boys, and that this in turn has an effect on their self-esteem, self-confidence and self-identities (Holland et al. 1998, Evans 2006a). This has been particularly evident in recent debates about childhood obesity (Evans 2006b, Colls and Evans 2007). Moreover, Gordon et al. (1998) highlight the desire of girls to be seen as 'typical' or 'normal'. They argue that girls must manage their bodies to stay on the right side of the slippery boundary between being acceptably attractive (not fat, no spots, no surplus hair, fashionable, etc.) without being overly sexualised (and labelled a 'slag' or a 'tart' – terms that imply sexual promiscuity). In this way, 'normality' is understood through its opposite: 'the place not to be, or more accurately as the girl not to be' (Hey 1997: 135).

In the case of boys, it has been argued that bodily performance is crucial to their ability to maintain a hegemonic, heterosexual (masculine) identity (Mac an Ghaill 1996). Coakley and White (1992) argue that boys associate sporting prowess with being a 'successful' male, and gain kudos from participating in competitive and aggressive leisure activities. In particular, boys are expected to be tough and be able to 'handle' themselves physically or to be able to occupy and take up space through verbal or intellectual performance. Compulsory heterosexuality, misogyny and homophobia, therefore, play an important role in policing and legitimising such hegemonic male heterosexual identities. Like girls, boys experience pressure to conform to what is a narrow and constraining conception of sexuality. Haywood and Mac an Ghaill

(1995) argue that it is dis-identification with other male students – to be 'a poof' or 'a paki', for example is also to be a non-proper boy – that enables heterosexual males to produce their own identity. Through such peer group relations masculine identities are therefore differentiated to produce a hegemonic masculinity in relation to subordinated racialised masculinities as well as femininities.

In an in-depth study of 11–14-year-old boys in London schools, Frosh et al. (2002) demonstrated the power of a particular hegemonic social narrative of black masculinity as the 'boy to be'. This located African Caribbean boys as smart and tough: the 'cool pose'. Frosh et al. argue that some white boys are 'black wannabes' who aspire to the cultural trappings associated with being black. In contrast, Asian is the 'boy *not* to be': Asian boys are the focus through which other boys develop and assert their masculinity. Black and white boys regarded themselves as more like each other than Asian boys, who were picked on and disparaged in implicitly Islamaphobic ways because of perceived differences, such as their language and culture, strong family ties and a sense of togetherness. Other research with Somali children in the UK has shown how this group negotiate the complex ambiguities of their positioning as British, black and Muslim. It identified the importance of the young people's emotional investment in the subject position Muslim as an explanation for why Somali children prioritise their faith above their racial, gender or ethno-national identities in their narratives of the self (Valentine and Sporton 2009, Valentine et al. 2009). The highly embodied, gendered and racialised character of school cultures described here can also have significant consequences for both girls' and boys' educational outcomes. Hyams argues that for young Latina women in Los Angeles, completing high school – with all that this achievement represents in terms of future employment opportunities – is dependent on the way that the girls negotiate their gender identities and sexual morality. In exploring the way they talk about their experiences of be(com)ing high school students, she suggests that for the young Latina women, 'There is an integral relationship between their gender and sexual identities conceived in terms of "victimisation" and "loss of control" and their historically low academic achievement and attainment' (2000: 652).

The places children's bodies cannot let them go

Reflecting on how people have viewed and treated her because she is white and female, Rich (1986: 216) writes that to locate herself in her own body means recognising 'the places it [her body] has taken me, the places it has not let me go'. Corporeal differences are the basis of prejudice, discrimination, social oppression and cultural imperialism (Young 1990). These exclusionary geographies operate at every scale, from the individual to the nation: discursively defining what different bodies can and cannot do, dividing conceptual space and operating materially to structure physical and institutional spaces.

For example, within families parents develop their own norms about appropriate spatial boundaries according to children's perceived age and bodily competencies. Negotiating greater spatial freedoms from their parents is part of the process through which children make the transition to adulthood (Matthews et al. 2000). Here, it is worth noting that the meanings of children's biological age and spatial freedoms can vary considerably according to their age, gender, environmental setting and household type (Katz and Monk 1993). In the wider adult world children's bodies are socially and spatially segregated from grown-ups, not only through parents' boundaries and the schooling system, but also through age-specific laws (which e.g. dictate when children can enter certain public spaces, bars, cinemas), curfews and informal regulations (e.g. shops which do not permit more than two or three children to entering at any one time), which bar them from certain public spaces at specific times. The purpose of these regulations is to protect children from physical harm (e.g. stranger-danger violence) and social harm (e.g. being exposed to adult sexuality, alcohol, drugs, and so on).

In many contemporary North American and European societies, attempts to restrict children and young people's movements or to control their bodies reflect growing concerns about the unruliness of young people in public space as evidenced in different contexts by graffiti and vandalism, gangs and alcohol-induced disorder (Valentine 1996a). The blame for this problem has been placed at the door of parents, schooling and the state. All three stand accused of having made children ungovernable by eroding the hierarchical relationship between adults and children. It is argued that parents have traditionally had 'natural' authority over their offspring as a result of their superior size, strength, age and command of material resources. This is an authority which, it is argued, has traditionally been sustained by the law and religion but also by everyday norms about the appropriate behaviours of adults and children (Jamieson and Toynbee 1989). However, towards the end of the twentieth century understandings about what it means to be a parent are alleged to have changed, with adults voluntarily giving up some of their 'natural' authority in favour of a closer and more equal relationship with their offspring. This has been accompanied in the twenty-first century by a general shift in both legal and popular attitudes to young people, away from an adults-know-best approach towards an emphasis on the personhood of the child and children's rights. In addition, the more liberal line adopted by the state towards the corporal punishment of children has also removed this tool, which adults could previously use to enforce their authority.

The moral panic about the ungovernability of children is being used to justify adults' perceptions that contemporary young people – particularly teenagers – are a threat to their hegemony on the street. Teenagers value the street as the only autonomous space they are able to carve out for themselves away from the surveillance of parents and teachers (Valentine 1996b). Hanging around on street corners, underage drinking, petty vandalism, graffiti and larking about are some of the ways that young people can deliberately or unintentionally resist adult power and disrupt the adult order of the streets and the suburbs. These uses of space are read by adults as a threat to their property and the safety of children and the elderly, but at the same time they believe that they no longer have the authority to regulate or control teenagers' behaviour. As a result, moral panic is being used to mobilise a consensus which is being employed to justify various strategies to restrict young people's access to, and freedoms in, 'public' space (Valentine 1996a, 1996b). In the US this has been extended to the imposition of curfews. Over 1,000 American cities and smaller communities have imposed curfews on teenagers, which require youths under the age of 17 year to be off the streets by 10.30–11 pm. In the first two months following the introduction of a curfew in New Orleans, 1,600 teenagers were picked up and detained until they could be collected by their parents. (It is worth noting that adult fears of and hostility towards the younger generation are not just a contemporary phenomenon but have been widespread over the centuries.) In this sense, the social meanings attributed to children's bodies matter because they shape children's individual and collective experiences of and exclusions from public space and have important implications for children's sense of place in the world.

Conclusion

This chapter has demonstrated how the body has been a fundamental, yet rarely explicitly acknowledged, cornerstone of research on children's geographies. It has been shown, however, that research within the particular field of children's geographies does include children's bodies by highlighting research that considers the ways that bodies have been imagined and constructed historically, how children are understood, regulated and controlled by adults, the importance of their relationships with their peers and their exclusion from public space in particular social and political contexts (see also Colls and Hörschelmann 2009 on 'the body'). In short, this chapter has sought to make the absent presence of the child's body 'present'. In concluding, this chapter draws attention to the specific sub-disciplinary context that has shaped geographers' engagement with children's bodies and then suggest ways that geographers and others might further their understandings of children's bodies through considering the family and relations of 'intimacy'.

In understanding children's bodies and identities, children's geographers have primarily borrowed theoretical concepts from mainstream social science disciplines which have been employed but not developed by this field. This is perhaps because, as a field, children's geographies are relatively empirical and lack a substantive theoretical foundation (Horton and Kraftl 2005) that might be pertinent to other sub-disciplinary areas of geography (Katz's 2004 is perhaps the only significant example to date of an attempt to employ research with and about children's lives, to address a substantive geographical concept such as globalisation). As such, children's geographies have not challenged geography or introduced new ways of thinking in the discipline in the way that other sub-disciplinary areas have had an impact on mainstream thinking (e.g. the geography of gender and geographies of sexuality introduced feminist and queer theory into geography respectively and have had wider consequences for the development of the discipline). Indeed, the development of the journal *Children's Geographies*, launched in 2003, may have unwittingly played a part in the marginalisation of this area because research on this topic has become somewhat ghettoised within this journal, leaving the adultist nature of the discipline as a whole uncritiqued or untroubled. In turn, because of this relative isolation, children's geographies have unwittingly become quite insular and self-referential, rather than disseminating its message to a wider readership. As Horton and Kraftl have argued, the field is at risk 'of becoming too much of a *comfort zone*' (2005: 139, emphasis in original), focusing on the same set of enduring themes (e.g. children's use of space) and drawing on the work of the same core group of authors.

Indeed, much work in children geographies has only focused on relationships between children and their parents. This is, to a large extent, a geography of parenting, rather than family life in its broadest sense. Little or no consideration has been given by geographers in the global north to other forms of familial relationship beyond parent–child: for example, between adult children and their adult parents; siblings; grand-children and grandparents; and wider familial networks of aunts and uncles, cousins and step-children/step-parents (Valentine 2008). This relative absence is particularly significant in the context of growing numbers of fragmented and reconstituted families or intra-familial negotiations across multiple generations. In particular, Vanderbeck (2007: 16) has drawn attention to the need for geography to adopt what he terms 'a less compartmentalized approaches to issues of age within geography', and to consider 'the diverse geographies of intergenerational relationships existing both within and between societies'. Likewise, Ruddick (2007) has called for a move away from the study of the behaviour of children and adults as static categories towards an exploration of shifting norms and forms of childhood and ageing as dynamic processes that constitute, and are constituted by, a new political economy.

These authors hint at the challenge for the sub-discipline of children's geographies in the future, which is how to make children's bodies matter to the wider discipline; how to locate understandings of children's lives within a wider socio-political framework; and how to scale up theoretical insights from children's geographies to have a wider impact on the discipline, as a whole. One way to achieve this may be to recognise the connections between children's geographies, geographies of sexualities and work on the 'family', understood in the broadest, not just traditional, nuclear sense. All of these areas are effectively studies of bodies, affective structures and intimate relations, albeit manifest in increasingly diverse and complex ways. Taken together, these currently disparate research areas might represent an important 'intimate turn' within the discipline. At the same time, the scaling up of this research under the banner of geographies of intimacy might also have a political outcome, demonstrating more effectively the significance and power of affective and embodied relations within and to the global economy (Valentine 2008).

Note

1. The argument in this chapter has been developed through my work over several years and elements of this chapter have previously been published as part of G. Valentine (2001) *Social Geographies* (Harlow: Pearson) and G. Valentine (2008) 'The ties that bind: towards geographies of intimacy', *Geography Compass* 2(6): 2097–110.

References

Coakley, J. and White, A. (1992) 'Making decisions: gender and sport participation among British adolescents', *Sociology of Sport Journal* 9 : 20–5.

Colls, R. and Evans, B. (2008) Embodying responsibility: children's health and
supermarket interventions', *Environment and Planning A* 40(3): 615–31.

Colls, R. and Hörschelmann, K. (2009) 'Editorial: the geographies of children's
and young people's bodies', *Children's Geographies* 7(1): 1–6.

Elias, N. ([1939]1978/1982) *The Civilizing Process. Vol. I: The History of Manners*;
Vol. II, State Formation and Civilization (New York: Wiley Blackwell).

Epstein, D. and Johnston R. (1994) 'On the straight and narrow: the heterosexual
presumption, homophobia and schools', in D. Epstein (ed.) *Challenging Lesbian
and Gay Inequalities in Education* (Buckingham: Open University Press).

Evans, B. (2006a) ' "I'd feel ashamed": girls' bodies and sports participation',
Gender, Place and Culture 13: 547–61.

Evans B (2006b) ' "Gluttony or sloth?" Critical geographies of bodies and morality
in (anti)obesity policy', *Area* 38: 259–67.

Fielding, S. (2000) 'Walk on the left! Children's geographies and the primary
school', in S. L. Holloway and Valentine, G. (eds) *Children's Geographies*
(London: Routledge), pp. 230–44.

Frosh, S., Phoenix, A. and Pattman, R. (2002) *Young Masculinities: Understanding
Boys in Contemporary Society* (Basingstoke: Palgrave).

Gagen, E. (2000) 'Playing the part: performing gender in America's playgrounds',
in S. Holloway and G. Valentine (eds) *Children's Geographies: Playing, Living,
Learning* (London: Routledge), pp. 223–39.

Gilligan, C. (1982) *In a Different Voice* (Cambridge, MA: Harvard University Press).

Gordon, T., Holland, J. and Lahelma, E. (1998) 'Moving bodies/still bodies:
embodiment and agency in schools'. Paper presented at the British Sociological
Association Annual Conference, University of Edinburgh, 6–9 April.

Haywood, C. and Mac an Ghaill, M. (1995) 'The sexual politics of the curriculum:
contesting values', *International Studies in Sociology of Education* 5: 221–36.

Hemming P. J. (2007) 'Renegotiating the primary school: children's emotional
geographies of sport, exercise & active play', *Children's Geographies* 5(4): 353–71.

Hey, V. (1997) *The Company She Keeps: An Ethnography of Girls' Friendships.*
(Buckingham: Open University Press).

Holland, J., Ramazanoglu, C., Sharpe, S. and Thomson, R. (1994) 'Power and
desire: the embodiment of female sexuality', *Feminist Review*, 46: 21–38.

Holland, J. et al. (1998) *The Male in the Head: Young People, Heterosexuality and
Power* (London: Tufnell Press).

Holloway, S. L. and Valentine G. (eds) (2000) *Children's Geographies: Playing,
Living, Learning* (London: Routledge).

Horton, J. and Kraftl, P. (2005) 'For more-than-usefulness: six overlapping points
about children's geographies', editorial, *Children's Geographies* 3: 131–43.

Hyams, M. S. (2000) ' "Pay attention in class... [and] don't get pregnant":
a discourse of academic success among adolescent Latinas', *Environment and
Planning A* 32: 635–54.

James, A. (1993) *Childhood Identities* (Edinburgh: Edinburgh University Press).

James, A., Jenks, C. and Prout, A. (eds.) (1998) *Theorizing Childhood* (Cambridge:
Polity Press).

Jamieson, L. and Toynbee, C. (1989) 'Shifting patterns of parental authority, 1990–1980', in H. Corr and L. Jamieson (eds.) *The Politics of Everyday Life* (London: Macmillan).

Jenks, C. (1996) *Childhood* (London: Routledge).

Katz, C. (2004) *Growing up Global: Economic Restructuring and Children's Everyday Lives* (Minneapolis, MN: University of Minnesota Press).

Katz, C. and Monk, J. (eds.) (1993) *Full Circles: Geographies of Women over the Lifecourse* (London: Rourledge).

Krenichyn, K. (1999) 'Messages about adolescent identity: coded and contested spaces in a New York City high school', in E. K. Teather (ed.) *Embodied Geographies: Spaces, Bodies and Rites of Passage* (London: Routledge).

Longhurst, R. (1995) 'The body and geography', *Gender, Place and Culture* 2(1): 97–106.

Mac an Ghaill, N. (ed.) (1996) *Understanding Masculinities* (Buckingham: Open University Press).

Matthews, H., Taylor, M., Sherwood, K., Tucker, F. and Limb, M. (2000) 'Growing up in the countryside: children and the rural idyll', *Journal of Rural Studies*, 16: 141–54.

May, J. (1973) 'Innocence and experience: the evolution of the concept of juvenile delinquency in the mid-19th century', *Victorian Studies*, 17: 7–29.

McDowell, L. (2000a) 'Learning to serve? Employment aspirations and attitudes of young working class men in an era of labour market restructuring', *Gender, Place and Culture*, 7: 389–416.

McDowell, L. (2000b) 'The trouble with men? Young people, gender transformations and the crisis of masculinity', *International Journal of Urban and Regional Research* 24: 201–9.

McDowell, L. (2002) 'Transitions to work: masculine identities, youth inequality and labour market change', *Gender, Place and Culture*, 9: 39–60.

Nayak, A. (1999a) ' "White English ethnicities": racism, anti-racism and student perspectives', *Race Ethnicity and Education* 2: 177–202.

Nayak, A. (1999b) ' "Pale warriors": skinhead culture and the embodiment of white masculinities', in A. Braj, M. J. Hickman and M. Mac an Ghaill (eds) *Thinking Identities: Ethnicity, Racism and Culture* (Basingstoke: Macmillan).

Philo, C. and Parr, H. (2001) 'Institutional geographies: introductory remarks', *Geoforum* 31: 513–21.

Ploszajska, T. (1994) 'Moral landscapes and manipulated spaces: gender, class and space in Victorian reformatory schools', *Journal of Historical Geography* 20: 413–29.

Rich, A. (1986 [1984]) *Blood, Bread and Poetry: Selected Prose 1979–1985* (London: Norton).

Ruddick S. (2007) 'At the horizons of the subject: neo-liberalism, neo-conservatism and the rights of the child. part one: from "knowing" fetus to "confused" child', *Gender, Place and Culture* 14(5): 513–27.

Shilling, C. (1993) *The Body and Social Theory* (London: Sage).

Smith, F. and Barker, J. (2000) ' "Out of school", in school: a social geography of out of school childcare', in S. L. Holloway and G. Valentine (eds) *Children's Geographies: Playing, Living, Learning* (London: Routledge), pp. 245–56.

Stables, J. and Smith, F. (1999) ' "Caught in the Cinderella trap": narratives of disabled parents and young carers', in R. Butler and H. Parr (eds) *Mind and Body Spaces* (London: Routledge), pp. 256–68.

Stainton Rogers, R. and Stainton Rogers, W. (1992) *Stories of Childhood: Shifting Agendas of Childhood* (Hemel Hempstead: Harvester Wheatsheaf).

Thorne, B. (1994) *Gender Play* (New Brunswick, NJ: Rutgers University Press).

Valentine, G. (1996a) 'Angels and devils: the moral landscape of childhood', *Environment and Planning D: Society and Space* 14: 581–99.

Valentine, G. (1996b) 'Children should be seen and not heard? The role of children in public space', *Urban Geography* 17: 205–20.

Valentine, G. (1997) 'A safe place to grow up? Parenting, perceptions of children's safety and the rural idyll', *Journal of Rural Studies* 13(2): 137–48.

Valentine, G. (2000) 'Exploring children and young people's narratives of identity', *Geoforum* 31: 257–67.

Valentine, G. (2008) 'The Ties that Bind: Towards Geographies of Intimacy', *Geography Compass* 2: 1–14.

Valentine, G. and Sporton, D. (2009) ' "How other people see you, it like's nothing that's inside": the impact of processes of disidentification and disavowal on young people's subjectivities', *Sociology* 43(4): 737–53.

Valentine, G., Sporton, D. and Nielsen K. B. (2009) 'Identities and belonging: a study of Somali refugee and asylum seekers living in the UK and Denmark', *Environment & Planning D: Society & Space* 27(2): 234–50.

Vanderbeck, R. M. (2007) 'Intergenerational geographies: age relations, segregation and re-engagements', *Geography Compass* 2: 200–21.

Willis, P. (1977) *Learning to Labour: How Working-Class Kids Get Working-Class Jobs* (Westmead; Saxon House).

Young, I. (1990) *Throwing Like a Girl ad Other Essays in Feminist Philosophy and Social Theory* (Bloomington and Indianapolis, IN: Indiana University Press).

Part I
Imagining Bodies

3
Femininity and Body Image: Promoting Positive Body Image in the 'Culture of Slenderness'

Sarah Grogan

Introduction

Slimness is generally seen as a desirable attribute for girls and young women in prosperous western cultures. Being slender is associated with self-control, elegance, social attractiveness and youth, and girls as young as five aspire to a slender ideal (Grogan 2008). The adult ideal is epitomised in the slim but full-breasted figure of actors and models such as Angelina Jolie and Elle MacPherson – the body type that Marchessault (2000: 204) describes as 'the physically impossible, tall, thin and busty Barbie-doll stereotype'. Muscle tone is also important, and the feminine ideal in the 2000s is a firm-looking, toned body (Bordo 2003). Researchers from psychology, sociology and gender studies have shown that body image is socially constructed and that maintaining a positive body image in cultures that specify a narrow range of acceptable body types can be a challenge. This chapter aims to investigate what we know about body image in western cultures, where a slender body type is idealised, and proposes ways of promoting positive body image in girls and young women. As such it will provide a complementary, primarily psychological, approach to other perspectives on contested bodies of children and youth presented in this text.

Body image

Body image, which can be defined as 'a person's perceptions, thoughts and feelings about his or her body' (Grogan 2008), is subjective and altered significantly by social experiences. Girls and young women make sense of how their bodies look within a context where a narrow range of body types are considered acceptable and appropriately feminine. Being 'feminine' is linked with being slender, not taking up space (Orbach 1993; Bordo 2003), and there is evidence that three-year-old children raised in western cultures show prejudice against female body types that do not conform to this ideal (Cramer and Steinwert 1998). Tracing the social meanings attached to slimness over the years, Bordo (2003) shows how, starting at the end of the twentieth century, excess flesh, for both men and women, came to be linked with low morality, reflecting personal inadequacy and lack of will. This preference for thinness is historically-specific, and recent work suggests that a desire to be slender is becoming more and more common across cultures, particularly in girls and young women who have more contact with western media. Research in South America (Negrao and Cordas 1996), South Korea (Kim and Kim 2001) and Japan (Nagami 1997) indicates that, even in cultures where extreme thinness previously signified disease and poverty, many women and girls now aspire to the thin, western body shape ideal.

Most adult women in western societies have attempted to change their weight and shape at some time in their lives by reducing the amount of food they eat, and women's magazines continue to promote dieting as an effective way to lose weight. Data from surveys carried out in Britain in 2001 show that 86 per cent of adult women have dieted (Wykes and Gunter 2005). In interviews with women aged 16–63, we found that nearly all had used dieting to try to lose weight (Grogan 2008). The 1990s and 2000s also saw a significant increase in the numbers of women having cosmetic surgery in Britain, Australia, Canada and the United States, the most frequently requested operations worldwide being liposuction and breast augmentation (Viner 1997, Cepanec and Payne 2000, Villeneuve et al. 2006). Cosmetic procedures are now 'normal' and accessible, and the 2000s have seen the genesis of reality TV shows in which women receive 'extreme makeovers', including cosmetic surgery, to correct perceived flaws. Arguably, women and girls are under more social pressure to conform to a narrow range of body types than ever before, raising the question of the impact of such social pressure on body image.

Researchers in psychology, sociology and gender studies have used a variety of techniques to study how women evaluate their bodies and have concluded that most young women and girls in western cultures are dissatisfied with some aspect of their body weight and shape. Studies using Figural Rating Scales (silhouettes of the female body, ranging from very thin to very plump) have found that adult women, on average, show a reliable tendency to pick a thinner ideal than their current figure. This effect has been replicated in the United States, Australia and Britain (Cororve-Fingeret et al. 2004). Body image questionnaires have also shown reliably that women tend to show higher levels of body dissatisfaction than men and that the areas of the body that present most concern for women are mid-torso (stomach) and lower torso (hips and buttocks) (Cash 2000). In interviews, women also tend to report dissatisfaction with stomach, bottom and thighs, irrespective of their age and actual body size. For instance, in one of our interviews, when Sheila (age 34) was asked whether there was anything that she would change if she could, she said: 'All the blub around my belly. I don't like that one bit'; and in another Dawn (age 17) said: 'I'd like my thighs to be smaller. And my bottom's too big' (both taken from Grogan 2008). These are areas of the body where women store fat and also areas that are often the focus of media attention in advertisements for slimming products (Bordo 2003). Most studies find that women tend to objectify their body and are able to describe what is 'wrong' with it with no difficulty, but find it difficult to identify any part that is satisfactory. In our own work, we have found that feeling slender and feeling confident are intrinsically linked for most of the women we interviewed, and all the women interviewed could identify at least one body site where they wanted to lose weight, whatever their objective size (Grogan 2008).

Research from psychology, sociology and gender studies has shown that girls raised in the western 'Culture of Slenderness' (Chernin 1983) become critical of their bodies before adolescence, use similar discourses around embodiment to adult women and that, given a free choice, girls from the age of five choose thinner ideal body sizes than their perceived current size. In our focus groups, girls as young as eight reported dissatisfaction with their body weight and shape and showed a preference for a socially acceptably slim body (Grogan and Wainwright 1996, Grogan 2008), showing that girls from primary school age onwards were sensitive to cultural pressures to conform to a limited range of acceptable body shapes. When asked if there was anything that they would change about their body, girls reliably reported that they would like to be thinner. For instance, in one focus group with a group of eight-year-olds (Grogan 2008):

Interviewer: Is there anything you like to do to change your body shape?
Girl 3: Lose weight.
Interviewer: Would you like to lose weight?

Girl 3: Yeah.
Girl 1: Lose weight.
Girl 3: You're thin enough.
Girl 1: I'm fat.
Girl 2: Look at your legs.
Girl 1: They're fat.

Being 'fat', especially having fat legs and 'stomach', was common in young girls' accounts. This has been called 'fat talk' by Mimi Nichter, who argues that talking about being fat can be a mechanism for gaining social approval and reassurance among girls and young women (Nichter 2000). The response seen above, where others in the group respond with reassurance that the target girl is slim, was a frequent pattern in our focus groups. However, the existence of 'fat talk' does not mean that the concerns expressed are not real for these young women. Supporting this interview work, Truby and Paxton (2002) have produced evidence that 48 per cent of pre-adolescent girls, when asked to choose between age-appropriate silhouettes, wanted to be thinner compared to only 10 per cent who wanted to be larger. Williamson and Delin (2001) have shown that girls as young as five show a significant tendency to prefer thinner figures than their current size and are significantly less satisfied with their body size than are five-year-old boys. There is also growing evidence that five-year-old girls are aware of calorie counting as a means to lose weight (Wheatley 2006).

There has been a lot of interest in body satisfaction in adolescence. Adolescent girls in western societies are subject to powerful cultural pressures to be very thin (Nichter 2000, Smolak 2004) and many authors have argued that adolescence is a time when body image concern in young women is at its peak due to physical changes in shape that may move girls away from a slender ideal (Burgess et al. 2006). It has been suggested that many adolescent girls say that they feel fat and want to lose weight (Neumark-Sztainer et al. 2006). In focus groups with adolescent girls (Grogan and Wainwright 1996, Grogan 2008), we found that although most expressed a general desire to be of average size (neither too thin nor too fat), they also said that they wanted to be thinner than they currently were. For instance, in one focus group (Grogan 2008):

Adolescent Girl 1: I'd maybe change my tummy.
Adolescent Girl 3: Yeah, I'd like to be a bit thinner.
Adolescent Girl 4: Yeah, just got a bit of a bulge on my tummy.

They said that they disliked the body shape of models in magazines because they thought they were too thin ('I think they do sometimes look too thin, they look anorexic'; in Grogan 2008), but were envious of their friends who were thin. What struck us most when reading the transcripts was the similarity between the accounts given by these thirteen-year-olds and those given by adult women in terms of apparent contradictions in their reports. Although they said that they wanted to be an average weight rather than thin and were critical of the extreme slenderness of magazine models, they still wanted to be thinner.

Promoting positive body image

Promotion of positive body image is important in improving quality of life and physical health in girls and young women, and body image is implicated in a number of health-related behaviours (Grogan 2006). Although being dissatisfied with the way that they look and feeling fat can motivate girls to exercise, it may also prevent them engaging in sports activities due to concern about whether they are sufficiently toned and thin to wear body-exposing sports clothes (Burgess et al. 2006). Body image factors may also influence whether they eat healthily and whether they restrain their eating. Positive body evaluation has been linked with healthy eating, and girls are less likely to binge eat and engage in restrictive dieting and self-induced vomiting if they feel more satisfied with the way that they look (Neumark-Sztainer et al. 2006). Body concern can also affect the decision to start smoking (as a means to suppress appetite) and to quit smoking if they fear that they will gain weight as a result (Grogan 2008) and may lead them to undertake unnecessary cosmetic surgery when they reach young adulthood, also putting their health at risk.

Psychological factors

Psychologists have suggested various psychological factors that predict positive body image. Most important of these are self-esteem, resistance to internalisation of the thin ideal and beliefs about personal control and mastery over the body, all of which are linked. Understanding the role of these factors has led to the development of interventions designed to help individual girls and young women resist social pressure to conform to the western ideal and to develop a more positive view of their bodies.

Girls and young women higher in self-esteem in general tend to be more satisfied with their bodies (Mintz and Betz 1986, Avsec 2006,

Connors and Casey 2006). Interview work has also supported the link between self-esteem and body image. In interviews (Grogan and Wainwright 1986, Grogan et al. 2004, Grogan 2008), positive body image has been linked with positive feelings about the self and feelings of self-confidence and power in social situations. Research in Australia and in the United States has shown that programmes designed to raise body esteem in adolescents (O'Dea and Abraham 2000) and young adults (Springer et al. 1999) can be effective in improving body image. The idea behind these programmes is that once self-esteem has improved, body image will also improve as a consequence of the self-esteem intervention. O'Dea (2004) and Paxton (1993) both argue that interventions that focus directly on body image have the potential inadvertently to raise body concerns in some girls. The advantage of programmes that do not focus directly on body image is that they may avoid increasing body focus in vulnerable girls and young women. This may be particularly important in children who have not considered body image problematic prior to the intervention. More work is needed in this area to determine the effectiveness of programmes that aim to build self-esteem and resilience as an indirect method of improving body image, although current American and Australian work with children and adolescents is producing very positive results (O'Dea 1995, O'Dea and Abraham 2000, Steese et al. 2006).

Young women who reject the mainstream thin ideal may also be less sensitive to thin ideal media cues and less vulnerable to dissatisfaction caused by self-ideal discrepancies (e.g. Jones 2004, Ahern and Hetherington 2006). Yamamiya et al. (2005) have shown that body dissatisfaction can be increased by five minutes' exposure to thin and beautiful images in women high in thin ideal internalisation, showing that social comparison with media ideals can produce particular risks for this group. This raises the question of how some women resist internalising the thin/muscular ideal. One factor that seems protective against internalisation is having a personal feminist ideology. Research has shown that girls and young women who hold feminist attitudes relating to body image were more satisfied than those who do not identify with feminist values (Dionne et al. 1995, Snyder and Hansbrouck 1996). Intervention programmes have enabled girls to change the ways they interpret cultural messages through recognising and challenging unhealthy female body ideals and practices. Work by Piran and colleagues (e.g. Piran 1996, Piran et al. 2004) takes girls' and women's experiences as their starting point, enabling participants to evaluate critically the lived experience of being a female in the 'culture of slenderness', challenging the thin ideal.

Peterson and colleagues (2006) suggest that a feminist schema may operate as a buffer through which societal messages may be filtered to enable girls and young women to resist internalisation of the thin ideal.

Other work has suggested that women who feel greater mastery and personal control over their bodies are likely to be more satisfied. Adult women body-builders interviewed in our study (Grogan et al. 2004) indicated that body building had enabled them to take control over their bodies which had impacted positively on their body satisfaction, self-esteem and a feeling of mastery over all aspects of their lives. Stressing control and mastery over the body is a traditional feminine discourse, drawing on notions of restraint and control of the female body (Bordo 2003), although in this case women were talking about increasing rather than reducing the size of their bodies. Intervention studies have shown that engagement in group discussion about practical strategies for improving body satisfaction stressing 'taking control' may lead to improved body image. Huon (1994) found that discussion of strategies to improve body satisfaction over which young women felt that they had control (taking up sport, identifying goals, learning to value individuality) was experienced as positive and motivating. Discussion of factors over which they felt that they had no control (barriers such as media promotion of the thin image, social attitudes about weight and shape, such as are often covered in media literacy programmes) was experienced as demotivating. This suggests that the development of perceptions of control over the body may be a useful and effective strategy for girls and young women.

There is also a growing body of evidence that shows that moderate exercise, focusing on mastery rather than aesthetics, can improve perceptions of control, self-esteem and body satisfaction in girls. Exercise improves mood, well-being and perception of control, at least in the short term (Brown and Lawton 1986), and there is a growing body of evidence suggesting that exercise improves body satisfaction. Intervention studies where girls have been randomly allocated to exercise and non-exercise conditions have shown that exercise programmes are effective in terms of improving body image (Burgess et al. 2006). It seems likely that exercise enhances self-esteem and body image by giving girls a sense of competence and by encouraging a focus on body mastery and function rather than on aesthetics. Martin and Lichtenberger (2002) note that increases in physical fitness and muscle tone are not necessary in order for an intervention to improve body image. What is crucial is that the girl or young woman feels subjectively fitter and higher in self-efficacy.

These positive effects of exercise on mental health and well-being, and especially on body satisfaction, suggest that girls and young women should be encouraged to undertake moderate exercise as a way of improving self-esteem and body image. In fact, recent estimates of frequency of exercise have tended to find that relatively small numbers of girls and young women in Britain undertake regular exercise. According to the recent Health Survey for England (Office for National Statistics 2007), there has been a steady increase in the use of cars, and a decrease in walking and cycling to school and to work in England since the 1990s, so that the percentage of 5–10-year-old children walking to school had fallen from 61 per cent in 1992 to 52 per cent in 2003, and the percentage of adults driving to work had increased from 66 per cent to 71 per cent. In all age groups, women were undertaking less exercise than men, and less than 30 per cent of adult women were engaging in the recommended amount of exercise per week. Encouragement of enjoyment, rather than competition or appearance focus, in sports and exercise may improve girls' and young women's motivation to exercise (Burgess et al. 2005, Grogan et al. 2006), which will be likely to impact positively on body image for all the reasons noted above.

Social factors

In the previous section, various body image promotion strategies that can be used by individual girls and young women have been reviewed. Membership of groups who do not espouse the thin ideal may also be crucial for determining satisfaction. Data from women from subcultures where there is less pressure to be slender suggest that social support for alternative body shapes can be crucial in promoting body satisfaction. This is the case where a plumper body type is idealised, as in African-American girls (Nishina et al. 2006), a more muscular body is the ideal as in women body-builders (Grogan et al. 2004) and when a wider range of ideals is presented, as in lesbian groups (Morrison et al. 2004). Work with girls and young women from these groups suggests that contesting the dominant slender ideal can lead to feelings of empowerment. These women's experiences provide a model of how it is possible to resist mainstream cultural pressures to be slender, providing women and girls have support from a salient sub-cultural group. This work suggests that the most effective means of promoting positive body image in girls and young women may be a cultural shift in the ways that slenderness is understood in western societies so that a wider range of body types becomes acceptable and socially sanctioned.

Conclusions

Young women and girls in western cultures make sense of their bodies within a social context where slenderness is value and maintaining a positive evaluation of their own bodies may be challenging. In order to enable girls and young women to develop positive body images, there needs to be a cultural shift in acceptance of the wide variety of body shapes and sizes that represent the normal range, and the de-stigmatisation of overweight. Cultural factors are important in determining girls' experiences of their bodies, and evidence from groups that do not stigmatise large body sizes (plump or highly muscular) suggests that acceptance of diversity may lead to a reduction in body dissatisfaction. A reduction in cultural objectification of the body, a shift in body aesthetics to encompass a realistic and healthy range of body shapes and sizes, and social support for alternative body types to the prevailing slender aesthetic would enable girls and young women to develop and maintain a more positive view of their bodies. Self-esteem promotion, resistance to the slender ideal and control/mastery of the body can enable individual women and girls to feel better about their bodies in the short term. However, what is needed in the long term is a concerted challenge to the 'culture of slenderness'.

References

Ahern, A. L. and Hetherington, M. M. (2006) 'The thin ideal and body image: an experimental study of implicit attitudes', *Psychology of Addictive Behaviours* 20: 38–42.

Avsec, A. (2006) 'Gender differences in the structure of self-concept: are the self-conceptions about physical attractiveness really more important for women's self-esteem?', *Studia Psychologica* 48(1): 31–43.

Bordo, S. (2003) *Unbearable Weight: Feminism, Western Culture, and the Body* (tenth anniversary edition) (Berkeley, CA: University of California Press).

Brown, J. and Lawton, M. (1986) 'Stress and well-being in adolescence: the moderating role of physical exercise', *Journal of Human Stress* 12: 125–31.

Burgess, G., Grogan, S. and Burwitz, L. (2006) 'Effects of a 6-week aerobic dance intervention on body image and physical self-perceptions in adolescent girls', *Body Image: An International Journal of Research* 3: 57–67.

Cash, T. F. (2000) *Users' Manuals for the Multidimensional Body–Self Relations Questionnaire*. Available on http://www.body-images.com.

Cepanec, D. and Payne, B. (2000) ' "Old Bags" under the knife: facial cosmetic surgery among women', in B. Miedema, J. M. Stoppard and V. Anderson (eds) *Women's Bodies, Women's Lives* (Toronto: Sumach Press), pp. 121–41.

Chernin, K. (1983) *Womansize: The Tyranny of Slenderness* (London: The Women's Press).

Connors, J. and Casey, P. (2006) 'Sex, body-esteem and self-esteem', *Psychological Reports* 98: 699–704.

Cororve Fingeret, M., Gleaves, D. H. and Pearson, C. A. (2004) 'On the methodology of body image assessment: the use of figural scales to evaluate body dissatisfaction and the ideal body standards of women', *Body Image: An International Journal of Research*, 1: 207–12.

Cramer, P. and Steinwert, T. (1998) 'Thin is good, fat is bad: how early does it begin?' *Journal of Applied Developmental Psychology* 19: 429–51.

Dionne, M., Davis, C., Fox, J. and Gurevich, M. (1995) 'Feminist ideology as a predictor of body dissatisfaction in women', *Sex Roles* 33 (3/4): 277–87.

Grogan, S. (2006) 'Body image and health: contemporary perspectives', *Journal of Health Psychology* 11(4): 523–30.

Grogan, S. (2008) *Body Image: Understanding Body Dissatisfaction in Men, Women, and Children* (second edition) (New York and London: Taylor & Francis).

Grogan, S., Conner, M. and Smithson, H. (2006) Sexuality and exercise motivation: are gay men and heterosexual women most likely to be motivated by concern about weight and appearance?' *Sex Roles* 55 (7–8): 567–72.

Grogan, S., Evans, R., Wright, S. and Hunter, G. (2004) 'Femininity and muscularity: accounts of seven women body builders', *Journal of Gender Studies* 13(1): 49–63.

Grogan, S. and Richards, H. (2002) 'Body image; focus groups with boys and men', *Men and Masculinities*, 4: 219–33.

Grogan, S. and Wainwright, N. (1996) 'Growing up in the culture of slenderness: girls' experiences of body dissatisfaction', *Women's Studies International Forum* 19: 665–73.

Huon, G. (1994) 'Towards the prevention of dieting-induced disorders: modifying negative food- and body-related attitudes', *International Journal of Eating Disorders* 16(4): 395–9.

Jones, D. C. (2004) 'Body image in adolescent girls and boys: a longitudinal study', *Developmental Psychology* 40: 823–35.

Kim, O. and Kim, K. (2001) 'Body weight self-esteem and depression in Korean female adolescents', *Adolescence* 36: 315–22.

Marchessault, G. (2000) 'One mother and daughter approach to resisting weight preoccupation', in B. Miedema, J. M. Stoppard and V. Anderson (eds) *Women's Bodies, Women's Lives* (Toronto: Sumach Press), pp. 203–26.

Martin, K. A. and Lichtenberger, C. M. (2002) 'Fitness engagement an changes in body image', in T. F. Cash and T. Pruzinsky (eds) *Body Image. A Handbook of Theory, Research, and Clinical Practice* (New York: Guilford Press), pp. 414–21.

McCabe, M. P., Ricciardelli, L. A., Sitaram, G. and Mikhail, K. (2006) 'Accuracy of body size estimation: role of biopsychosocial variables', *Body Image: An International Journal of Research* 3: 163–73.

Mintz, L. and Betz, N. (1986) 'Sex differences in the nature, realism, and correlates of body image', *Sex Roles* 15: 185–95.

Morrisson, M. A., Morrison, T. G. and Sager, C-L. (2004) 'Does body satisfaction differ between gay men and lesbian women and heterosexual men and women?' *Body Image: An International Journal of Research* 1: 127–38.

Nagami, Y. (1997) 'Eating disorders in Japan: a review of the literature', *Psychiatry and Clinical Neuroscience* 51: 339–46.

Negrao, A. B. and Cordas, T. A. (1996) 'Clinical characteristics and course of anorexia nervosa in Latin America, a Brazilian sample', *Psychiatry Research* 62: 17–21.

Neumark-Sztainer, D., Paxton, S. J., Hannon, P. J., Haines, J. and Story, M. (2006) 'Does body satisfaction matter? Five-year longitudinal associations between body satisfaction and health behaviours in adolescent females and males', *Journal of Adolescent Health* 39: 244–51.

Nichter, M. (2000) *Fat Talk: What Girls and Their Parents Say about Dieting* (Cambridge, MA and London: Harvard University Press).

Nishina, A., Ammon, N. Y., Bellmore, A. D. and Graham, S. (2006) 'Body dissatisfaction and physical development among ethnic minority adolescents', *Journal of Youth and Adolescence* 35(2): 189–201.

O'Dea, J. (1995) *Everybody's Different – A Self Esteem Program for Young Adolescents* (Sydney: University of Sydney).

O'Dea, J. A. (2004) 'Evidence for a self-esteem approach in the prevention of body image and eating problems among children and adolescents', *Eating Disorders* 12: 225–41.

O'Dea, J. A. and Abraham, S. (2000) 'Improving the body image, eating attitudes and behaviors of young male and female adolescents: A new educational approach that focuses on self-esteem', *International Journal of Eating Disorders* 28: 43–57.

Office of National Statistics (2007) 'Health: eating and exercise', www.statistics.gov.uk/cci/nugget.asp?id=1329&Pos=&ColRank=1&Rank=224, accessed 23 October 2007.

Orbach, S. (1993) *Hunger Strike: The Anorectic's Struggle as a Metaphor for Our Age* (London: Penguin).

Paxton, S. J. (1993) 'A prevention programme for disturbed eating in adolescent girls: a one-year follow-up', *Health Education Research: Theory and Practice* 8: 43–51.

Paxton, S. J., Neumark-Sztainer, D., Hannon, P. J. and Eisenberg, M. E. (2006) 'Body dissatisfaction prospectively predicts depressive mood and low self-esteem in adolescent girls and boys', *Journal of Clinical Child and Adolescent Psychology* 35: 539–49.

Peterson, R. D., Tantleff-Dunn, S. and Bedwell, J. S. (2006) 'The effects of exposure to feminist ideology on women's body image', *Body Image: An International Journal of Research* 3: 237–46.

Piran, N. (1996) 'The reduction of preoccupation with body weight and shape in schools: a feminist approach', *Eating Disorders: The Journal of Treatment and Prevention* 4: 323–33.

Piran, N., Jasper, K. and Pinhas, L. (2004) 'Feminist therapy and eating disorders', in J. K. Thompson (ed.) *Handbook of Eating Disorders and Obesity* (Hoboken, NJ: John Wiley & Sons), pp. 263–78.

Skoutaris, H., Carr, R., Wertheim, E. H., Paxton, S. J. and Duncombe, D. (2005) 'A prospective study of factors that lead to body dissatisfaction during pregnancy', *Body Image: An International Journal of Research* 2: 347–61.

Smolak, L. (2004) 'Body image in children and adolescents: where do we go from here?' *Body Image: An International Journal of Research* 1: 15–28.

Snyder, R. and Hansbrouck, L. (1996) 'Feminist ideology, gender traits, and symptoms of disturbed eating among college women', *Psychology of Women Quarterly* 20: 593–8.

Springer, E. A., Winzelberg, A. J., Perkins, R. and Taylor, C. B. (1999) 'Effects of a body image curriculum for college students on improved body image', *International Journal of Easting Disorders* 26: 13–20.

Steese, S., Dollette, M., Phillips, W., Hossfeld, E., Matthews, G. and Taormina, G. (2006) 'Understanding girls' circle as an intervention on perceived social support, body image, self efficacy, locus of control, and self-esteem', *Adolescence* 41: 55–64.

Thompson, J. K., Penner, L. and Altabe, M. (1990) 'Procedures, problems, and progress in the assessment of body images', in Cash and T. Pruzinsky (eds) *Body Images: Development, Deviance and Change* (New York: Guilford Press), pp. 21–46.

Tiggemann, M. (2005) 'Body dissatisfaction and adolescent self-esteem: prospective findings', *Body Image: An International Journal of Research* 2: 129–36.

Truby, H. and Paxton, S. (2002) 'Development of the Children's Body Image Scale', *British Journal of Clinical Psychology* 41: 185–203.

Villeneuve, P. J., Holloway, E. J., Brisson, J., Xie, L., Ugnat, A., Latulippe, L. and Mao, Y. (2006) 'Mortality among Canadian women with cosmetic breast implants', *American Journal of Epidemiology* 164: 334–41.

Viner, K. (1997) 'The new plastic feminism', *The Guardian,* 4 July: 5.

Wheatley, J. (2006) 'Like mother like daughter: the young copycat dieters', *The Times,* 11 August: 6–7.

Williamson, S. and Delin, C. (2001) 'Young children's figural selections; accuracy of reporting and body size dissatisfaction', *International Journal of Eating Disorders* 29(1) 80–4.

Wykes, M. and Gunter, B. (2005) *The Media and Body Image* (London: Sage).

Yamimiya, Y., Cash, T. F., Melnyk, S. E., Posavak, H. D. and Posavac, S. S. (2005) 'Women's exposure to thin-and-beautiful media images: body image effects of media-ideal internalisation and impact-reduction interventions', *Body Image: An International Journal of Research* 2: 74–80.

4
Mimesis and Alterity: Representations of Race in Children's Films

Karen Wells

> Film is 'a new schooling for our mimetic powers'.
>
> (Buck-Morss 1989: 267, cited in Taussig 1993: 20)

Introduction: performativity, 'race' and children's animation

In this chapter I use the concept of mimesis (copying and reproduction) to show that contemporary animated children's films frequently depict race and gender as performative identities, the competent performance of which is learned through copying the child's intimate others, particularly their mothers/maternal figures and, to a lesser extent, their fathers. The question that guides this analysis is: how do children learn to take on a racialised identity? Work in the performativity of gender has been very important in developing an understanding of gender as a socially constructed subjectivity (Butler 1990, 1993). Empirical work on how children are constituted as gendered subjects has shown how boys and girls are interpellated as gendered subjects. There is nothing subtle about this. Thorne (1993), in her study of a kindergarten in the US, and Connolly (1998), in his study of a primary school in England, have shown how children in putatively progressive (at least about gender equality) institutional settings are constantly asked to identify themselves as boys or girls and to establish the performativity of their gendered identity in opposition to that of the other gender. Whilst race shares with gender this performative character, the interpellation of children as raced subjects cannot be directly compared with their interpellation as gendered subjects. The hailing of children as people with a gender remains normative, notwithstanding shifts in what might be meant by femininity or

masculinity. This is not the case for race. Increasingly, the continued per-
tinence of race to social worlds and the impact of racism on life-chances
are elided in favour of claims to contemporary racelessness (Goldberg
2001). The claim that contemporary liberal democratic societies are race-
less, in the sense that 'race' is no longer a meaningful identity, or is not
salient to how resources are distributed or to life-chances, is particularly
the case in relation to the racialisation of children who are considered
to be innocent of race and not to notice skin colour. Notwithstanding a body of scholarly work, principally in social psychology, which
establishes that children do 'see' race and deploy both racial identities and racist practices (Van Ausdale and Feagin 2001), the insistence
that race does not exist for children is a widely held, 'common-sense'
view. Children, especially white children, are not hailed as raced subjects
directly through language, outside of Apartheid and other segregation-
ist regimes, black children and white children in school are not asked to
group themselves racially in the ways that children are constantly asked
to group themselves by gender (although see Gilborn and Kirton 2000
and Van Ausdale and Feagin 2001 for how race is deployed in schools).
Linguistic references to race are oblique and visual representation –
whose interpretation is more contestable – replaces textual representation (Wells 2007). Notwithstanding discourses of racelessness, children –
like adults – are constituted as raced subjects and draw on multiple
resources to understand what it means to perform their racial identity
conventionally. My contention is that popular culture is one of those
resources that present children with representations of the signification
and performativity of race (Willis 1997: 3, Giroux 2001: 1–12).

Social theory on the body is polarised between the discursive and
the material (Prout 2000: 3–5). This chapter analyses film as a discursive resource for the embodied performativity of 'race' and gestures
towards how the discursive/material binary might be disrupted in ways
that advance our understanding of how racism is inscribed on the
human body. The analysis of a film cannot, of course, tell us anything about whether children watching film use it as a resource for
understanding and constructing the relationship between their social
identities and their bodies; nor, as a representation of the body, can
it tell us what material bodies do to perform 'race'. What it can do
is to make an opportunity or space for interrogating the relationship
between the discursive construction of 'race' and the material body. I do
not want to suggest that this is as straightforward a relationship as Disney would have us believe. It is not that colour and physiognomy are
the origins of a racial identity, which can then be misidentified and

this misidentification 'corrected' through the normativity of heterosexual desire. Tarzan's attempts to dissolve an (unacknowledged) alterity through mimesis are ultimately blocked by the corporeal differences between his body and that of the ape group he has believed himself to be part of. The thinly veiled racial discourse of the film forces the viewer to consider what exactly the relationship is between different bodies and the taking up/taking on of 'race' and gender and what part heterosexual and narcissistic desire (desiring the other who resembles the self) does play in the alignment of racialised identities.

Surprisingly little attention has been paid to the specific role of material and/or visual culture in the formation of racial or ethnic identities in young children. Although there are ethnographies of everyday culture – particularly music cultures – and its role in constructing racial and ethnic identities, these have mostly been about older teenagers and young adults (Hewitt 1986, Jones 1988, Back 1999, Nayak 2003) the role of visual culture as race-making resources for children and young people has been neglected (see Ali 2003 for a notable exception). Since the 1990s the study of children's television and computer games has shown that children are active users/readers (rather than passive consumers/viewers) of media (Bazalgette and Buckingham 1995, Buckingham 1996, Kinder 1999). There are important studies of children using media to construct their identity as children (Mitchell and Reid-Walsh 2002) and as working-class girls (Walkerdine 1997), but very little on race. If media studies have taken children's media seriously the same cannot be said of film studies, which has had little to say about children's films. Film studies has embraced popular films as worthy of serious critical attention, particularly in their representations of race and gender (Willis 1997), but children's films continue to be dismissed as mere entertainment (though with notable exceptions, e.g. Street 1983, Bazalgatte and Buckingham 1995, Wojcik-Andrews 2000). Disney(land) as a space has been the subject of studies in social geography (e.g. Zukin 1993, Marling 1997) and there has been some research into the political economy of the Disney studios (Smoodin 1994, Hiassen 1998), as well as critical assessments of Walt Disney himself (Eliot 1993), but there have been few studies of Disney films or films from other studios that focus on social representation. The few studies there are have paid significantly more attention to the representation of gender in film than to the representation of race (Bell et al. 1995, Giroux 2001). Given that watching film, either at the cinema or on video, is a far from negligible leisure activity for most children in the UK (Livingstone 2002), such critical neglect is undeserved.

Notwithstanding the limited scholarly attention that has been paid to children's films, watching animated film is a significant leisure activity for children if the size of the children's animated film market is taken as an indicator of their viewing habits. In 2002, 8 per cent of DVD sales and 20 per cent of VHS sales in Europe were for animated films. In the US, *The Lion King*, *Shrek* and *Toy Story 2* are three of the top 20 grossing films at box office (www.bbc.co.uk/i/hi/entertainment/film/700265.stm). The three Pixar Productions, *Shrek*, *Monsters Inc.* and *Toy Story*, have generated box office receipts of $US 769 million; three of the top ten animation sales – *Aladdin*, *Tarzan* and *The Lion King* – are Disney productions: these three films have grossed in excess of $US700 million (www.digitalmediafx.com/specialreports/animatedfilms.html). Increasingly, video and DVD animation production is targeting ethnically segmented markets, while attempting to retain crossover between market segments. This is in response to a large young Hispanic and African American population in the US, where in the next 20 years Hispanic children aged 2–11 will comprise 25 per cent of all children in the US (Cella 2001).

Representations of 'race' in children's animation

One of the main narrative devices that animated films use to tell the story of how social identities are taken up is that of a displaced child/animal rescued by adults of another species, who then more or less willingly protect and nurture the child until she or he can be or is reunited with the family of origin. I argue that some very complicated work about the signification of race and gender is done in these films and that they circulate multiple, often contradictory, discourses about and representations of 'race'. On the one hand, they propose that species (for which, in children's animated films, read racial) difference is easily transcended or erased by emotional attachment to an other; and further, the emotional mother–child attachments that these films set up between different species of animal or animals and people are signified through the child learning to be like the substitute/adoptive mother by copying and reproducing the sensibilities and behaviours of that mother and her family (now the orphan's family). Through this trope of mimesis we learn that not only can attachments be made across difference, but that difference itself can be dissolved by the infant becoming like the 'mother'. This discourse of race as a socially constructed identity might seem very familiar from social and cultural studies, but it is perhaps an unanticipated representation of race from one of the most conservative production companies in the US (Giroux 2001: 91). However contradictory its provenance is, this representation of race and gender as social and cultural constructions in popular children's films may be welcomed; however, it has not displaced biological discourses of race and gender that insist that the body sets limits on the capacity for mimesis to dissolve alterity, nor of a Romantic discourse that essentialises the connection between place and (racial) identity. In contrast to the representation of gender and race as performative accomplishments, heterosexuality is essentialised in these films as an innate, biological drive that finally trumps and undoes the performativity of race and gender by always making the object of sexual desire, when the child reaches adolescence, a character of a different gender and of the same 'race'.

Disney's *Tarzan*

My main object of analysis is the 1999 Disney animation *Tarzan*. I chose this film because of its particularly clear and sustained use of mimesis for the overcoming or dissolving of alterity. *Tarzan* is a sustained exploration of how children learn to perform their (racial) identity and of the limits that the phenomenology of the body places on the racial roles and scripts that people can successfully deploy. It is also explicitly about the learning of *white* masculinity and the possibility of being a white man and still being a good person. In this respect, *Tarzan* is an unusual film; for the exploration of the signification of 'race' for white people *qua whites* being almost entirely absent in western visual culture (Dyer 1997). Critical white studies has insisted on the importance of rendering the production of whiteness visible in order to undo its social/political/economic power (Ware and Back 2001), whatever the merits of that project, it is rather unexpected to find a film from the Disney studios engaging in a critical reading of whiteness. Before analysing *Tarzan*, I briefly detail the output of Disney animation since the 1990s, demonstrating that *Tarzan*, whilst being a particularly complex text, is an exemplar of a contemporary sub-genre of children's films that attend to difference and identity.

The earliest Disney animation to deal with the theme of identity and mimesis, in this case through the trope of the wolf-boy, was the 1968 *Jungle Book*. (A direct-to-video sequel, *Jungle Book 2*, was released in 2002.) However, it was not until the 1990s that Disney released a series of films dealing with difference, gender and 'race'. These include *Beauty and the Beast* (1991), *Aladdin* (1992), *The Lion King* (1994), *Pocahontas* (1995), *The Hunchback of Notre Dame* (1996), *Mulan* (1998) and *Tarzan* (1999). It is perhaps indicative of how central the theme of social identity was to Disney in the 1990s that only three other Disney animations were made in that decade (not including Pixar or Disneytoon productions, or live action/animation hybrids). In 2000, in a reworking of the wolf-boy trope, this time as an orphaned dinosaur raised by lemurs, Disney released *Dinosaur* (2000). In 2002 Twentieth Century Fox released *Ice Age* and in 2006 its sequel *Ice Age 2: The Meltdown*. In *Ice Age* the 'wolf-boy' is a motherless human who is cared for by a sloth, a mammoth and a sabre-toothed tiger making their way across the ice to return the infant to his father. A straight to video sequel of Tarzan was released in 2005. The theme of the sequel is the young Tarzan's search for an identity after he is made aware that he is not an ape. The film ends with his reintegration into his ape family with the identity of 'a Tarzan'.

In the 1999 Disney version of the Tarzan story, Tarzan and his mother and father are shipwrecked off the coast of Africa when he is a baby. Their treetop house is attacked by a tiger which kills both parents. A female ape, whose infant has recently been killed also by a tiger, rescues the infant. Her partner and the head of the extended ape family, Kerchak, objects to her adopting the infant saying, 'Kala, look at it, it's not our kind.' Nevertheless, she raises the boy and he learns to walk, eat, play and speak like other young gorillas. As he and his peers grow older it is clear that Tarzan, although believing that he is a gorilla, has different capacities from the 'other' gorillas. One of these is his ability to imitate other species and learn their languages; another is that he is physically slower than the gorillas, but he is able, being human and having a capacity for mimicry, to compensate for his slowness by copying how other animals use the environment as tools or prosthetic extensions of their own capacities. Kerchak never accepts Tarzan as part of the ape family. He shouts at Tarzan and his mother, 'You can't keep defending him. He will never learn. You can't learn to be one of us ... look at him, he will never be one of us.' Tarzan runs off, crying and angry.

'Why am I so different?' he asks his mother. 'Kerchak said I don't belong in the family.'

'Look at me.'

'I am and do you know what I see. I see two eyes, like mine, and a nose ... two ears. Lets' see what else?'

'Two hands,' says Tarzan, putting his hand against hers excitedly and then withdrawing them when he sees the difference between his hands and hers.

Having failed to establish their physical similarity, she tells him to close his eyes and, putting his hand against his heart, she tells him:

'Forget what you see, what do you feel?'

'My heart.'

'Come here,' she puts his face against her chest.

'Your heart,' he says.

'See,' Kala says. 'They're exactly the same.'

For now, Tarzan's fears that the differences between him and his family are unassailable are assuaged and he ends the conversation determined to be 'the best ape ever'.

It is not long after this that the film ends its depiction of Tarzan's childhood and turns to his adolescence/young adulthood. It is at this time that Tarzan meets three white humans: an elderly explorer and his adult daughter – both gorillaphiles – and a hunter, Clayton, whose sole purpose for being in Africa is to capture (rather than observe) gorillas for the profits they will realise him in Europe. Tarzan rescues Jane from an attack by a group of monkeys. She takes him to her camp where Tarzan learns the culture of humans and falls in love with Jane. When the time comes for Jane to leave, still not having found the gorillas they came to observe (or, in Clayton's case, capture), Clayton suggests to Tarzan that if Jane could see the gorillas she would stay in Africa. Tarzan, breaking his promise to Kerchak that he will not reveal the camp to the humans, takes them to see his family. When Kerchak returns, he attacks the humans and they only escape when Tarzan restrains him. Tarzan, realising that he has challenged Kerchak's authority before all the family, runs away. His mother finds him and, in response to his despairing comment that he is 'so confused', she takes him to the tree-house his parents built when he was an infant and shows him a picture of himself as a baby with his mother and father. 'Now you know,' she says, although what he knows is left opaque. Are we to understand that until this moment Tarzan hasn't realised he is human like Jane? Or does Kala mean that this explains his confusion about why he defended humans and betrayed his gorilla family? In any case, it is this moment that Tarzan (literally) puts on his father's clothes and leaves 'Africa' to go to England to be with Jane.

Once on the ship Clayton imprisons Tarzan, Jane and her father in the ship's hold before returning to the shore to capture Tarzan's family. Tarzan is furious with himself when he realises the danger that he has exposed his family to. He escapes from the ship and goes to their defence. His (gorilla) father is fatally injured defending Tarzan from Clayton and, in retaliation, Tarzan fights Clayton and takes his gun from of him. Putting the muzzle to Clayton's neck, Clayton taunts him: 'Go ahead, shoot me. Be a man.' 'Not a man like you,' retorts Tarzan, flinging the gun away from him. Clayton and Tarzan's fight ends with Clayton cutting himself free from the hanging branches that Tarzan uses to swing though the jungle. Clayton falls, the trellis twisted around his neck, and stops short of the ground: lynched by the forest. Tarzan now goes to his dying father, who asks for Tarzan's forgiveness for 'not understanding that you have always been one off us. Our family will look to you now... take care, my son.' Tarzan, as the son of the clan's now dead leader, takes up his role as leader of the family, with Jane as his partner.

The limits of mimesis; the limits of hybridity

One of the significant divergences between the original books and the early films and this version of *Tarzan* is the complete absence of Africans. Until Tarzan meets Jane, her father and Clayton he is not aware that there are others who resemble him. This device of depopulating Africa means that the rendering of Tarzan as alone takes on a different significance from that of the books, and would do here were the possibility of Tarzan making a human community with Africans available. In the books, as Torgovnick (1990) points out, Tarzan's first glimpse of another human, an African man who has killed Tarzan's gorilla father, is the first occasion on which he thinks about who he might share being different (from his gorilla family), being human, with. The second occasion is when he meets a white woman, Jane. Through Kerchak's murder, which Tarzan is implicated in through his betrayal of the location of the family to Clayton, Tarzan becomes the leader of the clan, with Jane as his partner, establishing himself at the apex of a hierarchy in which all other members are subordinate to him (Torgovnick 1990: 55) and to Jane.

To understand how race is treated in this film it is necessary to remind ourselves that this is a children's film, which deploys the well-worn book and film convention for children of anthropomorphising animals. Filmic and textual representations of animals are then coded through the use of dialect, idiom, actor's voice, gesture and demeanour to signify their 'race' and class location (Byrne and McQuillan 1999). Animated films are replete with instances where these devices are used: the donkey in *Shrek*; the blackbirds in *Dumbo*; the hyenas in *The Lion King* are all examples that readily spring to mind where this sort of coding is used to establish the identity of characters as black or urban (Giroux 2001: 105–6). There is a scene in the Disney's animation *Beauty and the Beast* (1991) when the curse on the Beast's house ends and all the objects in it are restored to their human form. This is a rare instance where the slipperiness of this kind of coding is fixed. In general, these moments of revelation are not available to the viewer and the signification of animals (and talking objects) remains slippery; one can only make a plausible case that a particular set of signs are intended to signify a particular ethnic, national or cultural identification. This slipperiness is not accidental, I suggest; it allows the producers to deal in cultural/racial stereotypes and controversial issues of contemporary identity formation whilst always having the defence that this is *only* a children's film, the figures are *only* cartoons and that any resemblance to the real world is unintentional (Byrne and McQuillan 1999: 100–1).

Having established that objects and animals in children's animations are racially coded, we can return to *Tarzan* and ask how the gorillas are coded. There is nothing here (in contrast to, say, *The Lion King*) that codes these animals as human, as Africans. There is no attempt to render their speech in any of the conventional codes Hollywood uses to depict 'African' speech, there are no attempts to construct a *faux* African tradition, as there is in *The Lion King*. They are not rendered as human (other than in the capacity for complex language), rather it is Tarzan who is rendered as animal-like. Yet it is Tarzan's human capacity that also allows him to take up his leadership of the clan – his combination of human capacities and his intimate knowledge of gorilla life means he possesses the leadership qualities for this new age of threats from white hunters. My argument is this: the gorillas are intended to be coded as animal and many of the messages of this telling of the Tarzan story speak directly to the environmental/ecological preoccupations of its intended audience, with its sentimental view of animal worlds as more 'humane' than human worlds (as, for example, in the trope that only humans kill wantonly). Nonetheless, there is a racial reading here that is impossible to ignore because Tarzan's identity crisis in being different from his gorilla family is not so much about what it means to be human as what it means to be a white man. To expose this reading most effectively we might ask: why is the human family that appears in Tarzan's 'Africa' not a black family, why are Jane and her father white, and also what difference would it make to this story and its account of race if they were depicted as black? I suggest that they could not be black because, despite the absence of racial coding, the difference between Tarzan and his (gorilla) family is intended to be read as a story of racial difference where race is taken as physical difference inscribed on the body which marks the limits to the possibility of dissolving alterity through mimesis. When Kala takes Tarzan back to his 'birth mother's' house she is affirming her identity as his 'adoptive' mother in a scene that echoes a familiar narrative of adoption as a crisis of (non-)resemblance between parents and children and purports to establish the limits to the plasticity or constructedness of 'race'. Because the only other humanoid in the film before Jane, her father and Clayton make their appearance is not a racial other but a species other, the limits to mixedness or hybridity that the film establishes can be simultaneously insisted on and disavowed. This, as Torgovnick remarks of the Tarzan books, is 'the threat of miscegenation disguised as species difference' (1990: 54).

Learning whiteness

Tarzan's corporeal differences are represented as initially marking the limits of his assimilation into the world of his gorilla family and peers, and it at this point in the film that Jane, her father and Clayton arrive in Tarzan's Africa carrying with them all the paraphernalia – both ideological and material – of Victorian English bourgeois culture. It is their camp that becomes the space in which Tarzan will learn to be a white man. Tarzan's lessons in white masculinity are beautifully and comically depicted in Disney's animation. In the original Tarzan stories Tarzan already knows how to read English when he meets Jane, having taught himself from infant readers left in his parents' tree house. In the animation Tarzan learns language and from that how to be a white man by mimicking Jane, through Jane's attempts to teach him language and – brilliantly represented – through his watching and imitating Daguerreotypes.

Tarzan's entry into whiteness coincides with his loss of childhood. Only when he has completed his transition to young adulthood does it become imperative that he learns to be a white man and, in an entirely related point, it is his whiteness that makes it possible *and* necessary for him to fall in love with a white woman, and it is his love for a white woman that finally undoes his ambivalent species/racial identity. This representation of whiteness as a learned/performed subjectivity is highly unusual. Critical whiteness studies have shown how the power of whiteness is partly located in its constant erasure of the acknowledgement of its own existence. Here, in a mainstream film from a production company renowned for its reactionary politics (Giroux 2001), is an exposure of whiteness as a social fact and a denaturalising of race. How can this be accounted for?

Tarzan does not only learn to be human, he also learns to be a white man, and chooses a particular kind of white man to be. The gaze that the film invites is that of the white child. This is not, of course, the same as saying that Disney only intends this film to be watched by white boys, any more than in Laura Mulvey's ([1975]2003) seminal article is she advancing the argument that Hollywood film is only intended to be looked at by white men. The power of the gaze as a concept is that it draws attention to how a particular kind of audience is conjured up by the representation of gender (and for our purposes 'race') deployed in the film. In the case of Disney's *Tarzan* not only is the central protagonist a white boy/man, he is one of only four humans in the film, all of whom are white. More significant, perhaps, than this representational erasure of black people (important as that is for an animation ostensibly set in Africa) is that the film is a narrative about finding a liveable, *white, masculine* identity. The struggle that Tarzan goes through invites the identification of a white boy viewer with his screen likeness.

In its address to this imagined audience the film argues for the limits of contact across difference, the limits to the appropriation/incorporation of another's culture, and it establishes those limits through the body and specifically the specular regime of race. It is after all by looking at his reflection that Tarzan initially apprehends what he later insists is the incommensurability of himself and his gorilla family. It then declares that racial identity – authentic racial identity derived from and located in the body – has to be learned. Finally, it counterpoises 'good' whiteness to 'bad' whiteness, in which the former is situated in the family and with the feminine and in which the taking up of good whiteness in no way diminishes the social/political authority of whiteness. It is this last point that reconciles a critical deconstruction of whiteness that the film attempts with its provenance from the ideologically conservative world of Disney.

Back to Africa

Disney's *Tarzan* might be thought of as a triptych on mimesis. The first panel is Tarzan's imitation of gorilla culture, which ends with the shocking realisation that his corporeal difference places limits on the completion of mimesis and his at-homeness with his gorilla family. The second panel explores the presumption that mimesis rests on physical similarities and, in particular, skin colour. It is this second panel that clarifies the point that, despite the species differences of the first panel, the question or problematic that Tarzan (the boy and the film) is dealing with is the construction (or otherwise) of race. The second panel establishes Tarzan's whiteness, the recognition of which is made possible by and necessitates his love for a white woman – Jane – and makes his whiteness/love for her drive him into exile from his family and home; which is no longer either family or home. The third panel disrupts this reading/watching, however, because in the last part of the film a theme that has been latent in the second panel is brought to the fore with great consequences for how the question of mimesis, alterity and belonging are resolved. This theme is that white masculinity is not monolithic and that there are different ways to take up whiteness.

It is in this third panel that Clayton and Tarzan directly oppose one another as models of white masculinity. Clayton – muscle-bound and violent – is opposed to Tarzan, who is strong, lithe and sympathetic. Tarzan refuses Clayton's challenge to 'be a man' with the response: 'Not a man like you'. His determination to be a different kind of white man does not, however, change the relationship between white people and Africa; it merely reformulates it. Here, Tarzan and Jane establish their dominance over Africa not through violence and coercion, but through sympathy and a more Gramscian kind of hegemony. Here, reforming whiteness and white masculinity is, for the white man at least, a win–win outcome: he becomes a decent person without relinquishing power.

Conclusion

From time to time Disney productions attract serious critical attention in social studies (Bell et al. 1995, Byrne and McQuillan 1999, Giroux 2001). Most of these studies attend to how Disney films represent gender and, less frequently, how they represent 'race' and class. Perhaps because of their sociological concerns, or perhaps because they are children's films, most of these studies have little or nothing to say about the pleasure young children derive from the (often repeated) viewing of these productions. I have tried to give a sense of the pleasure of watching Disney, of the (often very high) quality of the animation, of the sophistication of the story-telling and of the complex ways that it represents the social world. This is not, of course, because I think Disney needs my endorsement or because I want to endorse its conservatism. My attempt to convey the pleasure of viewing these films is done simply to suggest that children find these productions so inviting, not because they are 'cultural dopes' but because the films depict, in artful and often very beautiful ways, concerns that necessarily preoccupy children in the negotiation of the relationship between themselves and others in their cultural and social worlds, Disney's 'animated films provoke and inform children's imaginations, desires, roles, and dreams while simultaneously sedimenting affect and meaning' (Giroux 2001: 91). I have argued in this chapter that *Tarzan* is a particularly clear instance of how cultural productions encode and depict narratives and performativities of race which children may then take up in their negotiation of racialised identities. Despite the undoubtedly conservative ideological values of Disney (man and company), the multifarious and disparate tasks of producing animation films apparently break down the representation of any monolithic or singular account of social identities.

References

Ali, S. (2003) *Mixed-race, Post-race: Gender, New Ethnicities and Cultural Practices* (Oxford: Berg).

Back, L. (1999) *New Ethnicities and Urban Culture: Racisms and Multiculture in Young Lives* (London: UCL Press).

Bazalgatte, C. and Buckingham, D. (eds) (1995) *In Front of the Children: Screen Entertainment and Young Audiences* (London: British Film Institute).

Bell, E., Haas, L. and Sells, L. (1995) *From Mouse to Mermaid* (Bloomington, IN: Indiana University Press).

Buck-Morss, S. (1989) *The Dialectics of Seeing: Walter Benjamin and the Arcades Project* (Cambridge, MA: MIT Press).

Buckingham, D. (1996) *Moving Images: Understanding Children's Emotional Responses to Television* (Manchester: Manchester University Press).

Butler, J. (1990) *Gender Trouble: Feminism and the Subversions of Identity* (New York: Routledge).

Butler, J. (1993) *Bodies that Matter: On the Discursive Limits of 'Sex'* (New York: Routledge).

Byrne, E. and McQuillan, M. (1999) *Deconstructing Disney* (London: Pluto Press).

Cella, C. (2001) 'For kids video, ethnic titles are more than a niche market', *Billboard* 113(23): 76.

Connolly, P. (1998) *Racism, Gender Identities and Young Children: Social Relations in a Multi-Ethnic, Inner-City Primary School* (New York and London: Routledge).

Dyer, R. (1997) *White* (London and New York: Routledge).

Eliot, M. (1993) *Walt Disney, Hollywood's Dark Prince: A Biography* (New York: Birch Lane Press).

Frankenburg, R. (1994) *White Women, Race Matters: The Social Construction of Whiteness* (Minneapolis, MN: University of Minnesota Press).

Gillborn, D. and Kirton, A. (2000) 'White heat: racism, under-achievement and white working class boys', *International Journal of Inclusive Education* 4(4): 271–88.

Giroux, H. A. (2001) *Disney and the End of Innocence: The Mouse that Roared* (Lanham, MD: Rowman & Littlefield).

Goldberg, D. T. (2001) *The Racial State* (Malden, MA: Blackwell)

Hewitt, R. (1986) *White Talk. Black Talk: Interracial Friendship and Communication Amongst Adolescents* (Cambridge: Cambridge University Press).

Hiassen, C. (1998) *Team Rodent: How Disney Devours the World* (New York: Ballantine).

Hirschfeld, L. A. (1998) *Race in the Making: Cognition, Culture and the Child's Construction of Human Kinds* (Cambridge, MA: MIT Press).

Jones, S. (1988) *Black Culture, White Youth: The Reggae Tradition from JA to UK* (Basingstoke: Macmillan Education).

Kinder, M. (1999) *Kids' Media Culture* (Durham, NC and London: Duke University Press).

Lasker, B. (1929) *Race Attitudes in Children* (New York: Henry Holt).

Livingstone, S. (2002) *Young People and New Media* (London: Sage).

Marling, K. A. (1997) *Designing Disney's Theme Parks: The Architecture of Reassurance* (Paris: Flammarion).

Mitchell, C. and Reid-Walsh. J. (2002) *Researching Children's Popular Culture: The Cultural Spaces of Childhood* (New York: Routledge).

Mulvey, L ([1975] 2003) 'Visual pleasure and narrative cinema', in A. Jones (ed.) *The Feminism and Visual Culture Reader* (London: Routledge), pp. 44–53.

Nayak, A. (2003) '"Boyz to men": masculinities schooling and labour transitions in de-industrial times', *Educational Review* 55(2): 147–59.

Prout, A. (2000) 'Childhood bodies: construction, agency and hybridity', in A. Prout (ed.) *The Body, Childhood and Society* (Basingstoke: Macmillan).

Smoodin, E. (ed.) (1994) *Disney Discourse: Producing the Magic Kingdom* (New York: Routledge).

Street, D. (ed.) (1983) *Children's Novels and the Movies* (New York: Frederick Ungar).

Taussig, M. (1993) *Mimesis and Alterity: A Particular History of the Senses* (London and New York: Routledge).

Thorne, B. (1993) *Gender Play: Girls and Boys in School* (New Brunswick, NJ: Rutgers University Press).

Torgovnick, M. (1990) *Gone Primitive: Savage Intellects, Modern Lives American Ethnologist* (Chicago: University of Chicago Press).

Troyna, B. and Hatcher, R. (1992) *Racism in Children's Lives: A Study of Mainly White Primary Schools* (London: Routledge).

Van Ausdale, D. and Feagin, J. (2001) *The First R: How Children Learn Race and Racism* (Lanham, MD: Rowman & Littlefield).

Walkerdine, V. (1997) *Daddy's Girl* (London: Macmillan).

Willis, S. (1997) *High Contrast: Race and Gender in Contemporary Hollywood Film* (Durham, NC and London: Duke University Press).

Ware, V. and Back, L. (2001) *Out of Whiteness Color, Politics, and Culture* (Chicago: University of Chicago Press).

Wells, K. (2007) 'Diversity without difference: modelling "the real" in the social aesthetic of a London multicultural school', *Visual Studies* 22(3): 270–82.

Willis, S. (1997) *Race and Gender in Contemporary Hollywood Film* (Durham, NC and London: Duke University Press).

Wojcik-Andrews, I. (2000) *Children's Films: History, Ideology, Pedagogy, Theory* (New York: Garland).

Zukin, S. (1993) *Landscapes of Power: From Detroit to Disney World* (Berkeley, CA: University of California Press).

Filmography

Aladdin. Dir. John Musker and Ron Clements. Walt Disney Productions, 1992.

Beauty and the Beast. Dir. Kirk Wise and Gary Trousdale. Walt Disney Productions, Silver Screen Partners IV, 1991.

Dinosaur. Dir. Eric Leighton and Ralph Zondag. Buena Vista Pictures, 2000.

Ice Age. Dir Chris Wood and Carlos Saldanha. 20th Century Fox, 2002.

Ice Age: The Meltdown (2006). Dir. Carlos Saldanha. 20th Century Fox, 2006.

Mulan. Dir. Tony Bancroft and Barry Cook. Walt Disney Productions, 1998.

Pocahontas. Dir. Mike Gabriel and Eric Goldberg. Walt Disney Productions, 1995.

Tarzan. Dir. Chris Buck II and Kevin Lima. Walt Disney Productions, 1999.

The Hunchback of Notre Dame. Dir Gary Trousdale and Kirk Wise. Walt Disney Productions, 1996.

The Lion King. Dir. Roger Allers and Rob Minkoff. Walt Disney Productions, 1994.

5

Deviant Femininities: The Everyday Making and Unmaking of 'Criminal' Youth

Catherine Alexander

Introduction

This chapter presents an insight into some of the ways in which young people who have been convicted of criminal offences become essentialised as 'deviant' through media discourses and the reiterative practices of others in everyday life. It discusses how a group of young women aged 17–25, who have, by their own definition, been 'involved' in the youth justice system, are conceived, imagined and understood both within and outside their local neighbourhood. Using their own words and frameworks of understanding, the chapter demonstrates how these young bodies are both emotionally and metaphorically marked, recognised and categorised. Their narratives reveal the way they (often feel they have to) dress; the way they (sometimes feel they have to) 'carry' themselves; the people they (can be forced to) associate with – all have significant impacts on how they are perceived and identified on an everyday basis. To my reading, there are a number of fractions which, taken together, work to stigmatise them as a group. Their bodies are read as 'risky' and, as a consequence, their actions and daily movements can be misunderstood and misinterpreted. 'Youth' as a problem for society is the dominant discourse evoked here, and the chapter adds to existing literature on constructing youthful bodies as 'deviant' (Jenks 1996, Griffin 2001, Little and Leyshon 2003, Hörschelmann 2005), by arguing that this is part of a multidimensional process of making and manufacturing social class.

The ways in which power is practised and perceived are central to the (re)production and (re)working of everyday space (Massey 1999, Gregson and Rose 2000, Allen 2003). Social class as a construction is fundamentally about power. In relation to this research, class is 'so insinuated in the intimate marking of self and culture that it is even more ubiquitous than previously articulated, if more difficult to pin down, leaking beyond the traditional measures of classification' (Skeggs 2005b: 969). The chapter points towards the unspoken, omnipresent and everyday process of class-making and the localised, profoundly felt effects this has on the young people who participated in the research project. Media representations in particular can affect an individual on a deeply personal level. Thus the chapter demonstrates that, through both local and national media discourses, fear is cultivated and works to inform the public perception of 'young people' generally. One young woman conveys how she has been equated with the popular media stereotype 'Vicky Pollard'[1] on a number of occasions, which, to my reading, has had a powerful stigmatising effect, which she has deeply internalised. This is in line with Skeggs' (1997, 2005a) argument that the body is the most important marker of class. Her research on the formation of social class in Britain analyses media sources and, drawing on a diverse array of evidence – from feminist commentators to the Blair government – she traces the way that these narratives act to reproduce, recirculate and repeat the representation of white working-class women, so that 'we now have the loud, white, excessive, drunk, fat, vulgar, disgusting, hen-partying woman who exists to embody all the moral obsessions historically associated with the working class; contained in one body' (Skeggs 2005b: 967). National media representations such as these relate to other practices of marginalisation and exclusion by caricaturing young women's bodily appearance in particular ways, drawing on their clothing, speech and comportment. At the same time, on a more immediate level, I illustrate how the local media are also targeting the young women individually, which acts to keep their personal 'criminal record' vivid in the public imagination. One example of this is explored in the continual references to the names and photographs of these young people published in the local newspaper. Some individuals are still undergoing 'the performance of punishment', with restrictions to their everyday lives in the form of Anti-Social Behaviour Orders (ASBOs) and electronic tagging[2] mapping a visible, material layer onto their already 'risky bodies'. These echoes of their former offences are heard again and relayed sometimes many years after the events took place. They are powerful in cementing how these young women are understood as both 'offender' and 'criminal'.

The young women convey that the very process of being marked out as 'criminal' evokes in them anxiety and a significant sense of injustice.

The uncertainties related to fear and the discrimination related to these stereotypes are a dominant discourse in these young people's everyday lives. The chapter outlines the myriad ways in which fear is experienced individually and the ways the young women deal with their fears. By dressing and 'hanging out' in the neighbourhood in particular ways they respond to their fears, but ironically these actions can, at the same time, work to inspire new fears in others living in the area (see Pain 2003, Hopkins and Smith 2008). This essentialising of their identities is a vicious circle; the more they try to 'put on a front' as a defensive tactic to alleviate their fears, the more fearful they become. Yet, these young women are not merely passive victims of the essentialising process. The chapter shows how they actively employ a number of other strategies in order to feel safe and get a handle on their fears. They too have worked to resist and contest negative stereotyping in the neighbourhood, and I have observed how personally empowering this has been to the young women involved.

The underlying argument here is that these young women are essentialised as deviant through the process of class formation. Individual assemblages of how they dress, their regional accents and how they 'carry themselves' materialise within certain circumstances to essentialise criminality. In the concluding sections, I demonstrate that addressing these stigmatising tendencies may entail more than the consideration of class-based relations alone. Rather, the research project is revealing ways in which a generational orientation could be working to elude this class orientation of their identities. Inter-generational exchanges can be one way to contest the class-based construction of deviance as it allows new assemblages to be constructed and lived out.

Methodology

As part of my doctoral research, I worked with 30 young people from three youth groups in a west end neighbourhood of Newcastle upon Tyne in north-east England. The research was designed to explore the everyday hopes and fears of young people growing up in the area. In the 2007 *Index of Multiple Deprivation*, the estate was classified in the 10 per cent 'most deprived' areas of the UK and has long suffered the effects of social and economic disengagement. The estate supports large youth and older populations, but there is considerable tension and a distinct lack of contact between the generational groups. Having lived in the west end of Newcastle for five years, I have observed that the neighbourhood is highly stigmatised by outsiders and associated with anxiety and social decline. Local residents suffer considerably from the effects of this stigmatisation and prejudice (Alexander 2008).

I employed a range of qualitative methods during my research. In the initial stages participatory diagramming techniques such as mind mapping and photography were used to generate group discussions and to encourage the young people to suggest issues of relevance to the research (for details see Alexander et al. 2007). A second stage involved more in-depth, collaborative research with six young women from one particular youth group. We carried out focus groups, together with more relaxed, informal conversations, to gain a deeper insight into how the young women feel about living in the neighbourhood. Two of the women described experiences of being mistaken for a man – one also told of being targeted because of her sexuality. This, and various other ways in which the young women's bodies have been (mis)understood, is an emergent theme in the study. The young women felt strongly about how they were perceived both in the immediate neighbourhood and throughout the wider city. The group through which I met the young women responded directly to the issue of stigmatisation and encouraged them to become actively involved in their 'Giving Back' project, designed to 'make the area better'. The underlying aim of this was a decriminalising intervention – breaking the classed assemblage and offering new ways for these young people to practise their identity. As such, the project provided space for them to attempt to contest, challenge and ultimately change how their bodies are read, processed and understood in the neighbourhood. A number of intergenerational programmes, including community bingo and afternoon tea sessions, were designed in collaboration with the local Senior Action Group to strengthen contact between the groups. The expertise of individuals from both age cohorts was invaluable in taking into account the particular types of conflicts and the issues that were specific to the neighbourhood itself.

Constructing deviance

Gradually, over three years, I got to know individuals in the group and from them I learnt that their narratives overwhelmingly indicate the vulnerable and insecure trajectory of their everyday lives. The young women expressed much frustration about how their bodies are read, and as a consequence they experience incidents of targeting, harassment and victimisation.

CA: How is it for you, living round here?
Carly: I can't even walk the dog without them [the police] calling me: 'Where you off to, Carly? Show us your tag.' It's six months since it was taken off! They're always trying to, like, provoke me – even if I'm just off to the shops!

Carly felt she was judged wherever she went and on a daily basis treated with suspicion both inside and outside of the neighbourhood. When spending time in the city centre, for example, she tells of feeling watched, monitored and surveyed:

Carly: Y'can see it [CCTV camera] in every shop, man. You can actually see it following us around everywhere! That's if they let us inside [the shop] in the first place, like.

It is worth noting that the young women are not passive victims of these surveillance practices, and that they work together to support each other and at times to resist them. Carly explained that when she was 'tagged', the police officer unknowingly failed to secure the device tightly enough and as a consequence she was able to slip it off her ankle and put it on her dog, Snoopy, who was subsequently monitored pottering around her house for the rest of the evening.

In general, though, the constant suspicion which these young women feel they are under became a second dominant theme in the research. They felt strongly that people only saw them in light of the criminal offence they had committed. In one example, Sarah (aged 21) had actively been trying to get a job and made an appointment at the local jobcentre. On sight, she felt discriminated against and was further deflated when she was informed by the adviser that her considerable experience in paid employment at the youth centre was 'worthless' and that 'there's no point putting that on your CV'. Having low self-esteem and lacking confidence, Sarah had found it difficult to attend the appointment in the first place; and she told of how the event both devastated and demotivated her from seeking future employment. Sarah's narrative demonstrates that, despite her best efforts, she felt that people see her as 'criminal'; she was afraid that this was something she would never get past: 'I can't get a job without my record. What's the point in trying if you canna[3] even get past the dole?'

Negative experiences such as these outside of the neighbourhood have meant that everyday lives become all the more localised as a defensive strategy.

> Michelle: It's my confidence. I struggle to talk to new people. Most people take one look at you, and they jus divvn't wanna know. I canna be bothered with that. I'd rather just stay round here – everyone knows me, I get nee bother.

The young people spoke very territorially about the neighbourhood and, as was found in a similar study of Newcastle upon Tyne, everyday interactions with other young people outside their estate serve to 'accentuate difference felt between these young people and make their individual desire to feel a sense of belonging to the local neighbourhood all the more palpable' (Nayak 2006: 820).

Discussions with the young people revealed that they overwhelmingly wanted to 'blend in' with the crowd and not be ridiculed for looking different. They told me that this was an attempt to 'look hard' and engender the feeling that 'you can't mess with us'. I would suggest that this criminalised assemblage is a space they put themselves into as a way of coping with living with anxiety and fear. Yet, ironically, the clothes they choose to wear to 'blend in' – tracksuits, baseball caps and hooded tops – can mean that they are further excluded from mainstream society. As Nayak (2006) has outlined, Newcastle city centre has long targeted young people wearing this type of casual sportswear (trainers, tracksuits and baseball caps are banned from popular bars and clubs) specifically marketing itself as a 'charver free zone'.

Michelle had made the decision to shave her head in an attempt to look 'hard' and she said that she wore baggy clothing so that she wouldn't be seen as 'a girl', which to her implied personal weakness. Carly agreed: 'It's safer if they think y'look hard. Nee one will bother you if y'carry yourself right.' For this reason both young women describe how they are often mistaken for 'a bloke'. Browne (2004, 2005) has succinctly shown that women who are mistaken for men can contend the supposed 'natural' links between sex and how one's body is read. These moments of transgression may challenge the performative illusion of fixed sexes yet, importantly, 'the (re)formation of these categories can be painful, disconcerting and discriminatory for those whose embodiments do not 'fit' dichotomous gender norms' (Browne 2005: 245).

Ironically, despite deploying these bodily comportments as a strategy for 'staying safe' and avoiding confrontation, there is much evidence to show that people who fall outside of the 'common sense' of the man/woman binary are all the more likely to experience discrimination and verbal and physical abuse (Butler 1990, Halberstam 1998). The threat of physical violence has been, and continues to be, a part of these young women's everyday lives. Some spoke passionately about being deeply embedded in personal vendettas relating to associations with family members, friends and boyfriends. As a consequence, the young people told how personal disputes in the neighbourhood can escalate, and that they often get 'dragged in' and are called on to 'watch my back'. These young women felt that sometimes they had to resort to violence as a survival strategy. This, ironically, serves to reinforce the everyday risks that they face. They tend to 'hang out' together to form allegiances to resist their everyday fears, yet remain very insecure generally as they move about the neighbourhood. The women told how they go around in groups of three or four to reduce the risk of 'being jumped on' – something Michelle had experienced at first hand when she was punched in the face by a group of young people she did not know. Having been bullied at school because of her sexuality, she thinks rumours relating to this may have been the reason she was attacked.

Engaging with literatures on feminine masquerades and the instability of bodily signifiers, Browne (2004) has also introduced the possibility of 'genderism' to describe the subtle, nuanced, often unconscious and sometimes hostile readings of gender ambiguous bodies, and 'articulate often unnamed instances of discrimination based on the discontinuities between the sex/gender with which an individual identifies, and how others, in a variety of spaces, read their sex/gender' (ibid.: 332). Feeling 'exposed' and 'watched' was another dominant theme for the young women. This is important as it can play a part in (re)forming the identities and embodiments of those who are viewed (Bornstein 1995).

As 'New Labour' Britain more generally is increasingly rocked by moral panics concerning young people, the effects are experienced by individuals, who feel all the more visible and vulnerable as a consequence. The next section considers the effect popular media sources have had on how these young women have come to embody fear in the neighbourhood.

Representations of youth in UK popular media

Popular media have a powerful influence in helping to create and cement stereotyped imaginations. Drawing on news media, internet sources and popular television series, Tyler (2008) traces the increasing currency of terms such as 'chav'[4] or 'charver', and demonstrates how they are the principal means through which the 'chav figure' has been constituted and reproduced in contemporary Britain. Employing a figurative methodology to focus on the emotional and affectual value of the 'chav', she analyses the ways in which class identities are mediated and made. In this way, the media employ a 'combination of caricature and *serious intent* to produce abhorrence which is not simply reactive, but is constitutive of social class' (Tyler 2008: 24). The significance of all this media interest is that white working-class women in particular are being 'marked as the national constitutive limit to propriety' (Skeggs 2005b: 968).

The ways in which social class is imagined and observed have had a direct impact on the ways in which these young women are recognised and addressed in the city centre in particular. During a focus group discussion, one of the young women, Lisa (aged 21), spoke of harassment she has experienced several times:

> Lisa: They see me and start pointing... and then they all yell, 'Yeah but no but' and 'Where's yer Westlife CD Vicky?' Or something like that. It's happened three or four times now, and I'm sick of it.

The bodies of working-class young women are seen as 'troublesome' and 'dangerous', but also increasingly 'fair game' to be taunted and provoked. Indeed, the term 'Vicky Pollard' has itself become a term in common useage. Tyler gives the following example:

> The reason Vicky Pollard caught the public imagination is that she embodies with such fearful accuracy several of the great scourges of contemporary Britain: aggressive all-female gangs of embittered, hormonal, drunken teenagers; gym slip mums who choose to get pregnant as a career option; pasty-faced, lard-gutted slappers who'll drop their knickers in the blink of an eye... these people do exist and are every bit as ripe and just a target for social satire as were, say, the raddled working-class drunks sent up by Hogarth in Gin Lane. (James Delingpole, *The Times*, 13 April 2006: 25, quoted in Tyler 2008)

In this way, 'the movement of this fictional figure from scripted television comedy into news media political rhetoric and onto the streets, foregrounds the disturbing ease which the chav figure shapes social perception' (Tyler 2008: 35).

Although social class may rarely be discussed directly by young people, it 'continues to be threaded through the daily fabric of their lives: it is stitched into codes of respect, accent, dress, music, bodily adornment and comportment' (Nayak 2006: 828). In these young women's everyday lives, both within and outside their local neighbourhood, the 'affective politics of class is a felt practice, tacitly understood and deeply internalised' (ibid.).

These young women are taunted in the street because of their appearance; moral judgements are made wholly on the basis of their clothing, speech and comportment. Yet national media discourses are not the only prism through which their bodies are reflected. The next section considers the more immediate, individual effects of local media coverage.

Local media effects on individuals

The young women involved in the research have all featured in the local newspaper, in reports of their criminal activities. As with other sources, local media play a 'pivotal role in moral panics by representing deviant groups or events and their effects in an exaggerated way' (Valentine 2004: 181). The young women themselves are left to suffer the backlash of media representations of them, which are all the more personal, all the more specific and all the more damaging.

The Newcastle *Evening Chronicle* is the local newspaper in the northeast of England. With a readership approaching 32,000 it is the biggest selling daily newspaper in the region and the second best performing regional newspaper in the UK. In 2006, a particularly derogatory photo of Michelle – taken three years previously – was splashed across the front page, as part of a three-page spread. In the article, the paper revealed her personal details, including the street where she lives. The article refers to her 'yobbish behaviour' and an incident when her mother beat her in the street. The newspaper continued to publish the photograph every time she was involved in an incident in the local area.

The *Chronicle* also uses a particularly interesting journalism tactic – it gives the names and photographs of the young people when reporting an incident they have not been involved in. One particularly high-profile unsolved crime, when a young mother was stabbed to death in the city, attracted considerable media coverage. The paper could not associate these young people to this event in any way other than spatially; nonetheless in the article they included a reference to an occasion when Michelle was arrested 'with [a] blade in [her] pocket'. In fact, she on her way to a youth group redecorating project and was carrying a small 'Stanley' knife. This juxtaposition associates their names with violent, unsolved crimes and, to my reading, perpetuates the stigmatising process.

It should be noted that the newspaper has published a piece on the youth group's 'Giving Back' project, which was supposed to represent the young women in a positive light for the voluntary work they have contributed to in the area. Yet, the same, now recognisable photograph of Lisa was published, and the paper referred to her as an 'ex-yob':

> Youth worker: You were devastated by that article, weren't you, Lisa? I've never seen her like that. Cried herself to sleep. They just don't *think* about the effect these articles have on the kids – you were just a bairn when that was written! They forget you've got feelings too.
> Lisa: I never believe what I read in newspapers since then. I thought they'd print what I said, but there was only, like, two lines. The rest was made up!

A year later, the same photo of Lisa, and an equally stigmatising article was published in the national *Sun*. Since then, she has had to endure repeated verbal abuse and has received hate mail from residents in the neighbourhood.

I can only describe the way in which the young people reported to me their experience of repeatedly reading the words 'yob', 'criminal' and 'notorious offender' alongside derogatory pictures of themselves and the long-term effect this has had on their self-esteem. They express in powerful language exactly how these articles continue to affect them; the words they use and the sentiments expressed evoke a sense of marginalisation and the stigmatisation with which they are addressed. The presence of these young women in the street materialises a body that 'signals class through moral euphemism, rarely naming it directly, hence relying on the process of interpretation to do the work of association' (Skeggs 2005b: 968).

One way these young women have chosen to work to challenge victimisation and stereotyping is to engage in intergenerational work that seeks to bridge the divides between older and younger residents. I see 'intergenerationality' as a concept that could usefully be applied to reworking not only how these young women are read and understood, but also to create new social networks between generations living in the neighbourhood thereby actioning social change.

Crossing generational divides

Recent debates on the sociology and geography of childhood and youth have shifted towards conceptualising age as relational, meaning that individuals cannot be understood outside of their relationships, which are constituted both within and between social groups. Young people and older people are often seen to hold specific social positions which are defined in relation to each other, but, importantly, these can be redefined within specific social situations (Alanen and Mayall 2001: 8). For Hopkins and Pain (2007), conceptualising more relational geographies of age marks a fundamental difference in the way we approach and think about groups of young people more generally. If we think about age as being produced in the relations and interactions between generational groups, and view intergenerationality as an aspect of social identity, this suggests that individuals' and groups' sense of themselves and others is formed partly on the basis of generational difference or sameness. At the same time, 'without situating older people clearly within the social and political relations that connect them (and which they share) with the young, analysing issues such as the fear of crime runs the risk of imagining them as fearful, irrational victims' (Hopkins and Pain 2007: 288).

Within the situated context of the local neighbourhood, and with sometimes 40 or more years' experience in the area, some individuals in the older age cohort carry with them knowledge, assumptions and specific experiences related to the area acquired during their life trajectory (see Vanderbeck 2007) These understandings have 'roots in time past, which throw long shadows forward, and they are re-negotiated and transformed through interactions between groups' (Alanen and Mayall 2001: 8).

Yet, having spent some time working with the young women, it became clear that they often did not have much contact with their parents or grandparents, let alone their elderly neighbours. As described above, it would appear that the older people in the area have their own preconceptions about the young people, since the less contact there is 'between generations, the greater the stereotyping of age groups and the greater the reliance on the media for an understanding of the age groups' (Moore and Statham 2006: 472).

Within the research project, in the initial meeting between the two age cohorts, one of the young people, Sarah (aged 17) brought her four-year old son, Tony. The shared experience of 'bringing up' young children helped 'break the ice' and generated a number of humorous stories. Interestingly, in talking about what it was like to live in the area, both age groups expressed similar fears:

> Joan (65): Y'canna walk past the Gala neemore – y'never know who's behind there.
> Sarah (17): Yeah – I do feel scared sometimes there.
> Michelle (16): It's them druggies – they're up a height [high on drugs] half the time.
> Mary (70): Exactly – it's those few who go and spoil it for everyone. I remember when y'could be on that field any time, day or night, and we were. It's where we'd go courting! Trying t'catch ourselves a man!
> Sarah: Courtin'! Ye'd never catch us on there now!
> Michelle: Ye'd never know what y'might catch from them charvers! (*laughter*)

Although 'getting to know you' was a lengthy and difficult process, beset by sensitive issues and personal complexities, eventually more regular contact was established between the two groups and a number of barriers broken down, as relations between them were fostered. The extract above reveals intent on behalf of both groups to find common ground, with Mary remembering and sharing tales of herself as having engaged in 'illicit' 'courting' activities in her youth. More recently, the young people have been involved in gardening, painting and decorating for older residents of the neighbourhood. Word of mouth has advertised these young people's services, which have further helped the two age cohorts to get to know each other.

Although superficial, these initiatives have, so far, been thoroughly beneficial. A number of young people told me how important it is to them to have something worthwhile to do – how it gives them a sense of achievement and satisfaction when they see the results of activities such as restoring an overgrown garden or helping to renovate a derelict building. These conversations have also revealed that relationships are growing outside the organised group sessions – around the movements and motions of everyday life in the neighbourhood.

> Youth worker: Pat (78) can cope with her garden much easier now – it makes the whole street look better!
> Sarah: And she always has a lolly for Tony now, when she's passing, don't she?
> Michelle: Yeah – what does he call her again?
> Sarah: Patty Pan!! I divvn't know why!

The young people continue to organise social events with the older residents. More recently, Sarah has developed such a rapport with some of the older people that she has forged contacts which have helped her go on to gain full-time employment at the residential care home in the area – a fact I initially found out by 'word of mouth' when I bumped into Pat in the neighbourhood. This is a significant achievement, given the considerable barriers to employment she experienced 18 months earlier – the hostility from the Job Centre and her 'irrelevant' work experience; her lack of general qualifications; and the insecurity she lived through before taking part in the 'Giving Back' project. The underlying aim of these intergenerational programmes is beginning to materialise, by changing how individual bodies are read, processed and understood as relationships develop within, between and across the two generations.

Yet it is interesting to note that when presenting the 'Giving Back' project to an academic audience, I included a number of photos of the young women both 'hanging out' together and of them wearing smart black trousers with old-fashioned 'pinny' style aprons (a dress choice that they made themselves because they had decided to act as waitresses during the afternoon tea sessions). On sight, the audience, however, deemed the young people to be 'unrecognisable' and interpreted them as having changed so much of themselves as the only way they could fit in and be accepted by the older group. This was not the case, but it would seem that, even within the most critical academic circles, these young people are imagined to have only one style of dress so that seeing them dressed in anything other than the 'hooded top', the 'baseball cap' or the 'tracksuit' is uncomfortable, unacceptable, unimaginable even.

Conclusion

This chapter has demonstrated that taking everyday life seriously as a site of ethical practice and cultural politics can constitute a profoundly transgressive political act. The research project is demonstrating the ways in which local people are beginning to gain an understanding of each other's views, behaviour and intent. What is of significance at this stage of the research project is that it is often the same incidents, 'hotspots' and social problems in an area which cause both the older and the younger age cohorts concern.

The estate is part of a socially and economically disenfranchised area, where the impact of fear of crime is felt strongly by residents, both young and old. This chapter has demonstrated how local and national media discourses contribute to this cultivation of fear and work continually to construct, imagine and classify these youthful bodies as deviant. I have outlined a number of ways in which the effects of discrimination are experienced on a deeply personal level. The young women themselves adopt a number of practices in response to these threats in their daily lives, which work to resist and contest such stereotyping. The chapter has discussed how the process of contesting negative readings can be personally empowering and how the young women employ a number of strategies in order to feel safe and get a grip on their fears. Addressing the issue of intergenerational conflict has been a key part in beginning to resolve some of the fears expressed by older people about young people hanging about and engaging in what they defined as 'anti-social behaviour'. The way young people's bodies are read by the older age cohort is slowly changing and media stereotypes – which used to be the only source – come to be contested, as word of mouth spread alternative forms of 'news' throughout the neighbourhood. Although space does not allow for detail here, it is important to note that the young people, too, are challenging some of the stereotypes they once held about older people more generally, as they forge relationships with a generation they once lacked access to.

The chapter points to the ways in which we are able to claim a new identity and construct ourselves differently according to when, where and how we put ourselves. In this research, adding an age dimension introduces an intervention which is deliberately decriminalising. The circularity of the criminalised assemblage can be broken by the practice, manufacture and performance of another assemblage in a different time and place. 'Deviance' is thus challenged and contested as these young women go about their everyday lives. It is important to continue to recognise these strengths and diversities in disenfranchised neighbourhoods, in order to resist and overcome stereotyping tendencies.

Notes

1. 'Vicky Pollard' is one of the fictitious characters adopted by the BBC's popular comedy series *Little Britain* (2003–6). The character is depicted as an overweight, moody, teenage mother who is recognised in particular by a pink tracksuit and an incomprehensibly fast, regional (Midlands) accent.
2. Electronic tagging: an electronic device is attached to a person – usually round the ankle – allowing their whereabouts to be monitored by the police. Together with Anti-Social Behavior Orders, they form the Home Office's 2003 Intensive Supervision and Surveillance Programme.

3. Quotes are cited 'in the raw' in an attempt to capture the vernacular 'Geordie' accent of the area. The personal significance of the local dialect to the young people of the area is discussed in Alexander (forthcoming).
4. The term 'chav' was the word of 2004 (Oxford English Dictionary), yet is highly contested. It is thought to be derived from the Romany word for child – chavo or chavi – and is closely aligned with stereotypical disenfran chised white poor: 'a term of intense class-based abhorrence' (Haywood and Yar 2006: 16).

References

Alanen, L. and Mayall, B. (2001) *Conceptualising Child–Adult Relations* (London and New York: Taylor & Francis).

Alexander, C. (2008) 'Safety, fear and belonging: the everyday realities of civic identity formation in Fenham, Newcastle upon Tyne', *ACME* 7(2): 173–98.

Alexander, C., Beale, N., Kesby, M., Kindon, S., Pain, R., McMillan, J. and Ziegler, F. (2007) 'Participatory diagramming: a critical view from North East England', in S. Kindon, R. Pain and M. Kesby (eds) *Participatory Action Research Approaches and Methods: Connecting People, Participation and Place* (Routledge: London), pp. 112–21.

Allen, J. (2003) *Lost Geographies of Power* (Oxford: Blackwell).

Bornstein, K. (1995) *Gender Outlaw: On Men, Women and the Rest of Us* (New York: Routledge).

Browne, K. (2004) 'Genderism and the bathroom problem: (re)materialising sexed sites, (re)creating sexed bodies', *Gender, Place and Culture* 11(3): 331–46.

Browne, K. (2005) 'Stages and streets reading and (mis)reading female masculinities', in B. van Hoven and K. Hörschelmann (eds) *Spaces of Masculinities* (London and New York: Routledge), pp. 237–48.

Butler, J. (1990) *Gender Trouble* (London: Routledge).

Delamont, S. (2001) *Changing Women, Unchanged Men? Sociological Perspectives on Gender in a Post-Industrial Society* (Buckingham: Open University Press).

Delingpole, J. (2006) 'A conspiracy against chavs? Count me in', *The Times*, 13 April,: 25.

Gregson, N. and Rose, G. (2000) 'Taking Butler elsewhere: performativities, spatialities and subjectivities', *Environment and Planning D – Society and Space* 18: 433–52.

Griffin, C. (2001) 'Imagining new narratives of youth: youth research, the "new Europe" and global youth culture', *Childhood* 8(2): 147–66.

Halberstam, J. (1998) *Female Masculinity* (Durham, NC and London: Duke University Press).

Hayward, K. and Yar, M. (2006) 'The "chav" phenomenon: consumption, media and the construction of a new underclass', *Crime, Media, Culture* 2(1): 9–28.

Hopkins, P. and Pain, R. (2007) 'Geographies of age: thinking relationally', *Area* 39(3): 287–84.

Hopkins, P. and Smith, S. (2008) 'Scaling segregation; racialising fear', in R. Pain and S. J. Smith (ed.) *Fear: Critical Geopolitics and Everyday Life* (Aldershot: Ashgate).

Hörschelmann, K. (2005) 'Deviant masculinities: representations of neo-fascist youth in eastern Germany', in B. van Hoven and K. Hörschelmann (eds) *Spaces of Masculinities* (London and New York: Routledge), pp. 138–52.

Jenks, C. (1996) *Childhood* (London and New York: Routledge).

Lawson, D. (2006) quoted in 'Nurseries "fostering generation of Vicky Pollards"', *The Guardian*, 2 August.

Little, J. and Leyshon, M. (2003) 'Embodied ruralities: developing research agendas', *Progress in Human Geography* 27(3): 257–72.

Massey, D. (1999) *Power Geometries and the Politics of Space-Time*. Hettner Lectures 2 (Heidelberg: University of Heidelberg).

Moore, S. and Stratham, E. (2006) 'Can intergenerational practice offer a way of limiting anti-social behaviour and fear of crime?' *The Howard Journal of Criminal Justice* 45(5): 468–84.

Nayak, A. (2006) 'Displaced masculinities: chavs, youth and class in the post-industrial city', *Sociology* 40: 813–31.

Pain, R. (2003) 'Youth, age and the representation of fear', *Capital and Class* 60: 151–71.

Shirlow, P. and Pain, R. (2003) 'Introduction: the geographies and politics of fear', *Capital and Class* 60: 15–26.

Skeggs, B. (1997) 'Formations of class and gender: becoming respectable', *Theory, Culture and Society* (London: Sage).

Skeggs, B. (2005a) *Class, Self and Culture* (London: Routledge).

Skeggs, B. (2005b) 'The making of class and gender through visualizing moral subject formation', *Sociology* 39: 965–82.

Skeggs, B. and Wood, H. (2004) 'Notes on ethical scenarios of self on British reality TV', *Feminist Media Studies* 4 (1): 205–8.

Tyler, I. (2008) ' "Chav mum, chav scum": class disgust in contemporary Britain', *Feminist Media Studies* 8(2): 17–34.

Valentine, G. (2004) *Public Space and the Culture of Childhood* (London: Ashgate).

Vanderbeck, R. (2007) 'Intergenerational geographies: age relations, segregation and reengagements', *Geography Compass* 1: 200–21.

6
How *Do* Children Taste? Young People and the Production and Consumption of Food

Elspeth Probyn

> I have been assured by a very knowing American of my acquaintance in London, that a young healthy child well nursed, is, at a year old, a most delicious nourishing and wholesome food, whether stewed, roasted, baked, or boiled; and I make no doubt that it will equally serve in a fricasie, or a ragoust.
>
> Jonathan Swift 1729

Introduction

I've always been fond of Jonathon Swift's tone in his *A Modest Proposal*. The literalness with which he addresses the heated debates of his time – and they were large ones about the trade in human bodies and souls – zings down through the centuries. What to do with a burgeoning poor Catholic population – well, eat them. For us now in the midst of yet another heated battle about the young, this time over children's burgeoning bodies, that he attributes the flavoursome basis of his modest proposal to an American makes the irony all the more delicious. For, of course, many would blame the putative global epidemic of youth obesity on American media and food cultures. It bears emphasising that Swift's satire was first and foremost directed at the simplistic 'solutions' paraded by experts to the economic and social problems that faced Ireland and elsewhere at the time (Wittkowsky 1943). We might say that this trend continues in the various 'solutions' now being proposed about youth obesity, such as the banning of junk food ads. Food porn, food blame, food guilt, food catastrophe.

In this chapter I want to begin to address another way of figuring a response to youth obesity. While there are many polemical aspects that

I do not agree with in the dominant framing of youth obesity, which I will detail shortly, I do want to flag that there are serious problems and consequences about the current state of affairs as it concerns children, taste, eating and food knowledge. I am convinced that issues around food and eating are to be seen as a continuum, with eating disorders such as obesity and anorexia at the extreme ends (Probyn 2000, 2008). What concerns me here is the large middle of this problematic, whereby, for increasing numbers of children, food is a source of anxiety, fed by ignorance. This situation is exacerbated – if not produced – by the endless stream of injunctions directed at their parents, teachers and, more generally, the larger public. We could conduct an endless deconstruction of the expert disciplinary power at work in creating this discursive context. But I am saddened by studies that report on the extent of children's ignorance about where food comes from and what to do with it.

Consider these morsels from the mouths of babes:

> Rhubarb is like carrots, it's what kangaroos eat. Sometimes it grows on trees without any seeds.

> A lemon is from Birmingham and it grows in the ground. A kiwi is from Jamaica.

> White bread is made from milk but brown bread is from wheat.
> (cited in Sigman 2007)

> 60% of schoolchildren thought that potatoes grew on trees, while 11% of 8-year olds don't know the origin of pork chops.
> (www.soilassociation.org)

At one level these ideas are beautifully inventive, a taxonomy of food production that is so different that it beguiles. But placed in the bigger picture they begin to paint a depressing picture of a total disconnection from nature that speaks to an impoverishment of experience.

How to talk about taste?

> Taste is not only a part and index of morality, it is the only morality. The first, and last, and closest trial question to any living creature is 'What do you like?' Tell me what you like, I'll tell you what you are.
> (John Ruskin 1858)

While discussion of children's eating habits is rarely couched in terms of taste, there is a pervasive idea that children like things that are bad for them. In a recent paper by Italian nutritionists this is given scientific weight. Apparently humans have 'genetically determined predispositions to like sweet and salty and to dislike bitter and sour tastes' (Scaglioni et al. 2008: 522). The authors argue that parents who try to restrict or to pressure their children 'may contribute to childhood overweight'; the key to success lies in giving children opportunities for more self-control. However, the possibility for self-control is widely thought to be undermined by those bad entities such as fast-food chains, which promote bad eating habits by encouraging children – through inevitably nefarious means – to like the taste of bad things. This creates a corporate monster called 'pester power'. On paper it may be easy to dismiss its power and to mock Ronald McDonald. But I'm sure that many a tired mother has given up the unequal battle faced with kids screaming for 'Happy Meals'. And according to another nutritional study, it doesn't help if the kids are just going to their friends' homes: 'the percentage of food energy from fat was above the recommended 35% at other people's homes' (Burke et al. 2007). 'Other people's homes' is further imbued with menace. As if 'stranger danger' were not scary enough, now they're feeding your kids bad fat.

The notion that food that is supposedly bad for us tastes better goes deeper than the slogans of fast-food corporations, although they may benefit. Researchers in health education and behaviour have found that connotations of healthiness tend to be a consumer turn-off. In an experimental study, Jane Wardle and Gail Huon discovered that when they presented a new health drink and a new drink without any health qualification to children, they had far fewer positive responses about the health drink. Their recommendation is that 'parents should especially avoid invoking healthiness when a child is refusing or disliking a food' (2000: 43). To reframe Ruskin's phrase, what we *don't* like to eat seems to identify our very being. And as anyone who has tried to rationally counter the refrain of 'I don't like that' knows, it does little good to argue that if you haven't tasted it how do you know? As the quotations from children cited above attest, it seems that a lack of knowledge about foodstuffs and their preparation has become the norm. Or rather, as other health researchers argue, the widespread deploring of 'deficient' knowledge about food and eating always supposes a normative standard (Caraher et al. 2004).

Screening fat panic

That normative standard of general knowledge is becoming ever more difficult to locate, as we are continually overwhelmed with information and injunctions about eating. This is creating a situation where taste is becoming the only morality. As Jean Anthelem Brillat-Savarin's over-cited aphorism puts it: 'Tell me what you eat, and I will tell you what you are.' More to the point, the Swedish anthropologist Björn Kjellgren argues, 'we are what we have the means to eat' (2004: 14).

In the words of the French sociologist Pierre Bourdieu, 'taste classi-fies'. While to some extent eating practices have long been an index of one's social standing, tastes and diets have now become the stuff of shame, shaming and contempt. The latest sub-genre on television stages a meeting of Weight-Watchers with *Big Brother*. *The Biggest Loser*, now franchised around the world, is surreal to watch. Contestants are housed together, continually tempted by 'bad' food, and the pinnacle of emotion (in porn-speak, the 'money shot') comes with the weigh-in as each contestant mounts the blue flashing scales to have their cur-rent weight and how much they have lost or gained shown on a huge screen.

The cluster of emotions generated by this televisual form of classifying ranges from pathos to disgust. Two separate clips from the unofficial. com website demonstrate how surreal reality has become. One adver-tises itself as a *Biggest Loser* parody, produced by 'Dirty Taint', a small independent crew of filmmakers. It hangs on the song 'I'm Fat' by 'Weird Al' Yanovik from his 1988 'Even Worse' album. 'Weird Al' is certainly very strange. A takeoff of Michael Jackson's 'I'm bad', Weird Al's video shows a skinny white kid in a hoodie being confronted by very large black guys in black leather who taunt the white dude with pizza and doughnuts, singing 'the question is are you fat or what?' Al transforms into (a white) Michael Jackson with his own gang, and then, to the horror of all, he transmogrifies into a hugely obese version of Jackson, singing:

> Your butt is wide, well mine is too.
> Just watch your mouth or I'll sit on you.
> The word is out, better treat me right.
> 'Cause I'm the king of cellulite.
> Ham on, ham on, ham on whole wheat, all right.
> My zippers bust, my buckles break.
> I'm too much man for you to take.
> The pavement cracks when I fall down.
> I've got more chins than Chinatown...

You would think that it would be hard to rival Weird Al's parody of Jackson, and the *Biggest Loser* 'parody' turns out to be fairly tame by comparison. It features a young, large, white woman auditioning for the show. She gets out of bed and immediately eats pizza. Brushing her teeth she alternates between toothbrush and chocolate bar. She goes for a run only to collapse while smoking a cigarette. The parody, of course, plays on the stupidity of the TV show and is filled with a knowingness about how bad it all is: the contestants on the *Biggest Loser*, the show itself, Michael Jackson, Weird Al... the list goes on.

In contrast, the real casting tape is just sad. A young, white, American female nurse from Florida is obviously desperate to be on the show and to lose weight for her school reunion. Her sister films the audition tape and, to the young woman's constant degradation of herself, her sister tells how sexy she is. The theme of bad comes back as she is filmed with a glass of normal milk (good) and a carton of chocolate milk (bad). The chocolate milk wins out. She is filmed in a swimsuit and bathrobe drinking it, and as her sister says, she does look sexy. However, that shot is followed with deep self-loathing. Seated on a chair she calls herself 'the human elephant'. Trying to cross her legs she wails, 'I can't sit like a lady. I sit like a dude and that's disgusting.'

The *Biggest Loser* consistently delivers big ratings. In Australia last year's finale and weigh-in scored the highest in every demographic. The combination of competition and emotion revolving around the very common problem of how to lose weight obviously attracts viewers across age, location and gender. It has spawned others, such as the truly bizarre *Fat Teens Can't Hunt*. Produced by Cheetah Television, a sidekick of *Big Brother* producer Endemol, it features 'ten overweight teenagers [who] will embark on the adventure of a lifetime when they adopt a hunter-gatherer lifestyle in the Australian outback.' (www.endemoluk.com) According to their website:

> It tackles head on the ticking time bomb that is the UK's obesity problem.... For these ten teenagers Fat Tens Can't Hunt is a chance to understand and conquer their destructive relationship with food in an extraordinary and demanding environment.
>
> (accessed 20 April 2008)

As the Australian Aboriginal Labor politician Warren Mundine comments, 'it's so insulting it's almost funny. Here's big fat civilized people coming down to frolic with the natives. I just find that almost hilarious' (www.smh.com.au 2007). While Aboriginal Australians continue to have an expected lifespan that is 20 years less than non-Aboriginals, it's hard to know where to start in listing how offensive the concept of this programme is. Compared to *Fat Teens*, another of Cheetah/Endemol's offerings is merely strange. Airing in January 2008, *Supersize vs Superskinny* pairs the obese and the anorexic in a 'diet swap', and asks: 'Will they discover that they are both putting their health in danger with their current diet and lifestyle?' (www.endomoluk.com, acessed 22 April 2008).

Kids and class

My point is not to bemoan how tasteless current television is. Rather, I use these examples to sketch part of the context in which youth eating needs to be understood. But we mustn't overestimate the role of popular culture as all-determining. While the emotional manipulation and the ways in which television shows such as the ones I've described add to an emotionally charged culture of eating, they are but one factor in many. Popular culture is, of course, an important context, which offers frames of reference about eating and weight issues. And it injects into the public realm scenarios about eating, which involve heavily charged negative emotions. These meet other representations that constitute moral tales about food and eating, such as *Supersize Me* and *Mum and Dad Don't Supersize Me*, or *Fast Food Nation*. These tend towards a fairly simplistic view of the food system, where the individual faces off against the big bad fast-food corporations. In the case of *Fast Food Nation* the tenor is one of guilt-inducement, with the onus on the plight of migrant workers. The depictions inside the meat-processing factory are enough to turn anyone into a vegetarian, but this doesn't do much for opening young people's minds and palates to discovering other tastes. The choice becomes a moral one rather than a point of curiosity and pleasure.

Many might say that it is the family who should be responsible for introducing their children to different foods and tastes and for ensuring they eat well. Bourdieu argues that our educational and family backgrounds are incorporated into what he calls habitus:

> The habitus, a product of history produces individual and collective practices – more history – in accordance with the schemes generated by history ... [the habitus] ensures the active presence of past experiences, which, deposited in each organism in the form of schemes of perception, thought and action, tend to guarantee the 'correctness' of practices ... more reliably than all formal rules and explicit norms.
>
> (1990: 54)

Bourdieu uses this term to designate how objective social structures such as class become part of how we orient ourselves in the world – our dispositions to life-choices. The family gives us our primary habitus, which although it may be altered over a lifetime nonetheless remains pivotal to how we experience taste. In Bourdieu's words, 'to discover something to one's taste is to discover oneself, to discover what one wants... what one had to say and didn't know how to say and, consequently, didn't know' (1993: 108).

If this sounds complex it is because taste formation is increasingly fraught. On the one hand, we have a public sphere filled with contradictory messages. We have perhaps too much information about what's good for us and what's bad. And on the other, as we found out in a study of Australian young people,[1] kids feel bombarded with expert opinion. The anxiety about eating disorders spread by educational and health experts mean that young girls especially are hyper-aware of the dangers of eating disorders. This meets the more recent attention to overweight and obesity, with proposals that school children should be weighed. Then there is the peer pressure of youth culture in terms of what's cool and where it's cool to hang out – the food court of shopping centres is a favoured locale for school kids.

Several sociologists of consumption have argued that too much choice leads to anxiety. Alan Warde and his colleagues review what they call 'the problem of variety' (Warde et al. 1999). They start from the observation that 'one highly consequential feature of contemporary commodity culture is the enormous variety of cultural items in circulation' (ibid.: 106). Their particular interest is whether this characteristic 'omnivorousness' towards cultural choice equates to a lessening of social and class distinction. In a large-scale interview survey of British eating habits entitled *The Nation's Diet*, they found that the middle class had a wider repertoire about eating and food. While not greatly surprising, the reason behind it is interesting: 'If knowledge of food is an element in middle-class social competence, then it is probably largely because it is a topic of conversation... it is a form of communication that can be re-visited in conversation' (Murcott 1998: 122).

Succinctly this raises a number of issues about children's eating practices and tastes. The research I've cited and the examples from popular culture form a world-view where too much is on offer and anxieties loom large. 'Choices' come in unpalatable forms: public humiliation, the desire to emulate impossible cultural ideals, the dazzling array of fast food that lines every high street and byway. But for all this choice, it seems the cultural capital that actually accrues from being able to distinguish only serves the middle class.

In a recent issue of *Soundings*, Jonathan Rutherford attempts to depict the current form of the culture of capitalism, asking: 'how are new technologies and new modes of production transforming the cultures and social relations of class?' (2008: 8). He charts the well-known story of the rise of neo-liberalism from Thatcher to New Labour, arguing that 'new capitalism is extending commodification into the realms of subjective life'. While not a novel argument, Rutherford (ibid.: 14) reminds us of the stark figures that underlie 'the promises of economic success and the pleasures of consumption [which] casts a veil over the inequalities' of contemporary Britain – and elsewhere. The facts are grim and jar with the vaunted benefits of 'creative economies' and knowledge nations. 'One in six leaves school unable to read, write or add up properly.' The fastest growing sector is the low paid and potentially unhealthy employment of the data input and call centre sectors. Half the population shares 6 per cent of UK wealth. The social context is splintered, with no clear allegiance to a culture shared by the working class, migrants, the second or third generation of migrants, white poor, the working poor, single mothers, etc. As Rutherford (ibid.: 14) puts it, 'The culture of capitalism has depoliticized class while heightening the inequalities and social gulf between classes'.

Rutherford (ibid.: 16) argues that 'the question of hope is bound to the question of how to live'. In the context of such poignancy and an overarching picture of gloom it may seem trivial to talk about food. And yet it is precisely in terms of eating, food choice and supply that the realities hit home. The Low Income Diet and Nutrition Survey commissioned by the Food Standards Agency (2007) surprisingly did not find huge differences in actual nutritional intake between the poor and the middle class. However, they did find a considerable desire for change, understood as out of the hands of individuals:

> 30% of men and 29% of women reported that price/value/money available for food was the most important influence on their choice of food. Thirty-five percent of men and 44% of women wanted to change their diet. 60% of parents/carers wanted to change their children's diet.

Growing change

How can we intervene and change the seemingly intractable problem of cultural influence, choice, class and monetary restrictions, and children's eating habits? Governments around the world turn to 'solutions', such as taxes on junk food and banning advertisements for fast food during prime time. Motivated by logics of restriction and surveillance, these measures cannot promote change in any meaningful way. Much more promising are the different initiatives around the world, which place child obesity within the context of the production and consumption of food. As we shall see, they are not without limitations, which I address as I describe three programmes taken from Australia, the United States and France.

In 2001 one of Australia's most respected cooks and food writers, Stephanie Alexander, set up her Kitchen Garden Foundation in the working-class suburb of Collingwood, near Melbourne, Victoria. It works by embedding growing and cooking within primary schools. Since then it has expanded to take in 27 schools in the state of Victoria and has encouraged the Federal government to emulate its model around Australia. As Alexander says:

> To see them digging, planting and firming in seedlings they have propagated, and carefully watering and mulching, is to see future citizens aware of the need to care for the earth responsibly, together with the knowledge of how to grow some of their own food. To see these same children rolling their own delicate pasta, shredding silver beet leaves or pounding broad beans to make a dip, is to see future citizens fully aware of the value and flavours of fresh ingredients and of the pleasure in sharing food with others around the table.
>
> (www.kitchengardenfoundation.org.au,
> accessed 4 May 2008)

In the US the Farm-to-School programme started in 2003 as a pilot project at schools in lower socio-economic areas. 'Instead of the classic lecture on why students should eat five fruits and vegetables a day, the students were presented with a box of fruits and vegetables that had been ... picked the previous day and dropped off at the classroom by a farmer' (Vallianatos et al. 2004: 414). The plan works under the rubric of Community Supported Agriculture in the Classroom, whereby the schools subscribe for the boxes, allowing farmers a small but reliable source of income. It purports to be an 'effort to establish change in the food system as a whole' by guaranteeing local and edge-of-metropolitan farmers an income, and introducing fresh produce into the lives of poorer children, their parents and teachers. One of the immediate problems that the programme encountered was a lack of adequate kitchen and storage facilities at schools and widespread ignorance about how to prepare meals from fresh produce.

In France, where the mere possibility of overweight children is taken as a sign of national shame, a collective of mayors set up a programme with the acronym EPODE: Ensemble nous prevenons l'obesité des enfants (Together we will prevent childhood obesity). The key tenets are close connections between farmers and producers and schools, and supervised walking or cycling trips from home to school. Towns in France have to compete to be part of the programme and the accent is on inclusion, bringing together supermarkets, schools, parents, farmers, markets, etc. What seems to happen is that a web of information and support spreads across the town, and the effects of increased knowledge among the schoolchildren is passed on to their families. Compared to the other programmes, it seems to do the most to make the production and consumption of food part of the school learning, rather than being an add-on, extracurricular activity. The results have been good – less obesity in children and their parents – and it has been taken up in South Australia, which is coincidentally a leading wine- and food-producing state in Australia.

What these programmes all try to offer is a way of thinking about food and eating as a continuum, which goes from production through to preparation and consumption. They differ from the grandiose but often shortsighted programmes often offered by governments. For instance, compared to their aspirations the British government's response seems slight and even small-minded. Despite the enormous hype provided by Jamie Oliver's television programmes to both the issue of school dinners and to growing one's own food, the UK government came up with an additional funding to authorities for school dinners of £240 million for 2008–11 (www.schoolfoodtrust.org.uk). This comes to a fairly small amount but, more importantly, it came with a plethora of restrictions, which meant that it cannot be used to promote healthy eating or to train staff in different ways of preparing food. It does nothing to bring children into the food system or to learn about its different facets.

The omission of a systematised kitchen garden programme in British schools seems especially strange given the UK's flourishing network of farmers' markets. Seemingly in response to the takeover of the food system by supermarkets and superstores, the food scene in the UK is becoming schizophrenic, with half the population shopping for locally grown produce or producing their own food and the other half buying two-for-the-price-of-one chickens for a fiver. In William Skidelsky's (2006) words:

All this has caused a stereotype to emerge of Britain as a two-tier nation with the proles gorging themselves on fried chicken and the middle classes shopping at farmers' markets. It doesn't matter that this picture only vaguely relates to reality; in some sense, increasingly, it's what we believe.

Breaking down food classes

We certainly seem to be increasingly class-stratified by what we eat. The question is: how do we break through these solidified notions? Polly Toynbee (2004), writing in the *Guardian*, argues that 'it is inequality and disrespect that makes people fat'. While there is an obvious correlation between class and, more importantly poverty, and obesity, middle-class moralising to the middle class may not be the way forward. And increasingly the middle class is also being fingered within the obesity panic. In 2007,

> researchers from the Institute of Child Health at University College London and Great Ormond Street Hospital reported that obesity increases in direct correlation with family income. And in higher-income households the longer the mother works each week, the greater the chances of her child being overweight.
>
> (Davies 2007)

Perhaps it is time that we move from polemics and the obsessions with the consumption end of food. It is becoming clear that the food system is much more complicated than the western-led debates about consumption have framed it. While the onus of the morality that accompanies most discussion about eating and obesity has come to rest on the embattled figure of the child, young people constitute a resource for thinking about the future of eating. It is simplistic to deny the effects of encouraging them into the food system by painting this alternative as a solely middle-class concern. The structural impediments to getting kids into growing are not to be underestimated. The rampant privatisation of school properties has turned potential fields into concrete schoolyards, which are hard to turn into gardens. Nonetheless getting children into the production of food that they will cook and eat offers the only one of the few viable ways of opening up worlds of taste.

Note

1. E. Probyn and J. O'Dea, 'Youth cultures of eating'. A three-year quantitative and qualitative study of primary and high school children's attitudes towards food. Funded by the Australian Research Council, 2004–7.

References

Bourdieu, P. (1990) *In Other Words: Essays Towards a Reflexive Sociology*, trans. M. Adamson (Stanford, CA: Stanford University Press).

Bourdieu, P. (1993) 'The metamorphosis of tastes', in *Sociology in Question*, trans. R. Nice (London: Sage).

Burke, S. J., McCarthy, S. N., O'Neill, J. L., Hannon, E. M., Flynn, A. and Gibney, M. J. (2007) 'An examination of the influence of eating location n the diets of Irish children', *Public Health Nutrition* 10: 599–607.

Caraher, M., Baker, H. and Burns, M. (2004) 'Children's views of cooking and food preparation', *British Food Journal* 106(4): 255–73.

Davies, C. (2007) 'Middle class fuelling child obesity', *Daily Telegraph*, 23 July.

Food Standards Agency (2007) *Low Income Diet and Nutrition Survey* (London: Food Standards Agency).

Kjellgren, B. (2004) 'Drunken modernity: wine in China', *Anthropology of Food* 3, http://aof.revues.org/document249.htlm, accessed 16 July 2008.

Marc, R. and Marc, J. (2008) *Please Mum, Don't Supersize Me!* PleaseMumDontSupersizeMe.com & Marc Wellness International.

Murcott, A. (ed.) (1998) *The Nation's Diet: the Social Science of Food Choice* (Longman: London).

Probyn, E (2000) 'Eating disgust, feeding shame', in *Carnal Appetites: Foodsexidentities* (New York and London: Routledge).

Probyn, E (2008) 'Fat, feeling, bodies: critical approaches to obesity', in H. Malson and M. Burns (eds) *Critical Feminist Approaches to Eating Dis/Orders* (London: Psychology Press).

Ruskin, J. (1866) *The Crown of Wild Olive: Three Lectures on Work, Traffic and War* (London: Smith Elder).

Rutherford, J. (2008) 'The culture of capitalism', *Soundings* 38: 8–18.

Scaglioni, S., Salvioni, M. and Galimberti, C. (2008) 'Influence of parental attitudes in the development of children eating behaviour', *British Journal of Nutrition* 99 (Suppl 1): 522–5.

Sigman, A. (2007) *Agricultural Literacy: Giving Concrete Children Food for Thought* (London: EdComs/YOFF).

Skidelsky, W. (2006) 'Making a meal of it', *New Statesman*, London, 19 June.

Swift, J ([1729]1999) *A Modest Proposal*. Renascence Editions (Eugene, OR: University of Oregon).

Toynbee, P (2004) 'Inequality is fattening', *The Guardian*, 24 May.

Vallianatos, M., Gottlieb, R. and Haase, M. A. (2004) 'Farm-to-school: strategies for urban health, combating sprawl, and establishing a community food standards approach', *Journal of Planning Education and Research* 23: 414–23.

Warde, A., Martens, L. and Olsen, W. (1999) 'Consumption and the problem of variety: cultural omnivorousness, social distinction and dining out', *Sociology* 33(1): 105–27.

Wardle, J. and Huon, G. (2000) 'An experimental investigation of the influence of health information on children's taste preferences', *Health Education Research* 15(1): 39–44.

Wittkowsky, G. (1943) 'Swift's modest proposal: the biography of an early Georgian pamphlet', *Journal of the History of Ideas* 4(1): 75–104.

Filmography

Fast Food Nation, dir. Richard Linklater, BBC Films, 2006.
Supersize Me, dir. Morgan Spurlock, Kathbur Pictures, 2004.

7
Commentary: Imagining Bodies

Sue Ruddick

Cartographies of the flesh

It was Michel Foucault who suggested that the flesh was first 'pinned to the body' in the sixteenth century. At the time, the Church moved from interrogating sin through the *intentions* of the sinner to interrogating the sinner's relationship to his or her own body. The body itself was modulated, made guilty through a vast and complex cartography. This development signalled the resurgence of a diagram of power in which subjects were conditioned *through* their bodies. It complemented the simultaneous emergence of the body as a site of training, and a more generalised governance through populations (although we can find evidence of the production of citizenry through bodily training in earlier times). The narrow focus on these polarities of the flesh – simultaneously disciplined and guilty – was organised through a vast architecture: confessionals, barracks, schools, hospitals. Through the eighteenth and nineteenth centuries this *dispositif* focused more narrowly still on the child's body as a more intense object of scrutiny. It linked childhood illness to a newfound children's culpability: an idea at the time that childhood consumption or tuberculosis arose from the child's natural tendency to an illicit sexuality. This shift extended the arena of scrutiny beyond institutions, bringing into its disciplinary orbit the family, the bed, the household.

I begin with these observations because they mark a sequence of events that still resonate in the constitution of subjects *through* their bodies. Of course, we are no longer confronted solely with an overly inquisitive Church. Our sense of our own subjectivity, ourselves, is entangled in a fleshy cartography, which proliferates through a multiplicity of sites. Through these sites we are governed and disciplined, and within them – as the preceding chapters demonstrate – children's bodies have become a central organising principle.

The body of the child, and the sites through which it is produced, as the contributors suggest, resonate in complex ways through the constellation of technologies which govern the population at large. Sometimes these sites act by stealth; sometimes they operate in plain sight, in disciplinary schema that act like a connective tissue between a range of discourses which have been mobilised in the service of contemporary liberalism. Here the idea of child development anticipates and enacts arguments about economic development. We also confront new iterations of the idea of an inherently wayward children's 'nature' which must be corrected through exposure to the redeeming features of 'Nature'. And sometimes the child functions as a kind of absent presence within larger constructs, a disciplinary trope for the adult world in so far as qualities of child-likeness, or youthfulness, are revered, but actual living breathing children and youth are reviled.

These disciplinary practices do not form a coherent whole, but rather a shifting kaleidoscope of registers – a multiplication of schema through which we are striated. And so, appropriately, the chapters vary in focus from minute practices through site-specific assemblages, to pervasive tropes. Rather than treat each chapter in turn I shall address them through connecting themes and subtexts, logics that run through and animate them sometimes made explicit and sometimes implicit in the treatment.

Fat – the new pornography

Although Foucault was careful to note that the confessional was focused not solely on sexuality but on a whole host of misdemeanors, it is curious in our contemporary dealings with children and adults how fat has become the *sine qua non* marker of indecency. The presumed wayward nature of children, which, Foucault suggests, was fixated in the eighteenth and nineteenth centuries on illicit sexuality, on onanism (masturbation), has migrated, perhaps because the contemporary emergence of a secondary disciplinary figure – the paedophile – renders any admission of child sexuality problematic. Contemporary moral panics no longer focus on the sexuality of children, except in relation to predation.

The logic and structure of governance that it expressed has not disappeared, however; it has merely been relocated. The old constellation of tubercular illness/onanism in which children are positioned by nature to be architects of their own illness has been abandoned in favour of a new pairing: obesity/predisposition to junk food, with fat (as we shall see) replacing sex as the new pornography. Practices of shaming and blaming, central to the constitution of a guilty flesh, have migrated from a focus on sexuality (in our relatively liberal sexual times) to obesity as the new sin, with a moral calculus based on degrees of fatness, from merely overweight to morbidly obese.

This connection is revealed in Probyn's argument about the new array of 'bad food' television programmes such as the *Biggest Loser*. Here, as she observes, the contestants are housed in a 'Big Brother'-style community under constant surveillance. This sets the viewer up to participate in the shameful and titillating moment in which contestants are weighed on camera, or as Probyn so succinctly puts it, 'in porn speak, the money shot'. We might consider, reading Probyn's piece against Grogan's, that fat – at least the idea of fat as shameful – is a recent innovation since fat was once a marker of wealth, success and command, expressed in the full-figured bodies of men and women of the Edwardian bourgeoisie. Moreover it is a recent construct only in the West: fat persists in some countries, particularly on the African continent, as signifying health, set against the presumption of HIV/AIDS marked outwardly by thinness.

The couplet nature/Nature

A second component of this construct is the idea that a child by nature is somehow unruly and, if left untrained, will diverge from the path of appropriate development. The couplet nature/Nature is a feature of Probyn's chapter – the idea that children by nature are drawn to improper eating habits and the idea that children's nature can also be redeemed by Nature, with all its ironic consequences. Here children are returned to 'Nature' to relearn their relationship to their bodies, even as indigenous populations in that same Nature starve. In Well's chapter the nature/Nature couplet is rendered differently: we are invited to consider both the child's distance from and proximity to a kind of nature. This is a Cartesian framing of nature in which every species knows, or eventually learns, its place. Well's analysis of Disney's *Tarzan* uncovers a Cartesian residual of hierarchised others in which the (white male) child in proximity to 'nature' rediscovers his own distance and difference from that nature.

Governing through the child: absent presence and reservoir

If children themselves are governed through the flesh, it is also through 'the child' that the rest of the population is often governed, either as an idealised construct or a reservoir for unpopular or politically incorrect points of view. Grogan shows us that the absent presence of a kind of idealised child (or at the very least androgynously youthful slender body) operates to govern not only female children, but also young and adult women. And Wells demonstrates that even as the child is positioned explicitly, at times, as an organising site for a host of wider disciplinary practices, the child and activities associated with children continue to function as a kind of reserve for regressive discourses. Thus racialised tropes – apparently excoriated in a so-called post-racial society – nevertheless remain active in children's cartoons. Here, as Well's notes, the simultaneous rendering of the African continent as empty, and populated with animal stand-ins for racialised others, becomes a landscape wherein racialised tropes can persist. The seeming insignificance of sites of children's entertainment – games, films and such – belie the crucial role that they play in the constitution of consciousness, a point Well's drives home in her subsequent analysis of the positioning of the racialised animal 'side-kick' (such as the Donkey in *Shrek*). Children's cartoons function not simply as a residue, a hold-over from a less enlightened past, nor as a neutral ground that trades on the currency of the child's world as a space of innocence and play, one unrelated to the troubles of the adult world. This space is also a reservoir, a cache that allows racialised and other oppressive discourses to persist, animates them and activates them in the child's imagination, by stealth.

Surfaces sites and assemblages

Clearly, the body can be many things at once. We see it as a collection of fragments, any one (or several) of which can surface through a complex assemblage to overdetermine or over-code how the rest of the body is read. Probyn suggests, for instance, how a whole moral economy on the comportment of children emerges from the surface of the tongue – a set of presumptions around the way children taste. Probyn is careful to locate this construct within a larger constellation of constitutive practices: the difficulties in poorer neighborhoods to gain access to good food, the relentless pressures of the fast food industry, the ways food itself functions in a production of habitus overdetermined by class.

At the same time body fat (the presumed result of improper taste) is harnessed to a complex of spatialised behaviours, an entire assemblage. As Alexander notes, this fuses a range of corporeal excesses: fat bodies, modes of dress, manners of speech and forbidden places whereby, in the policing of young women in Newcastle upon Tyne, restrictive legislations and electronic tagging map 'a visible material layer onto their already "risky bodies"'. Taken together, these chapters raise questions about the new and pernicious ways in which liberalism's narratives about economic development and the corporeal development of young people have become fused: a fit, flexible and disciplined body presages adaptability to shifting markets, the capacity to withstand risk and an assumption of responsibility for health.

These insights themselves provide clues as to how the terrain of contestation must be negotiated. It is not enough to take up bodily constructs on their own terms; one must reimagine an entire panoply of practices. Thus the successful contestation of childhood or adult obesity cannot be limited to practices at the scales, or at the table or in the kitchen where food is prepared (although this narrative is most readily invoked). It must reimagine the relationship between farmer and city, between market and consumer, and contest the limits of distance whereby poorer communities struggle to access fresh and wholesome foods. Cultures of obsessive slimness can better be countered by refocusing the desire to discipline and control the body on exercises, which enhance a sense of well-being. Challenges to racialised tropes and other stereotypes in children's marketed entertainment must do more than simply confront these renderings; they must contend with the ways in which such renderings are harnessed to and invoked through pleasurable activities – the artistic beauty of images, the comfort of certainty found in children's stories. Alexander focuses on a complex interplay of practices that constrain young women's lives in Newcastle: the intersection of media stereotypes (Vicky Pollard and chavers) with practices of criminal sentencing, the imposition of Anti-Social Behaviour Orders and spatial control of young women through wearing of electronic ankle tags. Alexander provides us with insights into the ways a myriad of constrictions of these bodies play into a larger project of reshaping city spaces – in this case the creation of 'chav-free zones'.

Here strategies of contestation become complicated through multiple narratives – in this case of class and gender. Alexander's account reminds us that strategies of contestation can sometimes feed into the very structures they seek to challenge. Thus young women in Newcastle attempt to look 'hard' and hang out in groups in an attempt to blend in to the local neighbourhood and avoid the very real threat of physical violence. Their challenge to the weakness implied in conventional gender roles, their adoption of a gender-ambiguous style, is precisely the strategy that contributes to their criminalisation as it intersects uneasily with a dominant narrative that disparages working-class culture. These young women face a Catch-22: victimised in conventional gender roles and criminalised in attempts to circumvent them. Interestingly, however, their challenges are oblique rather than direct: new lines of flight if you will. They foster intergenerational contacts, collaborations with seniors groups, and initiate projects to give back to the neighbourhood. They chose to re-script their image on their own terms, rather than capitulate to dominant constructs.

Together, these chapters remind us that even as we are pinned through our bodies, contestation must be more than a bodily affair. It must confront a complex array of institutions and practices through which the body is made flesh, and through which the subject becomes located in specific ways.

Part II
Disciplining Bodies

Part II:

Imagining Bodies

8
Embodied Childhood in the Health-promoting School

Jo Pike and Derek Colquhoun

Introduction

In the UK over recent years, the issue of childhood obesity has dominated the public health agenda with a proliferation of government policies and initiatives aimed at stemming the year-on-year increase in childhood obesity and overweight. Underpinning much of these efforts is an approach which centres on modifying the lifestyles of individuals and which has been widely critiqued by academics for some time (Crawford 1986, Naidoo 1986, Rodmell and Watt 1986, Kickbusch 1989, Colquhoun and Robottom 1990). Attempts at lifestyle modification are regarded as explicitly rooted in a victim-blaming ethos, accompanied by a moral evangelism which demonises those whose bodies fail to conform to expected norms (Evans 2006, Leahy 2009). Conversely, health promotion literature has stressed the role that structural factors, such as the environment, play in contributing to health outcomes (Naidoo 1986, Dahlgren and Whitehead 1991). Health geographers have also extended their analysis beyond the immediate environment to explore the ways in which space relates to embodied experiences of health and illness (Parr and Butler 1999, Moss and Dyck 2002). Others have proposed the concept of the 'obesogenic' environment to explore the effects of the physical environment on children's bodies (Egger and Swinburn 1997, Lake and Townsend 2006).

This chapter explores the relationship between childhood obesity, bodies and space, drawing on experiences from a three-year trans-European project, 'Shape Up', which ran from 2005 to 2008. The project worked with children and young people aged 4–16 years in schools in 20 European cities, funded by the European Commission Directorate General for Health and Consumer Affairs (DG Sanco) within its public health strand. 'Shape Up' adopted a positive, holistic approach to health, aiming to engage children in addressing the wider structural determinants of obesity, particularly through enacting environmental changes. In presenting experiences from this project, we acknowledge the importance of environmental and spatial factors in influencing health and welcome a departure from traditional biomedical and individualistic lifestyle approaches. Nevertheless, we maintain a critical perspective, suggesting that, while the project succeeded in enacting changes in health-related behaviour at the individual level and, to a lesser extent, changes to the physical environment at the school level, very little impact on the determinants of health was discerned beyond children's individual bodies and immediate environment. We suggest that this is of interest on two counts. First, that in failing to move beyond individualistic lifestyle interventions, health projects continue to position children's bodies as passive, malleable, 'bodies at risk'. This may be problematic if we consider the need for children's participation or authentic engagement a priority for future policy development in this area. Second, that a focus on children's bodies exclusively within the school environment continues to advance an approach which sees children as disconnected from the macro-level forces which shape their lives at the local level. Children's embodied subjectivity is isolated from the social, cultural and environmental contexts through which subjective experiences are made tangible.

In conclusion, we call for a more nuanced understanding of space that attempts to address the tensions between the macro-level forces shaping the structural determinants of health and the micro-spaces of children's day-to-day embodied existence.

Childhood obesity

Across Europe and much of the developed world, obesity has emerged as one of the most significant issues for public health policy in a generation. Globally, an estimated 1.2 billion people are classified as overweight, of whom 300 million are categorised as obese (Butland et al. 2007). Adult obesity rates in the UK have doubled in the last 25 years and childhood obesity is increasing. In 2004 around 10 per cent of children aged 6–10 years were classified as obese. It is predicted that by 2050 around 25 per cent of people under 20 years could be obese while 50 per cent of adult women and 60 per cent of adult men could also be classified as obese (Butland et al. 2007). These trends are consistent across Europe and such is the level of concern over the associated detrimental health effects of childhood obesity that the European Commission has responded with alacrity to attempt to avert an emerging public health crisis, launching the EU platform on Diet, Physical Activity and Health in 2005. The increase in childhood obesity is concomitant with a rapid proliferation of policies and interventions aimed at halting the year-on-year rise in childhood obesity. Consequently, the medical and policy gaze has been firmly directed towards the measurement, assessment and scrutiny of children's bodies in an almost unprecedented way.

This upsurge in interest has not escaped the attention of academics, some of whom have questioned the extent of the 'obesity epidemic' (Gard and Wright 2005, Evans 2006, Cole 2007) or 'obesity hysteria' (Pike and Colquhoun, 2007) and challenged the use of the body mass index (BMI, weight in kilograms divided by height in metres squared) as a monitoring/surveillance/diagnostic tool (Campos 2004, Ross 2005). Others have noted the tendency to equate overweight with obesity in public health literature (Courtnay Botterill 2006). The issue of measurement is not uncontroversial, and while a full discussion of this debate is beyond the scope of this chapter, suffice to say that the issue becomes increasingly complex in relation to the assessment of childhood obesity and the ability to compare rates of prevalence across international borders. The standard definition of childhood overweight and obesity are different from those of adults. BMI is used, but children are classified as overweight or obese according to their position on a BMI percentile chart taking account of their age and gender. In spite of an acknowledged difficulty in the classification and monitoring of childhood obesity (Flegal et al. 2006, Butland et al. 2007), anti-obesity initiatives remain a priority for many governments, for whom the existence of an obesity pandemic (Lake and Townsend 2006) is regarded as axiomatic.

There has been an exponential rise in the number of public health initiatives that attempt to treat and prevent childhood obesity. These initiatives can be loosely categorised as falling under the auspices of health education or health promotion, although some programmes attempt to combine elements of both. Health education programmes inform the public of the detrimental or positive health effects associated with particular lifestyle choices in the hope that the public will choose to modify their behaviour accordingly. The term lifestyle is generally taken to mean the behaviours and practices which individuals engage in, which are connected to particular health outcomes. Thus, teaching children about the causal link between the consumption of saturated fat and heart disease has the ultimate aim of discouraging them from consuming foods high in saturated fat. Significantly, health education

programmes aimed at children are also believed to be effective at preventing the onset of disease in adulthood, although there is little robust
evidence to support this (Flegal et al. 2006). Health promotion programmes are underpinned by a desire to empower individuals to be able
to change the determinants of health. Thus, individuals gain knowledge
and skills to be able to take action collectively to influence those factors
which contribute to particular health outcomes (WHO 1986).

In relation to childhood obesity, the health education approach
continues to dominate public health thinking in spite of numerous
criticisms. Over 20 years ago Robert Crawford (1986) alerted us to the
problems with the prevailing orthodoxy of lifestyle modification in
determining our own health. His words remain pertinent within our
current societal health consciousness. He suggested that

> we experienced a pre-occupation with personal health as a primary –
> often *the* primary – focus for the definition and achievement of per-
> sonal well being; a goal which is attained primarily through the
> modification of lifestyles… the aetiology of disease may be seen as
> complex, but healthism treats individual behaviour, attitudes and
> emotions as the relevant symptoms needing attention.
>
> (Crawford 1986: 368; original emphasis)

Here Crawford identifies a focus on individuals and their health
behaviours as problematic, suggesting that while the causes of disease
are complex, the prescribed solutions are too simplistic. There are several
things we can comment on in this statement in relation to childhood
obesity. First, perhaps because of the burgeoning influence of the medical profession on more and more areas of life, obesity is now defined
as a medical problem, especially in its more 'extreme' cases, with medical intervention considered the only way to address the 'problem' of
obesity. Second, obesity is seen as a cause of other health problems,
including type 2 diabetes, cancer and heart disease. Obese children
therefore represent a potential drain on the public purse in terms of
future expenditure on the NHS. Third, a focus on obesity as a prod-
uct of an individual's choice of 'lifestyle' is that it – or its associated
health problems – is easily 'measured', with obesity, for example, the
most common and technically easy indicator to measure, using the BMI
(Evans 2004). Fourth, despite recent suggestions that obesity is 'socially
contagious' (Christakis 2007, Blanchflower, Oswald and Landeghem
2008), one cannot 'catch' obesity and therefore the reason why people become obese, and a public spectacle according the prevailing

healthist discourse, is because of an inappropriate lifestyle or moral failing (Naidoo 1986, Lupton 1996, Evans 2004, Leahy 2009, Probyn this volume, chapter 6). Fifth, a focus on individual lifestyle in relation to childhood obesity and a preoccupation with the individual as a major determinant of personal health sees us largely concerned with behaviour change and often neglects other avenues for improving health, such as upgrading the conditions in which we live, work and play. Sixth, the debate around obesity and health in general centres on the notion of individual choice. This implies that people choose to be obese through their lifestyle and behavioural choices and individuals need to exert control and exercise responsibility in order to stay healthy. Of course, if individuals do not appear to exert self-control and willpower, then they are blamed for being unhealthy. This is what is often termed a victim-blaming approach (Naidoo 1986). The focus of blame for childhood obesity is often the parents and family of the individual child, particularly where children are deemed incapable of making rational choices (Colls and Evans 2007). Seventh, a healthy lifestyle is presented as simply a matter of 'balance'. Nowhere is this more pertinent than with obese bodies, which are produced by an imbalance between calorie intake and calories used. Eighth, as a discourse, healthism serves to depoliticise other attempts to improve health – it appears 'natural' and 'given' that individuals should take responsibility for their own health. Finally, health messages aimed at preventing and reducing obesity are reinforced in a number of ways: through schools, workplace initiatives, media campaigns and in supermarkets. According to Zola (1978), obesity is an omnipresent disorder, pervading all aspects of our lives.

It is in the context of health education-inspired understandings of and approaches to obesity that many childhood obesity programmes are implemented. For example, the MEND (Mind, Exercise, Nutrition, Do It!)[1] project, based in the UK, aims to teach children and their families how to treat and prevent childhood overweight and obesity by implementing a ten-week programme of physical activity, nutritional education and psychological motivation. Similarly, 'Watch It' in the UK is described as

> a programme that aims to motivate children and parents to lead a healthier lifestyle with the intention of addressing the child's current problems and their later risks for adult obesity. The programme is designed for children and teenagers aged 8 to 16 years and their parents, who can refer themselves or be referred by a professional.
> (Rudolph 2006: 9)

By using approaches which aim to change the health behaviours of individual children, children's bodies are represented in these programmes as works in progress, as 'becomings rather than beings' (James et al. 1998), which are nevertheless problematic in the present since they have the potential to, or are 'at risk' of, developing diseases in adulthood. Individual children and young people, and their families, are therefore held accountable for their own obese bodies and are thus responsible for the amelioration of their condition. By choosing to eat more healthily and exercise more, children will not become obese. This approach takes no account of the social, cultural and environmental contexts in which we make our lifestyle 'choices'. The spatial and structural factors that influence our day-to-day practices are overlooked as attention is directed towards individual children's bodies. However, the 'Shape Up' project attempted to address some of these broader, structural determinants of health.

'Shape Up': towards a healthy and balanced growing up

'Shape Up' arose from a concern with the dominant approaches to addressing children's health in schools across Europe and was essentially underpinned by three theoretical principles that attempted to move the project beyond the preoccupation with lifestyle and individualism that dominates current public health obesity policy. First, it was based on a positive view of health, which regarded the concept of health as something more than simply the absence of disease and which takes account of its multifaceted nature, encompassing physical, spiritual, emotional and mental, sexual and social aspects of health and well-being (Naidoo and Wills 2000). In seeking to relate childhood obesity to this broader spectrum of health, the stigmatisation of overweight and obese children would be avoided, as it was considered that improvements to physical health should not detrimentally impact on other aspects of health, such as emotional and mental well-being. Second, a focus on structural determinants of health aimed to depart from a focus on individual behaviour modification and to acknowledge the complexity of the causes of childhood obesity. This would allow for a consideration of the interplay between individual health-related behaviour and the 'obesogenic' (Egger and Swinburn 1997) nature of particular environments. Third, the principle of children's participation was regarded as a key driver for enacting health-promoting change for individuals, their schools and their local communities aiming to empower children to deliver sustainable health promoting actions.

Shape Up aimed to:

> develop children and young people's capacity to critically explore
> and improve the health-related conditions, practices and choices or
> possibilities at different levels: family, school, community, city and
> even wider.
>
> (Simovska et al. 2006: 9)

Using participatory techniques children would work within their
schools to investigate health topics and identify structural barriers to
health. They would develop ideas and action plans to tackle these
barriers and then monitor the changes that occurred as a result. By
focusing on the social and structural determinants of health, 'Shape Up'
was a very different health promotion project from those that simply
focus on individual lifestyles. It recognised that children's behaviour
occurs within a context, place, setting or environment and understood that any project addressing children's health needs to recognise
the interplay between health-related behaviour and social, cultural and
environmental contexts.

Methods

This chapter draws on data generated from the evaluation of the project,
which employed a realistic evaluation framework (Pawson and Tilley
1997) to explore the particular contexts and mechanisms that influenced specific outcomes. The overall aim of the evaluation was to assess
activities in each of the 20 cities to determine levels of children's participation and children's views of health. Nevertheless, because of the
complex nature of the project, which was implemented in line with
priorities identified by children in each city, it was important to take
account of a range of contextual factors affecting project outcomes.
In essence, the questions underpinning much of the evaluation were:
'What works, for whom and under what circumstances?' While the
evaluation used a mixture of methods, including surveys with pupils,
teachers and key stakeholders, here we present a number of thematic
reflections from case studies of cities participating in the project undertaken over the period September 2006–June 2008. Six case study cities
were selected to represent different geographical areas in north, south
and central Europe. Data-generation methods included researchers conducting observations of project activities in schools, semi-structured
interviews with teachers, pupils and key project staff, and reviewing

portfolios of evidence collected by project staff in all the cities in line with project requirements. We consider the extent to which the project was able to fulfil its objectives in relation to two central themes of food and nutrition and spatiality and regulation before proceeding to relate these to children's bodies.

Nutrition and children's bodies

In traditional approaches to obesity, food is often represented in terms of its calorific value and nutritional content. Particular foods may be categorised as healthy or unhealthy relative to their ability to cause weight gain, or as foods which should be eaten often, a little or occasionally (Food Standards Agency 2007). According to the 'Shape Up' guidelines, we do not eat nutrition; therefore, the concept of food and eating should take into account

> children and young people's perceptions concerning: the aesthetic or visual appeal of meals and the environment in which meals take place; the taste and texture of food; the social aspects of eating together or sharing a meal; accessibility and the price of fresh, organic and healthy food; the ways in which food is produced and distributed.
>
> (Simovska et al. 2006: 26)

Project staff were encouraged to work with children on a range of participatory exercises to investigate the social and aesthetic aspects of food and the production and availability of fresh produce, alongside a consideration of nutrition. Questions such as 'What is the caloric [*sic*] value of a daily meal?' are suggested in the support materials to guide discussions among young people. However, this aspect is not discussed in detail and no further guidance is given about how this comprehensive view of food and eating can be taken up by project staff beyond suggestions of questions to prompt discussions.

In reviewing the types of food-related activities undertaken in the cities, it is clear that the wider influences on food and eating were not generally covered by the project and the majority of activities involved promoting healthy eating messages to children. In case study C, children explored the concept of the Mediterranean diet and the importance of food in defining their national identity through cultural and religious festivals. However, in most other cases food-related activities were limited to the nutritional. For example, in case study A isolated events were held, including special 'vitamin days', in which children were told the benefits of eating particular fruits and vegetables, or 'no chips days', when crisps would not be sold at the school canteen (in Europe crisps are called 'chips'). Children also dressed up as cows to explain the benefits of drinking milk to other pupils and, on another occasion, dressed as carrots and gave out carrots to fellow pupils in an attempt to persuade them to eat healthier snacks. In this particular case study, it was clear that the nutritional aspects of food and eating occluded all the other elements. Furthermore, the emphasis on equipping children to distinguish between 'healthy' and 'unhealthy' food meant that children's bodies were simultaneously the target of and the vehicle through which healthier eating messages were transmitted. The dressing up of children's bodies constitutes a peculiarly embodied method of promulgating dominant discourses of nutrition. Through receiving knowledge about healthy eating, children's bodies are transformed from ignorant, at risk and potentially excessive to knowledgeable, safe and regulated.

While there is a growing trend for peer-led health initiatives, these are often restricted to the delivery of fairly simplistic messages and it is often assumed that children lack sufficient knowledge to deliver more complex information regarding food and health (Colls and Evans 2007). In some cases knowledgeable 'experts', such as public health officials and dieticians, were recruited to teach children and their parents about healthy food. In case studies A and S activities included cookery demonstrations by experts using simple recipes that parents and children could try at home and nutritionists were recruited to inform children about the nutritional content of food. This strategy positions children and their parents as responsible for the regulation of children's bodies and neglects to consider the structural influences of food producers, retailers and governments on food availability and food choices.

> Thanks to the Shape Up educational procedure, pupils were informed about what constitutes a healthy snack and how to differentiate between a nutritious and unhealthy choice...By the end of the lessons, one of the basic conclusions reached was that successful healthy eating begins at home.
>
> (PAU Education 2008: 64)

Here, there is no discussion of the social and aesthetic aspects of food, nor of issues relating to food provenance and availability. Once skills and knowledge of healthy cooking are inculcated, the assumption is that this will translate into healthy eating behaviour in the home. In short, children will demand healthier food and parents will know how to cook it. One local facilitator working on the project states that, in her city, 'We have children thinking for themselves so we can change the habits of their families' (ibid.: 58).

This notion seems at odds with the project's ethos of changing the broader environmental and structural determinants of health. Here responsibility for children's bodies rests with parents and families. As Colls and Evans (2007) point out, children are at once 'responsible for' and 'responsible as' bodies. On the one hand, they are responsible for regulating their own consumption and ultimately their body size, but they are also responsible as bodies for transmitting health messages to other children and their parents. The home is positioned as a crucial site for governing the nutritional intake of children's bodies, and parents are regarded as deficient in health knowledge without the intervention of experts. This model is predicated on an assumption that health behaviour occurs in a social and spatial vacuum, that healthy food is available locally, and that parents have the means to purchase it, the time to cook it and the means to persuade children to eat it. It represents a typical health education model which aims to correct the behaviour of individual children and their families.

Spatiality and the regulation of children's bodies

In terms of obesity, the concept of the obesogenic environment (Lake and Townsend 2006, Procter et al. 2008), defined as 'the sum of influences that the surroundings, opportunities, or conditions of life have on promoting obesity in individuals or populations' (Egger and Swinburn 1997), has been developed to explore the environmental determinants of obesity. Studies have explored the factors that influence levels of childhood obesity in order to identify 'at risk' populations (Procter et al. 2008) and thus to enable interventions to be targeted in specific geographical areas. These include assessing food access, using Geographic Information Systems mapping, tracking children's daily movements using pedometers, heart rate meters and global positioning systems, assessing barriers and enablers to physical activity and healthy food consumption, and exploring children's and young people's use of space. Lake and Townsend (2006) suggest that interventions which focus solely on individual behaviour change need to take account of environmental factors.

'Shape Up' endeavoured to do this by encouraging children to enact change within their local schools, communities and cities:

Shape Up suggests that it is of vital importance that children and young people explore and reflect upon the ways in which the living conditions, surrounding environment and society affect their health and lifestyle choices. Moreover Shape Up aims to enhance young people's awareness and capacity to change these conditions.

(Simovska et al. 2006: 16)

The most frequent change that occurred in relation to the physical environment involved opportunities for increased physical activity in school playgrounds. These included activities ranging from the purchase of playground equipment such as balls, skipping ropes and hoops in case study C, to more radical transformations of playground spaces, such as the construction of a tyre park in case study H, a nursery school playground in case study A and the construction of a Viking ship in case study D. Where major construction work took place, in every case, this was planned prior to the commencement of the project. For example, the idea for the Viking ship was 'given a new lease of life' by the 'Shape Up' project (PAU Education 2008: 41); in case study H, 'Shape Up' provided a vehicle for consultation with children over design preference for the proposed tyre park; and in all other cases, the funding provided by the project enabled work to be completed.

We do not take issue with improvements to school play spaces, particularly where children have identified this as a priority and can express their preferences in terms of equipment and design. Rather, we question the extent to which children were able to influence the determinants of health beyond the school gates in a project which envisaged changes on a much broader scale: 'family, school, community, city and even wider' (Simovska et al. 2006: 9). The Social Studies of Childhood has much to say about the construction of children as local rather than global actors, but as Holloway and Valentine (2000) point out, children's social worlds are shaped by global factors, which are made meaningful at the local level. Consequently, they reject the traditional dichotomy between the two scales. Here, a useful view of children's embodied spatiality is offered which creates the potential for understanding the ways in which macro-level forces influence children's embodied experience at a local level. While supporting this understanding of scale, we maintain that an exclusive focus on school playgrounds perpetuates a conception of children's (healthy) bodies as existing solely within the conventionally prescribed parameters of the school and the home. Thus, issues such as children's ability to use public spaces safely, for example, are not interrogated in any meaningful way through this project.

In her study of school playgrounds in the UK, Thompson (2005) notes an increasing demand on and for playground spaces as they become subject to an array of policy initiatives, particularly in relation to physical activity and healthy playtime schemes. Thompson argues that playgrounds represent a specific territory in which spatialised strategies for the control and regulation of children's bodies are practised and contested. This includes the restricting of access to certain areas of playgrounds at various times through zoning and setting boundaries, regulating the use of equipment and stipulating particular forms of appropriate bodily deportment and activity. While many commentators have noted the capacity of schools to constrain children's embodied activity using spatial strategies (Aitken 1994, James et al. 1998, Holloway and Valentine 2000), Thompson's assertion that 'the playground is, by its very nature, a unit of containment' (2005: 68) suggests that children's ability to use the new playgrounds and equipment made available through 'Shape Up' may be curtailed by adult regulation. Furthermore, her point that this curtailment is often legitimised through a discourse of health and safety reveals an interesting paradox between the need for increased physical activity or freedom of movement of children's bodies on the grounds of health, and the need to protect children's bodies from physical harm on the grounds of health and safety.

Conclusion

This chapter presents two thematic reflections on the types of activities undertaken on a children's health promotion project in Europe, which sought to depart from traditional models of health education based on individual behaviour modification. We have suggested that rather than achieving the stated aims of addressing the structural determinants of health and specifically childhood obesity, in the vast majority of cases, activities revolved around changing the health-related behaviour of individual children and regulating their bodies in a restricted spatial context. Not only does this counter the specific intentions of the project, it also shifts responsibility for children's bodies onto children's bodies. In part, we suggest that the pervasiveness of nutritional discourse in relation to food and eating, the spatially restricted nature of environmental changes and the absence of a coherent alternative model for health promotion make it difficult for the project to move beyond a focus on the lifestyles of individuals and concern for educating and regulating children's bodies.

Twenty years ago Ilona Kickbusch, one of the architects of the Ottowa Charter and one-time Director of the WHO (Europe), prefigured this discussion and called for greater theoretical insights into our understanding of health and illness. In her classic article 'Self care in health promotion' (1989), she criticised traditional healthist research:

> the [healthism] approach focuses on modification of behaviour for reasons of health rather than on enabling healthier life patterns for reasons of wellbeing. The difference is crucial, as has been outlined by Coreil et al that reminds us of the origins of the concept of lifestyle. It outlines for epidemiological notions of lifestyle research what can be stated for functionalist notions of self care research: the lack of linkages to overall sociological theory results in oversimplified, non-scrutinized use of a sociological concept, which can in the end – as has happened to the term lifestyle – turn the term into its exact opposite which gave primacy to context and meaning.
>
> (Kickbusch 1989: 126)

Of relevance to us in this chapter is that Kickbusch suggests we need a better theoretical understanding of lifestyle which advocates a positioning of lifestyle within a broader social context where it

> constitutes part of the pattern that people establish for their behaviours, the meaning they attach to them, it is eased or made more difficult by cultural and structural elements and it will be influenced by overall cultures of health and illness...This implies that when studying human actions, we must relate the actions to the meanings people attach to them, the norms they are subject to and the power of decision making available [to them].
>
> (ibid.: 55)

In essence, 'Shape Up''s focus on the individual serves to decontextualise health-related behaviour from the social and spatial contexts in which it occurs. There is little regard for the ways that space and environment influence health outcomes for children. Space is merely conceived of as a 'passive container' for individuals' health-related behaviour rather than integral to the process of (re)producing health and illness. The social structure of the playground is overlooked and is simply regarded as an area in which children's bodies can be exercised. Within health promotion, the notion that social context and space have an important and often overlooked part to play in the delivery of these initiatives is acknowledged by many commentators (Popay 1998, Morrow 1999). While there have been calls to 'come up with concepts related to where people interact face-to-face on a daily basis' (Wenzel 1997), analysis of the relationship between space and health has tended to occur at a macro level within epidemiological research rather than focusing on individuals existing and interacting within ordinary, day-to-day spaces.

In summary, we suggest that a more nuanced understanding of children's ((un)healthy) embodiments, and the spaces which are con-stitutive of and constituted by children's bodies, is necessary if health promotion is ever to move away from lifestylism and nutrition-based models towards a more healthy and balanced growing up.

Note

1. MEND www.ich.ucl.ac.uk/website/ich/academicunits/Nutrition/Custom per cent20Menu_01/The_MEND_Project_Child_leaflet.pdf

References

Aitken, S. C. (1994) *Putting Children in Their Place* (Washington, DC: Association of American Geographers).

Blanchflower, D. G., Oswald, A. J. and Landeghem, B. van (2008) Imi-tative Obesity Relative Utility. Paper given at NBER Summer Institute on Health Economics. www2.ac.uk/fac/soc/economics/staff/faculty/Oswald/ao23julyobesity08.pdf, accessed 8 June 2009.

Butland, B. et al. (2007) *Foresight Tackling Obesities: Future Choices Project Report* (London: HMSO).

Campos, P. (2004) *The Obesity Myth: Why America's Obsession with Weight is Hazardous to your Health* (New York: Gotham Books).

Christakis, N. (2007) 'The spread of obesity in large social networks over 32 years', *New England Journal of Medicine* 357.

Cole, T. (2007) 'The truth about obesity', *The Investigation*, BBC Radio 4, available at http://news.bbc.co.uk/1/hi/magazine/7105630.stm, accessed 3 March 2009.

Colls, R. and Evans, B. (2007) 'Embodying responsibility: children's health and supermarket initiatives', *Environment and Planning A*, 40(3), 615–31.

Colquhoun, D. and Robottom, I. (1990) 'Health education and environmental education: towards a shared agenda and a shared discourse', *Unicorn* 16(2), 109–18.

Courtenay Botterill, L. (2006) 'Leaps of faith in the obesity debate: a cautionary tale for policy makers', *The Political Quarterly* 77(1): 199–203.

Crawford, R. (1986) 'A cultural account of "health", control, release and the social body', in J. B. McKinlay (ed.) *Issues in the Political Economy of Health Care* (London: Tavistock).

Dahlgren, G. and Whitehead, M. (1991) *Policies and Strategies to Promote Social Equity in Health* (Stockholm: Institute of Fiscal Studies).

Egger, G. and Swinburn, B. (1997) 'An "ecological" approach to the obesity pandemic', *British Medical Journal* 315: 477–80.

Evans, B. (2004) 'Be fit not fat: broadening the childhood obesity debate beyond dualisms', *Children's Geographies* 2(2): 288–91.

Evans, B. (2006) 'Gluttony or sloth? Critical geographies of bodies and morality in (anti)obesity policy', *Area* 38(3): 259–67.

Flegal, K. M., Tabak, C. J. and Ogden, C. L. (2006) 'Overweight in children: definitions and interpretation', *Health Education Research Theory and Practice* 21: 755–60.

Food Standards Agency (2007) *Eat Well Plate*, available at www.eatwell.gov.uk/healthydiet/eatwellplate, accessed 3 February 2009.

Gard, J. and Wright, M. (2005) *The Obesity Epidemic: Science, Morality and Ideology* (London: Routledge).

Holloway, S. and Valentine, G. (2000) 'Spatiality and the new social studies of childhood', *Sociology* 34(4): 763–83.

James, A., Jenks, C. and Prout, A. (1998) *Theorizing Childhood* (Cambridge: Polity Press).

Kickbusch, I. (1989) 'Self care in health promotion', *Social Science and Medicine*, 22(2): 125–30.

Lake, A. and Townsend, T. (2006) 'Obesogenic environments: exploring the built and food environments', *Journal of the Royal Society for the Promotion of Health*, 126(6): 262–7.

Leahy, D. (2009) 'Disgusting pedagogies', in J. Wright and V. Harwood (eds) *Biopolitics and the Obesity Epidemic* (New York: Routledge).

Lupton, D. (1996) *Food, Body and the Self* (London: Sage).

Morrow, V. (1999, 2005) 'Conceptualising social capital in relation to the well-being of children and young people: a critical review', *The Sociological Review*, 47(4): 744–65.

Moss, P. and Dyck, I. (2002) *Women, Body, Illness: Space and Identity in the Everyday Lives of Women with Chronic Illness* (Lanham, MD: Rowman & Littlefield).

Naidoo, J. (1986) 'Limits to individualism', in S. Rodmell and A. Watt (eds) *The Politics of Health Education* (London: Routledge & Kegan Paul), pp. 17–37.

Naidoo, J. and Wills, J. (2000) *Health Promotion: Foundations for Practice* (Edinburgh: Baillière Tindall).

Parr, H. and Butler, R. (1999) 'New geographies of illness, impairment and disability', in R. Butler and H. Parr (eds) *Mind and Body Spaces: Geographies of Illness, Impairment and Disability* (London: Routledge), pp. 1–24.

PAU Education (2008) *Shape Up Stories* (Barcelona: PAU Education), available at www.shapeupeurope.net/files/media/media407.pdf, accessed 3 February 2009.

Pawson, R. and Tilley, N. (1997) *Realistic Evaluation* (London: Sage).

Pike, J. and Colquhoun, D. (2007) 'Beyond the School Gates: School Food and Parenting Practice'. Oral presentation, University of Queensland, Australia.

Popay, J., Williams, G., Thomas, C. and Gatrell, A. (1998) 'Theorising inequalities in health: the place of lay knowledge', *Sociology of Health And Illness* 20(5): 619–44.

Procter, K. L., Clarke, G. P., Ransley, J. K. and Cade, J. (2008) 'Micro-level analysis of childhood obesity, diet, physical activity, residential socioeconomic and social capital variables: where are the obesogenic environments in Leeds?' *Area* 40(3): 323–40.

Rodmell, S. and Watt, A. (1986) *The Politics of Health Education* (London: Routledge & Kegan Paul).

Ross, B. (2005) 'Fat or fiction: weighing the obesity epidemic', in M. Gard and J. Wright (eds) *The Obesity Epidemic: Science, Morality and Ideology* (London: Routledge).

Rudolph, M. C. J. (2006) 'Watch it! An NHS community service for obese children', *Cambridge Medicine* 20(1): 8–10.

Simovska V. et al. (2006) *Towards a Healthy and Balanced Growing Up: Shape Up Methdological Guidebook* (Barcelona: PAU Education).

Thompson, S. (2005) ' "Territorialising" the primary school playground: deconstructing the geography of playtime', *Children's Geographies* 3(1): 63–78.

Wenzel, E. (1997) 'A comment on settings in health promotion', *Internet Journal of Health Promotion*, available at www.rhpeo.org/ijhp-articles/1997/1/index.htm.

World Health Organisation, Ottawa Charter (1986), available at www.who.int/hpr/NPH/docs/ottawa_charter_hp.pdf, accessed 3 February 2009.

Zola, I. K. (1978) 'Medicine as an institution of social control', in J. Ehrenreich, *The Cultural Crisis of Modern Medicine* (New York: Monthly Review Press).

9
Health Visiting in Anxious Times

Pamela Dale

Introduction

In recent years the challenges of globalisation have provided a new critical lens for viewing social, economic and political problems. Harry Hendrick draws a direct correlation between the rise of the social investment state and heightened concern about promoting and protecting the international competitiveness of the economy. In Britain, Hendrick notes that the New Labour government, which came to power in 1997, adopted the language and policies of social investment, thereby making children and childhood a focus of popular anxieties as well as state intervention (Hendrick 2003: 205–53). For Hendrick these emerging issues and debates served to resurrect a number of long-standing dualisms apparent in discussions about child welfare since at least the 1880s. These included children's bodies and minds, children as victims and threats, and the identification and management of the normal and the abnormal (Hendrick 1994: 1–15). These ideas provide a backdrop for the evaluation of health visiting practices, which are the focus of this chapter. The intention is to suggest that current critiques of early twentieth-century models of health visiting, which concentrate on controlling practices and elitism among practitioners, miss the important contribution such services could make to improving child welfare.

The historiography examining child welfare since 1880 has become increasingly dominated by narratives of disciplinary control, which have seen the working-class child and its family targeted for intrusive state interventions (Hendrick, 1997: 1–9). This idea of a contested child body created by and subject to external control (Armstrong 1983, 1986) is in marked contrast to an earlier interpretation, which had placed emphasis on the benefits accruing to children and their families from the development of health and welfare services. Historians, and interested policy-makers and practitioners keen to assert their own contribution to the reform process, amassed evidence that even before the creation of the classic welfare state in the 1940s, working-class children were better fed and clothed, received improved education and health services, and were recognised as a vulnerable group requiring additional state protection (Harris 2004: 216–18). New literature, adopting a Marxist, feminist and/or Foucauldian perspective, emerging from the 1970s, maintained the focus on the child and its family, but tended to view any improvements in care and material circumstances as largely incidental when compared to the real intention of imposing control (Donzelot 1979).

This emphasis on control was reinforced by the discovery of an apparent shift in official concerns in the 1920s, a development that saw existing controls on children's bodies extended to embrace their minds and bodies. For Hendrick, state interest in the body of the child centred on 'food and feeding, medical inspection and treatment, the ordering of the body in movement and of the tongue in speech' and the infliction of physical pain as a disciplinary tool (Hendrick 2003: 2). Such interventions were controversial, but arguably easier to accept or resist than subtle forms of normalisation that targeted the mind of the child and/or its parents. David Armstrong (1983) and Nikolas Rose (1999) are just two of the more influential exponents of what Mathew Thomson terms the 'disciplinary narrative' (Thomson 2006: 5). This sees 'psychological subjectivity... either imposed on the individual... [or] internalised in the individual through the growing influence of experts and their advice within private life' (ibid.). Thomson argues that the child was seen as a particularly good subject for psychological interventions, and identifies a number of programmes where elite groups attempted to discover and define normality. Efforts to apply such knowledge appear to support arguments about controlling intentions and disciplinary practices.

Yet, new research by Thomson points to the limitations as well as the strength of the 'disciplinary narrative' in the British context and argues that its focus on the 'aims, ideas and even the practical tools of the professionals' misses the vital negotiations and compromises that operate to translate policy into practice (ibid.: 7). It is also probable that practitioners were motivated by a number of conflicting agendas, combining aspects of care and control, and were willing to engage with a variety of what are now termed 'stakeholders'. These included parents and community groups allowing bottom-up as well as top-down influences on their work. Recognising at least the potential for client participation and shared concerns may allow a reassessment of one of the more maligned professional groups, health visitors, who emerged in their modern form against a backdrop of anxieties about the state of the nation around the turn of the twentieth century. Their current and future role is being explicitly adapted to respond to the needs of the social investment state in the new millennium. A useful discussion about the origins of Sure Start and its relationship to some of the issues raised in this chapter can be found in *Saving Lives: Our Healthier Nation* (Cm. 4386, 1999: 38).

Health visiting in theory and practice

There are surprisingly few detailed studies of health visiting theory or practice, but contributors to the debate on child welfare from a number of academic disciplines usually make some reference to the profession. Two key themes merge. The first is genuine uncertainty about what health visitors did, making it difficult for contemporaries and historians to evaluate what, if any, contribution their work made to improving child health (Smith 1979: 114–17). The second, dominant, narrative is one of controlling intentions with a subtext of client resistance. Feminists are especially critical of the way infant deaths, a multi-causal problem that evoked deep-seated fears about the social, economic and political health of the nation, were apparently recast in the Edwardian period to a simplistic concern with the behaviour of the mother. The mantra of 'saving babies' thus became a strategy of 'controlling mothers', which diverted attention away from social and economic inequalities in support of a conservative, maternalist agenda. In this interpretation visits by middle-class women working as professional health visitors to the homes of the poor were bound to be resented and resisted, even if the health visitors had sensible advice and practical help to offer; under this interpretation this was seen as unlikely because of class-based antipathy between visitor and visited (Ross 1993: 204–9).

This view has become surprisingly hegemonic, but can be challenged through a detailed examination of services. Deborah Dwork (1987) uses her survey of developing provision, including the appointment of professional health visitors, for mothers and infants before 1918, to argue that war is good for babies and young children. This was because increased state concerns with infant welfare led to the development of real services that, despite concerns about some of the paternalistic language and surveillance practices adopted, were in some crucial respects recognising and responding to the needs of poor families. Lara

Marks makes this case very strongly in terms of the maternity care made available to poor mothers in parts of London, but is less certain about the impact of health visitors (Marks 1996: 195, 200–1). Dwork (1987: 226–30) expresses serious concerns about the merits of the social control thesis (Davin 1978, Dyhouse 1979, Lewis 1980) and instead turns to a range of contemporary medical theories used to explain the infant mortality rate and the variety of public health strategies that developed from them. In a retrospective analysis from the 1960s, Margot Jefferys concluded that 'a great deal of the credit' for reduced infant mortality and a fall in the number of children of children 'permanently crippled by serious illness or nutritional deprivation' between 1900 and 1948 must be given to the 'educative work of health visitors' tasked with avoiding gastro-intestinal and respiratory infections in babies and rickets in toddlers (Jefferys 1965: 64).

A factor that can easily be overlooked is that although infant welfare was identified as an urgent national problem by contemporary commentators, statutory and voluntary services targeting babies and their mothers were organised at a local level. This meant there were wide variations in policy and practice, and the chronology of local developments. Dwork is correct to highlight the way war served both to heighten anxieties about children and stimulate specialist services. Councils that had been slow to adopt a coherent plan to improve infant welfare before 1914 started to develop new services, often in partnership with the voluntary sector, and these schemes were formalised and expanded after the passing of the Maternity and Child Welfare Act 1918. A good example is the Exeter Maternity and Child Welfare Committee. This was established in 1916 and its records demonstrate the importance of partnerships between the statutory and voluntary sectors in the city throughout the interwar period (Exeter MCWC minutes, 1916–35). More progressive councils that had acted earlier and developed more comprehensive provision present a more complex picture. While war undoubtedly heightened concern about babies and increased infant welfare activities, it also acted as a major disrupting influence which redirected effort to meet national rather than local agendas and cope with the exigencies of the time. Specialist provision tended to flourish, but many of the links to other services were lost, and even when re-established in peacetime some of the earlier dynamism appears to have been lost.

Halifax Corporation, a county borough council serving a town located in the West Riding of Yorkshire, with a population of about 100,000 in the period 1900–30, provides a useful case study of a progressive local authority struggling with these issues (Fraser 1982: 56–74, Digby 2006). Its elected and appointed officials sought to maintain a clear focus on child health within a wider agenda to improve the health and well-being of all local residents. Health visitors were seen as a local solution to this dilemma because they could operate within a number of health improvement schemes and coordinate services. They were also conceived as conduits for information to flow from the Health Department to the people and were simultaneously tasked with learning more about the population and its health concerns. There is no doubt that this approach, if handled insensitively, risked intrusive interventions by officious health visitors doing the bidding of the council, but their contribution to efforts to reveal and remedy health inequalities were not necessarily unwelcome to client groups and certainly not without benefits to child health.

The origins of the health visiting service in Halifax

Halifax was not a pioneer of health visiting services and deliberated carefully on the best scheme to adopt (Halifax Health Com, 30 October 1907: 102, 18 December 1907: 232). In this case geographical proximity to urban centres like Manchester and Huddersfield credited with developing alternative models of health visiting seems to have delayed a final decision (Davies 1988, Marland 1993). A discussion about the merits of lady health visitors enters the Halifax records from 1906 and the first appointment was made in 1908. Miss Watson Wayne resigned after just a few months in post, but her replacement, Miss A. M. Thompson, oversaw longer-term developments (Halifax Health Com, 15 July 1908: 1005–6). She was the sole salaried practitioner until 1916 and acted as senior health visitor until her retirement in 1921. Her successor, Miss Elsie Oram, was promoted from within the ranks of the Halifax health visitors and led a growing team of staff into the era of the National Health Service.

What is interesting about Miss Thompson's appointment is that her main qualification for the post, quite distinct from her professional status, was the fact that she was a local woman. In fact, the council minutes just record her Halifax address, while her professional qualifications appear only in later reports. Other staff were also drawn from the local area. This policy helped to recruit and retain health visitors when there was a national shortage of trained staff, but it also had distinct benefits for the practice of health visiting. The Halifax health visitors were meant to know the area intimately and understand its unique health problems.

They were also meant to be part of the local community and appreciate the qualities of the local population. According to J. T. Neech, Halifax's Medical Officer of Health (MOH) 1900–21, the people of Halifax were thrifty, sober and receptive to health messages.

It was Neech and his successors who identified Halifax as a predominantly working-class town, where health risks were shared and the citizens had a duty to help each other. This gave rise to a distinct pattern to the supply of, as well as demand for, health services. The social and political elite of the town were prepared to act philanthropically, but they also recognised the importance of the contribution of the working people. The local voluntary hospital, rebuilt in 1896, relied on a few large donations for its capital projects, but regular contributions from the working population met a significant proportion of its running costs (RHI Report 1928: 6–8, 16, Washington 1996). Some elite figures were prepared to channel their reform efforts through the Halifax Corporation. The council had established a nineteenth-century tradition of innovative sanitary improvement and, from about 1900, came under the control of a determinedly progressive group operating a Lib-Lab pact (Dawson 1994).

Left-wing politics did not preclude interest in the imperialist projects, national efficiency arguments and eugenic concerns, which Anna Davin and other critics of health visiting have aligned the infant welfare movement with, but in areas like Halifax there was more emphasis on providing services to families rather than simply offering advice to mothers (Davin 1978). Studies of London and the more conservative rural counties and provincial cities have tended to conclude that contemporary actors saw the latter as a substitute for the former and present the advice-givers as agents of social control giving only a top-down assessment of health and welfare problems (Peretz 1995). A slightly different interpretation is, however, offered in the case of Bradford, a city a few miles from Halifax and an important point of reference for Halifax's schemes.

In Bradford, elected members, like Margaret McMillan, and officials, such as James Kerr, are understood to have foreground a concern with the welfare of the child and a need to maximise its potential by developing its body and mind (Steedman 1990, Harris 1995: 21). This approach introduced a strong critique of existing statutory and voluntary services in Bradford (Dale and Mills 2007). This did not deflect attention away from concerns about the ignorance of parents who unwittingly, or otherwise, exposed infants to the dangers of cold, poor nutrition, germs and poor quality childminders. Yet records kept by the

Bradford Female Sanitary Inspectors (FSIs), later renamed health visitors, gradually reformulated their arguments to take into account the fact that most parents acted on realistic advice when it was made available to them. The FSIs found that the most serious obstacle to better childrearing was acute poverty, and started to suggest that the main difficulty was people's ignorance of their 'rights as human beings' rather than simply a lack of knowledge about domestic hygiene (Bradford FSI Report, 30 September 1908: 7). These ideas were linked to a wider reform movement in the city, which started a number of practical schemes to feed and otherwise improve the health of children, with concern moving back from the schoolchild, to the baby and then the infant before birth (Bradford Council of Social Service 1923: 42).

These programmes were explicitly used as a reference point when councillors and officials in Halifax started to address the questions of child welfare and maternal health in the Edwardian period. The schemes developed in Halifax, which included health visiting, had three distinct influences: national debates about the health of the nation, programmes initiated by other local authorities, and a need to respond to the distinctive problems of the town in a way that took account of local priorities and available resources. Two local actors played a vital role in mediating all three influences. They were the MOH and Alderman Coe, the chairman of the health committee, whose cooperative approach and commitment to health improvement were celebrated in Neech's final report as Halifax MOH. Neech and Coe went to important public health conferences together and used these opportunities to learn about developments elsewhere while making sure that Halifax's innovations reached a wide audience. Their written and verbal conference reports, sensitively attuned to local circumstances, pressed for expanded and reconfigured health services. Child health was a distinct part of these concerns but was also seen to benefit from wider programmes that advanced sanitary reform, slum clearance and the control of infectious disease.

In Halifax, councillors and officials were keen to respond to evidence of local need. Compulsory education brought poor children into contact with teachers and school attendance officers, who reported that many were too sick and hungry to benefit from education (Halifax Ed Com, 22 May 1905: 471–2). Following the Bradford model concerns were projected backwards to early life, but until the health visitors made detailed reports on infant health both the extent of any problems and their possible solution tended to elude official analysis and the first Halifax schemes explicitly addressed the health of school-age children.

A local, albeit limited, scheme of school medical inspection pre-dated national legislation (Halifax Ed Com, 15 January 1906: 160–1) and was later brought into conformity with national guidelines (Halifax Ed Com, 21 December 1908: 151, minute 97). School meals were quickly introduced, despite some opposition, following the Education (Provision of Meals) Act 1906 with some earlier provision under the Relief (School Children) Order 1905 (Halifax Ed Com, 17 July 1905: 632, 9 September 1907: 909, 7 October 1907: 1016–17, 16 December 1907: 158).

The idea that adequate nutrition was a foundation for health played into wider debates about national efficiency, but the concern in Halifax was more local and immediate. When councillors were alerted to the presence of hundreds of hungry children in Halifax they determined they should be fed. This was first conceived as a short-term response to periodic economic crises but later became institutionalised. The programme extended to breakfasts for exceptionally poor children, and during particularly harsh winters the central kitchen was kept open during the school holidays. Three members of the education committee were surcharged in 1909 for allowing this unauthorised expenditure (this was ultimately remitted by the Local Government Board; Halifax Ed Com, 20 December 1909: 210, 20 June 1910: 854–5, 19 September 1910: 1147). This concern for hungry children needs to be understood as genuine, although attempts to recover the costs of school meals from parents, the Halifax Guardians and charitable donations points to the complexity of the mixed economy of welfare at this time and a desire to enforce family and community responsibilities within national guidelines as well as extend services to people who might benefit from them (Halifax Ed Com, 10 February 1908: 394–5).

Evaluating Edwardian services and plans for the future

While a number of motivations – some of them probably more about control than care – undoubtedly lay behind the evolution of various services, it was the day-to-day concern with service provision rather than unifying ideologies that most concerned the Halifax Health Department. Thus the report presented by Coe and Neech on the 1902 annual congress of the Royal Institute of Public Health, Exeter, mentioned visits to see gas, electric and sewerage plants, artisans dwellings and a hospital. There was a discussion about a paper calling for the teaching of hygiene in schools, but attention also focused on debates about the causes of cancer and methods for controlling infectious diseases. The report noted that the Halifax delegation had been praised for the low death rate they had achieved that year and the promising state of the council's various municipal enterprises (Halifax Health Com, 17 September 1902: 670–4).

These services formed the core of the response to the problem of infant mortality when this was highlighted by later conference papers, circulars from the Local Government Board and trends in vital statistics recorded for the town (Halifax MOH Report 1906: 5–6). It is probably no coincidence that the first lady health visitor was appointed between the first two national conferences on infant mortality in 1906 and 1908, but discussions about this post continued to draw attention to local factors (Halifax Health Com, 4 July 1906: 607–12, 6 May 1908: 786–92). These included a desire to create better contacts with the Guild of Help (Laybourn 1994) and arrange the duties of the health visitor so that her work would support existing and planned council services. In Halifax, advice and instruction by the health visitor were conceived as just one part of a greater municipal enterprise. Responsibilities for health promotion and protection transcended several departments, allowing a comprehensive response to problems. Thus during epidemics of summer diarrhoea, when infant mortality typically rose, the health visitor distributed advice leaflets to parents suggesting that all milk should be kept covered and boiled before use. To back up these efforts the MOH arranged for additional street cleaning and refuse collection to suppress the dust and flies blamed for the diarrhoea and maintained careful vigilance over the supply and sale of milk. This was in marked contrast to the limited and belated efforts made elsewhere. As late as 1931, the Ministry of Health criticised Devon County Council for 'preaching to housewives' about the dangers of flies near milk jugs when the local authority made only token efforts to protect that same milk supply from adulteration and contamination (Devon Survey Report, 1931: 38).

Neech believed that all infant deaths from diarrhoea were preventable, and he viewed the low rates achieved in Halifax as evidence that parents could be trusted to take their responsibilities seriously if offered suitable support from the department (Halifax MOH Report, 1907: 42). A special campaign against deaths from diarrhoea was run in the hot summer of 1911 and Neech reproduced an example of his information leaflet in his annual report, together with an extended discussion on the subject (Halifax MOH Report, 1911: 22, 31–2, 57–9). If deaths from diarrhoea were preventable, there was less certainty about other causes of infant deaths. Here Neech's thinking developed along two parallel lines. He tended to see an irreducible minimum of non-preventable infant deaths – for example, those associated with congenital defects – but thought there was no reason why the worst performing areas within Halifax could not keep pace with the best given a sufficient commitment to public health. In the long term Neech advocated social progress and advances in medical knowledge as the most promising solutions to the infant mortality problem (Halifax MOH Report, 1920: 11–12).

In the short to medium term local reform suggested a way forward. Neech and the health committee were very interested in comparative, ward-level data which the MOH contrasted with the borough figure and national averages (Halifax Health Com, 17 November 1909: 150, minute 159). This type of analysis can create significant political difficulties when used in support of radical social and economic change. Charles Webster (1982), amongst others, suggests it is the suppression of this kind of data in the 1930s that concealed the true and disproportionate impact of the Great Depression. For Neech it revealed need. Rather than claim that the poorest people were the most ignorant about health and hygiene, and so largely to blame for their own problems, he drew attention to other factors, which condemned poor children to unacceptably high mortality rates. These included poor housing, overcrowding and chronic ill-health.

In Halifax there were 15 wards. Skircoat, an affluent area with plenty of open space, enjoyed the best infant mortality rate (IMR) figures; the worst, East ward, returned IMRs of over 200 per 1,000 live births in three out of seven years before 1914. The idea was that improved housing would reduce this level towards the average of 76 achieved by Akroyden, where working people lived in a kind of model urban village. Hence municipal priorities centred on slum clearance, together with efforts to improve the institutional and community health services available for vulnerable children. Advice-giving in Halifax was not seen as an end in itself but part of an effort to bring people into contact with expanding council services.

In a limited way, given that there was just one salaried visitor serving a population of about 100,000 in 1908, the first lady health visitor was meant to offer individual mothers advice and instruction when visiting newborns. The MOH created the Halifax Public Health Union (PHU) to supplement her efforts by developing a team of female volunteers to do follow-up visits and assist the health visitor. The MOH saw these activities as a natural extension of his own health information campaigns, and they also encouraged the statutory and voluntary sectors to develop new services (Halifax MOH Report 1906, introduction).

It was the PHU that started to develop instruction on hygiene alongside sewing and cooking classes for mothers. The PHU also encouraged the establishment of a municipal infant welfare centre. This opened in 1916, but in Halifax tended to function as a centre for the distribution of cheap milk and food, and operate as a clinic for sick infants. This alarmed Neech's successor, Cyril Banks, who wanted to concentrate efforts on the supervision of well babies and health education. Yet neither he nor his successor was able to divert the woman medical officer or the growing team of health visitors at the clinic from work they justified as desperately needed and appreciated by clients. A visiting medical inspector from the Ministry of Health in the 1930s found the Halifax clinic arrangements idiosyncratic, but agreed that they were effective and praised the way the clinics were closely integrated into an impressive array of municipal services, including a showpiece general hospital (Halifax Survey Report 1932, paragraphs 350–97).

At this time the clinic and the health office were sites of health surveillance, but they were also places where people could go voluntarily to get help and advice, access council services or secure a referral to other organisations (Pickstone 2000: 1–19). This had been something of a dream for Neech, though his personal aspirations had been curtailed during the difficult war years when local hospitals were taken over by the military, and vital services, including refuse collection, broke down as medical staff, male inspectors and manual workers were conscripted into the armed forces (Halifax Health Com, 21 February 1917: 398). In the short term the infant clinic provided a new focus and something of an alternative strategy, but it took many years to recover lost ground, a problem compounded by the national situation as the Ministry of Health, established in 1919, sought to control health expenditure and encouraged local councils to work in conformity with centrally approved schemes.

Discussion

Against a backdrop of severe economic depression in local industries throughout the inter-war period, the celebration of low Edwardian death rates in Halifax gave way to local and national concern about excessive mortality in the town. This was despite the fact that the acknowledged quality and quantity of local health services continued to provide some grounds for optimism (Halifax Survey 1932, letter). One problem was that councillors and officials tended to view health holistically, and while this led to comprehensive improvement schemes, their evaluation tended to confound conventional measurement. Neech had been MOH during a period that saw infant mortality rates in Halifax fall from an average of more than 159 for the period 1890–9 to just 96 in 1920 (Halifax MOH Report 1925: 11–12). Yet he remained ambivalent about whether this represented success or failure and took the opportunity of his final report to highlight the concrete legacy provided by his record on sanitary reform and combating lead poisoning (Halifax MOH Report 1920, introduction). Other local actors believed that the attention paid to providing clean water, preventing the contamination or adulteration of food and milk, improving sanitation, initiating slum clearance and house-building schemes, and developing a comprehensive array of institutional and community health services had contributed to the health and happiness of the population but were unable to quantify exactly what their impact had been.

This fuelled a number of anxieties about the future of health policy, especially where vulnerable groups like young children and pregnant women were concerned. It was in the 1930s that Halifax records adopted the rhetoric of impending crisis, fears about the future of the nation and the eugenic arguments which Davin and others have seen as the driving force behind the early infant welfare movement. This shifting concern was particularly noticeable after George Roe was appointed MOH in 1929. He was keen to develop a whole spectrum of services and sought to harness disparate concerns behind his own agenda for health improvement, while noting that 'the ultimate success or failure of a public health service depends not so much upon Acts of Parliament as upon the desire of the public to be healthy' (Halifax MOH Report 1929: 5).

Roe was something of a mental specialist as well as a public health practitioner and seems to have become frustrated that the scale of the mortality and morbidity crisis in Halifax concentrated local attention on physical health at a time when elsewhere it was the mind rather than the body of the child that was coming under scrutiny. It is misleading, however, to suggest that Roe either tried or succeeded in concentrating attention on children as a distinct group. His period in office was noteworthy instead for the development of institutional care. Less attention was given to established community services, though health visitors found a new role in hospital liaison work and continued to extend their visits to new groups of children and adults. There was a feeling they were doing good, but in Halifax and elsewhere there was no possibility of quantitatively assessing this because outcomes were hard to measure and the work was indivisible from the contributions of other health and welfare services and prevailing economic and social conditions. Client responses proved even more elusive, although under the crude measures of visits completed and clinic attendances, used by contemporary service providers, the health visitors were reaching increasing numbers of clients, who made more frequent use of available services.

Turning to the present, these are all points that have complicated attempts to evaluate today's Sure Start schemes, whose local organisation and responsiveness to the priorities of local 'stakeholders' means there are no standard criteria to measure them against. In the absence of early and concrete data, commentators have concentrated on the motivations for establishing such programmes and speculated about their effectiveness at a local and national level (Toynbee and Walker 2005: 28, 310–12). Elite and popular anxieties about citizens of the future within the social investment state have been highlighted, while concerns about obesity and anti-social behaviour have refocused attention on the body and mind of the child and the quality of modern parenting. Some commentators have expressed concern that programmes like Sure Start explicitly target deprived communities. This can lead to concerns about the surveillance and control functions of health visitors and other staff operating the schemes, but other researchers point to the way sensitive work that understands the needs of impoverished communities can be particularly rewarding for practitioners and clients (Symonds 2003: 171–94). Mapping and politicising the body of the child remains an important national project, but examination of health visiting services usefully highlights opportunities for negotiation. While emphasis can be placed on controlling impulses, there is also value in exploring shared goals. The body and mind of the child arguably were and continued to be a unique interface between the family and the state, where both could make reciprocal demands.

Acknowledgement

The research for this chapter was generously supported by the Wellcome Trust, grant 074999. This was for a personal fellowship titled 'The Medical Officer of Health and the organisation of health visiting as a comprehensive community health service, 1906–1974'.

References

Armstrong, D. (1983) *The Political Anatomy of the Body* (Cambridge: Cambridge University Press).

Armstrong, D. (1986) 'The invention of infant mortality', *Sociology of Health and Illness* 8: 211–32.

Bradford Council of Social Service (1923) *The Texture of Welfare: A Survey of Social Service in Bradford* (Bradford: P. S. King & Son).

Dale, P. and Mills, C. (2007) 'Revealing and concealing personal and social problems: family coping strategies and a new engagement with officials and welfare
agencies c. 1900–1912', *Family and Community History* 10: 111–25.

Davies, C. (1988) 'The health visitor as mother's friend: a woman's place in public
health, 1900–1914', *Social History of Medicine* 1: 39–59.

Davin, A. (1978) 'Imperialism and motherhood', *History Workshop Journal* 5: 9–65.

Dawson, P. A. (1994) 'Liberalism and the challenge of labour: the 1906 progressive election in Halifax', *Halifax Antiquarian Society Transactions*, new series 2:
107–24.

Digby, A. (2006) 'Changing welfare cultures in region and state', *Twentieth Century
British History* 17: 297–322.

Donzelot, J. (1979) *The Policing of Families*, trans. Robert Hurley (London:
Hutchinson).

Dwork, D. (1987) *War is Good for Babies and Other Young Children: A History of the
Infant and Child Welfare Movement in England 1898–1918* (London: Tavistock).

Dyhouse, C. (1979) 'Working-class mothers and infant mortality in England,
1895–1914', *Journal of Social History* 12: 248–67.

Fraser, D. (1982) 'The Edwardian city', in D. Read (ed.) *Edwardian England*
(London: Croom Helm).

Harris, B. (1995) *The Health of the Schoolchild: A History of the School Medical Service
in England and Wales* (Buckingham: Open University Press).

Harris, B. (2004) *The Origins of the British Welfare State: Social Welfare in England
and Wales, 1800–1945* (Basingstoke: Palgrave Macmillan).

Hendrick, H. (1994) *Child Welfare: England 1872–1989* (London: Routledge).

Hendrick, H. (1997) *Children, Childhood and English Society, 1880–1990*
(Cambridge: Cambridge University Press).

Hendrick, H. (2003) *Child Welfare: Historical Dimensions, Contemporary Debates*
(Bristol: Policy Press).

Jefferys, M. (1965) *An Anatomy of Social Welfare Services: A Survey of Social Welfare
Staff and their Clients in the County of Buckinghamshire* (London: Michael Joseph).

Laybourn, K. (1994) *The Guild of Help and the Changing Face of Edwardian Philan-
thropy: The Guild of Help, Voluntary Work and the State, 1904–1919* (Lampeter:
Edward Mellen Press).

Lewis, J. (1980) *The Politics of Motherhood: Child and Maternal Welfare in England,
1900–1939* (London: Croom Helm).

Marks, L. V. (1996) *Metropolitan Maternity: Maternal and Infant Welfare Services in
Early Twentieth Century London* (Amsterdam: Rodopi).

Marland, H. (1993) 'A pioneer in infant welfare: the Huddersfield scheme 1903–
1920', *Social History of Medicine* 6: 25–50.

Peretz, E. (1995) 'Infant welfare in inter-war Oxford', *International History of
Nursing Journal* 1: 5–18.

Pickstone, J. (2000) 'Production, community and consumption: the political
economy of twentieth-century medicine', in R. Cooter and J. Pickstone (eds)
Medicine in the Twentieth Century (Amsterdam: Harwood Academic).

Rose, N. (1999) *Governing the Soul: The Shaping of the Private Self* (second edition)
(London: Free Association Books).

Ross, E. (1993) *Love and Toil: Motherhood in Outcast London, 1870–1918* (Oxford:
Oxford University Press).

Smith, F. B. (1979) *The People's Health 1830–1910* (London: Croom Helm).

Steedman, C. (1990) *Childhood, Culture and Class in Britain: Margaret McMillan, 1860–1931* (London: Virago).

Symonds, A. (2003) ' "It's a funny job really": the contradictions of health visiting', in A. Borsay (ed.) *Medicine in Wales c. 1800–2000: Public Service or Private Commodity?* (Cardiff: University of Wales Press).

Thomson, M. (2006) *Psychological Subjects: Identity, Culture and Health in Twentieth-Century Britain* (Oxford: Oxford University Press).

Toynbee, P. and Walker, D. (2005) *Better or Worse? Has Labour Delivered?* (London: Bloomsbury).

Washington, J. G. (1996) 'The origins and development of the Royal Halifax Infirmary', *Halifax Antiquarian Society Transactions*, new series 4: 68–86.

Webster, C. (1982) 'Healthy or hungry thirties?' *History Workshop Journal* 13: 110–29.

Primary sources

Bradford Local Studies Centre, City of Bradford Central Library, B614 FEM, Reports of the Work of the Female Sanitary Inspectors (Bradford FSI Reports).

Devon County Record Office, ECA/27/1, Exeter Maternity and Child Welfare Committee (Exeter MCWC), Minutes and Reports 1916–35.

Halifax Local Studies Centre (HLSC), 352 Hal, Halifax County Borough Council Minutes (Halifax CB Minutes) 1907–8. These volumes include minutes and reports for different committees. The health and education committees and sub-committees (Halifax Health Com and Halifax Ed Com) provide the main sources for this chapter.

HLSC, 614 Hal, County Borough of Halifax, Report of the Medical Officer of Health (Halifax MOH Report).

National Archives, Kew (NA), MH 66/58, Administrative County of Devon, Survey Report by A. C. Parsons (Devon Survey), January–February 1931.

NA, MH 66/1071, Halifax County Borough, Survey Report by Dr D. J. Williamson (Halifax Survey), 1932. This file includes a letter addressed to Halifax Town Clerk, 8 December 1932.

Saving Lives: Our Healthier Nation (Cm. 4386) (1999), presented to Parliament by the Secretary of State for Health by Command of her Majesty, July 1999 (London: The Stationery Office).

Wellcome Library, Royal Halifax Infirmary, 121st Annual Report (RHI Report), 1928 (Halifax, 1929).

10
Contested Bodies of Asylum-seeking Children

Peter Hopkins and Malcolm Hill

Introduction

In this chapter, we draw on evidence from research with unaccompanied asylum-seeking children to explore the multiple ways in which the contested features of unaccompanied minors' bodies work to influence and shape their everyday lives. During our research, it quickly became clear that their bodies are contested sites. In a variety of ways, their status as asylum-seekers, their skin colour and their perceived age marked them out, structured their experiences and regulated the resources available to them. We focus here on three issues. First, we examine issues associated with the asylum system and the cultural politics of asylum in order to demonstrate the negative influence that the workings of this system and the stereotypes associated with those seeking asylum have on the experiences of unaccompanied minors. Second, the racialising of unaccompanied minors' bodies is outlined, showing how there appears to be a racialised hierarchy that influences their everyday experiences and structures how they use services and are treated by others. Third, we explore the issue of official age assessment to highlight the complexity of this process and the risks associated with it in terms of the children's experiences of and access to services.

Unaccompanied asylum-seeking children (also referred to as 'unaccompanied minors') are 'children under the age of 18 years of age who have been separated from both parents and are not being cared for by an adult, who by law or custom, has a responsibility to do so' (UNHCR 2004: 2). Our research with unaccompanied asylum-seeking children took place in Scotland. It has been recorded by the Convention of Scottish Local Authorities (COSLA) that, in early 2005, 109 unaccompanied minors seeking asylum were living in Scotland, most in Glasgow, with over 180 arriving in Scotland since 2001. Nearly all are aged over 14, with most being 16 or 17. While they are in the process of becoming young adults, they are still children according to the UN Convention on the Rights of the Child and certain UK legislation. Approximately two-thirds of them are male. The majority are from Africa, with smaller numbers from Asia and Eastern Europe. The largest group of unaccompanied minors in Scotland are originally from Somalia.

In this project, we conducted interviews with 30 unaccompanied minors and over 70 service providers. A broad range of professionals who took part worked directly with or for unaccompanied minors and so were closely acquainted with their lives. They included social workers, teachers, health professionals, youth workers, advocacy workers, voluntary sector employees and local authority staff. Recruitment followed a process of snowballing, whereby initial contacts were asked to identify other organisations, agencies and individuals who work with or for unaccompanied minors. The contacts gained through interviewing service providers were then used to request access to unaccompanied asylum-seeking children who might be interested in participating in the research. In this chapter, participants are identified by pseudonyms in order to protect confidentiality.

Like previous studies (Thomas et al. 2004), we found that the primary reasons for the children fleeing from their countries of origin included the death or persecution of family members, the persecution of the young people themselves as well as issues such as forced recruitment as child soldiers, war and generally tense political circumstances (Hopkins and Hill 2008). Although this chapter focuses on unaccompanied minors' experiences of living in Scotland, it is important to recognise that some of the young people had fled from persecution as a result of the ways in which perceptions of their bodily characteristics/appearance had already resulted in them experiencing extreme hardship and discrimination, often relating to the political or religious affiliation of family members. Awareness of their bodies as markers of social identity and group affiliation were already significant aspects of their everyday lives. For others who fled on political or personal safety grounds, racial differentiation as a basis for social action was, by contrast, a novel experience on arrival in the UK. Processes of embodiment therefore influence the experiences of unaccompanied minors in complex ways; their bodies are read and interpreted by others in particular ways, whilst the young people simultaneously choose to adopt certain forms of embodiment, such as through dress, as an expression of their identity (Longhurst 1995).

Cultural politics of asylum

Young (1990: 124) notes that 'the interactive dynamics and cultural stereotypes that define groups as the ugly other have much to do with the oppressive harassment and physical violence that endangers the peace and bodies of most members of most of these groups'. The everyday experiences of many unaccompanied children are influenced by the cultural politics of asylum and general frustration with the asylum system. By 'cultural politics of asylum' we are referring first to the ways in which the status of asylum-seekers are politicised particularly through the media, often by invoking negative bodily images of the potentially tainting outsider (cf. Hubbard et al. 2005). Their bodies are stereotyped as a result of the ways in which their bodily markers associate them with the status of asylum-seeker and the asylum system. These stereotypes work in powerful ways to stigmatise unaccompanied children as less deserving and less important than other children. Furthermore, some physical markings, such as those gained during war and conflict in their countries of origin (e.g. scars, wounds, etc.), or other aspects of mental and physical health also result in unaccompanied minors' bodies being read, interpreted and stigmatised in different ways.

A service provider working in social services described such exclusionary discourses:

I just think the biggest downfall at the moment is the suspicion and the negativity that is around this group of young people and they need to be seen as having the rights and the same eligibility for services and support as every other looked after and accommodated young person in the country.

Unaccompanied minors' bodies are thereby negatively stereotyped, socially excluded and geographically segregated as a result of the stigma associated with their status as asylum-seekers.

A second form of cultural politicisation involves the impact of the separate and uncertain legal status of asylum-seekers. This requires them to be recipients of particular forms of state benefit, reside in particular (stigmatised) locations and become stereotypically associated with certain behaviours and customs, which may bear little relation to their customs or current everyday practices.

Generally speaking, respondents disliked the thrust of the legislative framework for unaccompanied asylum-seekers. A legal representative described it as 'horrendous' and an educationalist thought it was 'draconian'. Similarly, a health professional said, 'I think it is crap...appalling...slow, cumbersome and unfair', and suggested that 'we should stop pretending that we are, in any way, observing human rights'. Another health worker felt that 'the mechanism and decisions seem inconsistently applied, bewildering, decisions seem to be erratic, the legal framework can change very suddenly with no apparent reason'. Many service providers saw it as constraining rather than enabling, so holding them back from concentrating on what they saw as the more significant aspects of their job, promoting the best interests of the children they were working with.

Many service providers bemoaned both the quantity of legislation and the pace of legislative change as a frustrating aspect in their work. A number said they were unable to keep up with what a legal representative referred to as 'constantly changing legislation'. Furthermore, the decision-making process was slow and cumbersome. As an education worker noted: 'you've got children that have maybe been here for three or four years and they have not had a decision'. As a result of this often protracted process, many unaccompanied minors have to endure a situation where their bodies are regarded as out-of-place, illegal and awaiting confirmation. This process marginalises them, increases their anxiety and insecurity, and contributes to worries about the threat of being sent home.

Racialised hierarchies

During interviews with service providers and unaccompanied minors, it was unsurprising that racism – which often took the form of verbal abuse based on negative reactions to bodily appearance and skin colour in particular – was a common issue which many of the young people experienced on a daily basis as these statements testify:

Sabir   Well, some people, you know, speak racist words...you know, 'black bastard', 'go to your country', all that stuff.
Prince   There are people who treat me differently because I am black – in the street, they call me 'fuckin' black'.
Junior   ...see I have got different skin. I am black. Some pupils, they say things. Some swear, some abuse me.

Similar accounts arose in many individual interviews with unaccompanied minors as well as during part of participatory diagramming exercises with a group of young people exploring 'bad things about

Scotland'. Professionals, too, mentioned young people being 'picked on' by police on account of their appearance. They also referred to instances of racism among asylum-seekers themselves, with some fights occurring when hostilities arose in relation to differences in country of origin.

Clearly, unaccompanied asylum-seeking children need assistance in dealing with racism. However, the research revealed a hierarchy of racial-isation linked to the ways in which their bodies were marked out and read in relation to favoured and disfavoured body images, ways of dress-ing and self-presentation. The unaccompanied minors from Eastern Europe were the least likely to recall experiences of racism on the basis of experience, although there were comments about how their accents led to discrimination against them. However, the intersection of accent with other markers of social identities was often important. They 'bene-fited' from having skin colour and phenotypical features less obviously different from the majority population, but at the same time suffered as a result of their language use. As Nayak et al. observe:

> As migration patterns become increasingly varied and ethnic divides grow ever more complex we may yet witness the production of new racisms as demonstrated against asylum-seekers, Eastern Europeans, gypsies, travellers and other communities deemed 'beyond the pale' or 'not-quite-white'.
>
> (2006: 84)

Unaccompanied minors from Eastern Europe were often identified as 'white' or, in Nayak's phrase, 'not-quite-white'. So although they were sometimes identified as being slightly different from other young white people, they were also sometimes viewed as belonging to indigenous Scottish youth culture because of their bodily features.

A different kind of ambiguity surrounded those from Africa. Some of the young Africans observed how their very visible blackness marked them out as different and elicited derogatory responses. On the other hand, they may also experience less racism and be more likely to be highly regarded by their classmates on account of their association with 'cool' behaviour, demeanour and clothing. When thinking about unaccompanied minors' experiences of racism, a health professional noted:

> In my experience working with young people, African boys seems to fare best in the peer group because they...there's a racism but it's a...sometimes, an inverse one where they're idealised a bit. I think that's based on American culture and often the young people

adopt mannerisms that are more like American mannerisms – getting into basketball, wearing what I would regard, stereotypically, as American-type rap culture, sort of thing. They're often held in very high regard by Scottish boys... Arabic people fair less well... I've had fewer complaints of racism from African males.

Sallie Westwood (1990: 56) has observed that 'for black men of African descent the stereotypes have been fixed on the body, on physicality, physical strength, and as a site for European fantasies about black male sexuality'. Unaccompanied males from Africa, then, may experience racism, such as being picked out by the police as a threat (as suggested above); however, they may also be revered by their peer group as a result of stereotypes associated with their cultural background. Many of the young African men adopted such characteristics, such as style of dress and bodily deportment, in order to gain respect from their peers. This may be seen as a form of positive resistance to the geography of exclusion (Holloway and Hubbard 2001).

It is therefore the unaccompanied asylum-seeking children from the Asian continent who were most likely to experience racism and marginalisation, and this relates both to their positioning in relation to other unaccompanied minors as well as to stereotypes associated with being Asian. O'Donnell and Sharpe (2000: 79) have observed that stereotypes of Asian youth as weak and effeminate have been fed by 'the apparent tendency of Asian boys to be physically smaller', and so, especially when compared with the stereotypes of black men, unaccompanied young men of Asian origin are often more likely to be marginalised. Furthermore, particularly as a result of their skin colour as well as other bodily markings and adornments such as dress and facial hair, unaccompanied minors from Asia may also often be assumed to be Muslim and so suffer from similar forms of marginalisation experienced by Muslim young people (Hopkins 2004).

Overall, then, as a result of the ways in which unaccompanied minors' skin colour and other phenotypical features are marked out, read and responded to, there appears to be a racialised hierarchy within this group of young people. This can have a profound influence on their experiences of resettlement and their everyday experiences and sense of well-being.

Age assessment

Unaccompanied minors' bodies are also contested terrains in the process of age assessment by Immigration and other personnel. Age assessment (sometimes referred to as age determination) is the process of attempting to establish the age of an individual. The need for official age assessment arises because many unaccompanied asylum-seeking children do not have documents or papers confirming their age or date of birth, and many come from cultures where birthdays are not celebrated. Crawley (2004: 76) notes that 'a third of all births worldwide are not registered and many countries do not issue contemporaneous birth certificates'. Therefore, children who are unsure of their age and have no documentation connected with this are not necessarily concealing their age. Judgements about age, then, become reliant on a young person's bodily appearance. However, 'children and young people may look older than they are because of their experience in the country of origin' (ibid.: 76). Some may have taken on adult responsibilities from a young age and may appear mature as a result of their experiences of trauma, migration and culture. Young men from certain parts of the world grow facial hair from a younger age that typically occurs in the UK. Also, some service providers noted how some of the African young men appear physically taller and bigger and hence apparently older than Asian young men of the same age. Overall, 'age determination is a process, not a single event. It is an inexact science and the margin of error can sometimes be as much as five years on either side' (ibid.: 78).

Age assessment has vital implications for their right to stay and other entitlements. In the short term, it means that young people may have to stay apart from their peers until their age is established. Assessing the age of an individual also has a direct influence on the services that will be available to them. In the long run, an adverse decision may result in return to their home country. Age assessment is therefore a key issue for service providers and unaccompanied asylum-seeking children. As a policy worker provocatively suggested, a number of service providers are unprofessional in their assumptions about the ages of some of the unaccompanied minors they work with:

> I hate this, but I have heard these comments before – [Someone says] 'aye, 16, but he is shaving twice a day!'

Another example of this was Apollo who revealed how immigration officials suggested that he was 22 or 23, and hence lying when he said he was 16.

In terms of the process of age assessment, Melzak and Avigad suggest that the practice of service providers should be informed by need and not by political concerns. They suggest:

To avoid being re-traumatised, humiliated and embarrassed, most of all those who have survived do not want to be disbelieved as is so often their experience with professionals in this country. Any assessment technique will therefore be useful only to the extent that the person carrying out the assessment actively conveys respect, acceptance and validation during the assessment process and is attuned to the client's need for safety and control over the answering of difficult questions.

(2005: 2)

Overall, then, it is important to emphasise that age assessment is a process that should be conducted with great care, and children should be fully informed of all stages of the process. If there is any uncertainty, the benefit of doubt should be given to the child. Furthermore, in the process of conducting age assessment, 'it is very important to ensure that vulnerable children are not left without services while their age is being determined by professionals' (Kidane 2001: 19).

The Separated Children in Europe programme suggests the following about age assessment procedures:

Age-assessment includes physical, developmental, psychological and cultural factors. If an age assessment is thought to be necessary, independent professionals with appropriate expertise and familiarity with the child's ethnic/cultural background should carry it out. Examination should never be forced or culturally inappropriate. Particular care should be taken to ensure that they are gender-appropriate.

In cases of doubt, there should be a presumption that someone claiming to be less than 18 years of age, will provisionally be treated as such.

It is important to note that age assessment is not an exact science and a considerable margin or error is called for. In making age an age determination, separated children should be given the benefit of the doubt.

(Save the Children 2004: 18)

Clearly, age assessment is not a precise procedure and there may be considerable margin of error. Judith Dennis clarifies that when in doubt it is better to age band a child rather than assign an exact age (Research in Practice 2005).

Age assessment was raised by a number of service providers, and their concerns here were directed at children who were receiving poorer care and consideration than other children due to an inaccurate age determination decision. An advocacy and advice worker intimated that 'age dispute issues can be very difficult', and a policy worker was worried about the age assessments that unaccompanied asylum-seeking children often 'have to endure'. It was clear from the views of a number of service providers that they were unsure about the age determination process, which led to some suspicion associated with certain unaccompanied asylum-seeking children who appeared to be older than they claimed to be. This demonstrates the significance of the ways in which unaccompanied minors' bodies are read, interpreted and responded to, and the often unsafe consequences this may have for the young person. Service providers were concerned about the many risks of placing a child in adult services (or vice versa), and some children were upset and stigmatised as a result of the lack of trust arising from their claim to be a particular age.

Conclusions

In summary, the bodies of unaccompanied asylum-seeking children – in particular their skin colour, their perceived age and their status as asylum-seekers – mark them out in certain ways, work to determine their place of abode, structure everyday experiences and regulate the resources available to them. It circumscribes the places they can go and kinds of services they can access. The first of these processes is shared by the indigenous black and minority ethnic population, but experienced in a different way by newcomers depending on the extent to which racialisation of the body shaped their pre-flight experiences. The second two processes represent an interaction between responses to bodily markers and specifics of their asylum status. This has implications for their everyday experiences of different spaces, their access to and use of particular services and their general well-being. By way of conclusion, we would like to make three general observations about the processes connected with the ways in which unaccompanied minors' bodies become contested sites of belonging, identity and difference.

First, contestations over unaccompanied minors' bodies – whether these relate to perceptions about their age, how much welfare benefit they receive or the facilities they are granted access to – are almost always controlled by the state. Many of the service providers consulted in this research worked exceptionally hard to maximise the well-being of the children they worked with, but many of their efforts were restricted as a result of the ways in which legislation and government policy worked to limit and constrain them. Examples include frequent government revision of legislation (making it very challenging for lawyers and other service providers to work in an informed way to assist unaccompanied minors) and the ways in which the persistent threat of 'dawn raids' heightened unaccompanied children's sense of being unsafe and insecure. Furthermore, as children and asylum-seekers, unaccompanied minors in Scotland are also the subject of different levels of government policy such as children's legislation in Scotland and asylum and immigration legislation in the UK, which further complicates their overall status and is challenging for many people who work with or for them. Generally, many of these negative outcomes are controlled by the state with service providers and unaccompanied minors having little or no say in such matters.

Second, a major challenge for the ways in which unaccompanied minors' bodies are read, interpreted and responded to relates to the negative coverage that asylum-seekers and refugees receive in the media and the lack of understanding associated with this. Lewis (2006) reported that the general lack of understanding about asylum as well as the influence the media have on informing opinions are two of the main factors that influence people's attitudes to asylum and asylum-seekers. A key conclusion of the research we conducted was that unaccompanied minors should be regarded as children first and foremost rather than asylum-seekers, since taking such a perspective radically changes people's perceptions of them. It is crucial that the media start to offer accurate accounts of issues relating to asylum, and that more information is made available in order to better inform people's perspectives on the experiences and circumstances of asylum-seekers, including unaccompanied asylum-seeking children and young people.

Many aspects of unaccompanied minors' experiences are strongly influenced by practices and discourses dictated by society, service providers and government legislation and policy. However, it is also important to acknowledge the active role that these young people play in their own embodiment and the resilience they regularly show in dealing with their experiences (see also Watters 2008). In many respects, unaccompanied minors are not simply victims of various forms of social and structural inequality but are competent negotiators of their everyday lives. Many of them displayed high levels of resourcefulness in getting on with their lives and were committed to giving something back to Scottish society. They were very passionate about the opportunities available to them in schools and colleges, and were eager to work hard to gain qualifications and new skills. Many also displayed compassion and warmth for the service providers who worked with them. All in all, despite the negative factors associated with their embodied experiences, the resourcefulness of the unaccompanied minors consulted in this study is evidence of their continuing resilience.

References

Crawley, H. (2004) *Working with Children and Young People Subject to Immigration Control: Guidelines for Best Practice* (London: Immigration Law Practitioner Association).

Holloway, L. and Hubbard, P. (2001) *People and Place: The Extraordinary Geographies of Everyday Life* (London: Pearson Hall).

Hopkins, P. (2004) 'Young Muslim men in Scotland: inclusions and exclusions', *Children's Geographies* 2(2): 257–72.

Hopkins, P. and Hill, M. (2006) *'This is a Good Place to Live and Think About the Future': The Needs and Experiences of Unaccompanied Asylum-Seeking Children and Young People in Scotland* (Glasgow: Scottish Refugee Council).

Hopkins, P. and Hill, M. (2008) 'Pre-flight experiences and migration stories: the accounts of unaccompanied asylum-seeking children', *Children's Geographies* 6(1): 257–68.

Hubbard, P., Kitchin, R., Bartley, B. and Fuller, D. (2005) *Thinking Geographically: Space, Theory and Contemporary Human Geography* (London: Continuum).

Kidane, S. (2001) *Food, Shelter and Half a Chance: Assessing the Needs of Unaccompanied Asylum-seeking and Refugee Children* (London: British Assocation for Adoption and Fostering).

Lewis, M. (2006) *Warm Welcome? Understanding Public Attitudes to Asylum-seekers in Scotland* (Southampton: Institute for Public Policy Research).

Longhurst, R. (1995) 'The body and geography', *Gender, Place and Culture* 2(1): 97–105.

Longhurst, R. (2005) 'Situating bodies', in L. Nelson and J. Seager (eds) *A Companion to Feminist Geography* (Oxford: Blackwell), pp. 337–49.

Melzak, S. and Avigad, J. (2005) *Thinking about Assessment of Asylum-seeker and Refugee Children Both Unaccompanied and Accompanied by Family Members* (London: Medical Foundation).

Nayak, A. with Welamedage, L., Brown, R. and Humphrey, L. (2006) *'Beneath the Skin': The Future of Race Equality in Tyne and Wear* (Newcastle: School of Geography, Politics and Sociology, Newcastle University).

O'Donnell, M. and Sharpe, S. (2000) *Uncertain Masculinities: Youth, Ethnicity and Class in Contemporary Britain* (London: Routledge).

Research in Practice (2005) 'On New Ground: Supporting Unaccompanied Asylum-Seeking Children and Young People' (transcript), Audio Series 9.

Save The Children (2004) *Separated Children in Europe Programme: Statement of Good Practice* (third edition) (London: Save the Children).

Thomas, S., Thomas, S., Nafees, B. and Bhugra, D. (2004) ' "I was running away from death" – the pre-flight experiences of unaccompanied asylum-seeking children in the UK', *Child: Care, Health and Development* 20(2): 112–22.

UNHCR (2004) *Trends in Unaccompanied and Separated Children Seeking Asylum in Industrialised Countries 2001–2003* (Geneva: UNHCR).

Watters, C. (2008) *Refugee Children* (London: Routledge).

Westwood, S. (1990) 'Racism, black masculinity and the politics of space', in J. Hearn and D. Morgan (eds.) *Men, Masculinities and Social Theory* (London: Unwin Hyman), pp. 55–71.

Young, I. M. (1990) *Justice and the Politics of Difference* (Princeton, NJ: Princeton University Press).

11
Children's Bodies: Working and Caring in Sub-Saharan Africa

Elsbeth Robson

Introduction

Most ordinary Majority world[1] children in sub-Saharan Africa under-take heavy (paid and unpaid) burdens of work (Schildkrout 1981, Kayongo-Male and Walji 1984, Reynolds 1991, Robson 1996, 2004a, 2004b, Bourdillon 2000, Katz 2004). Children's everyday work includes domestic chores, head-loading, working on farms, estates and in family businesses, trading, collecting water and firewood, herding livestock and caring for the sick, disabled or elderly and younger siblings. Their young working bodies perform necessary productive and reproductive work for the survival and well-being of themselves and their households. The responsibilities carried by the bodies of African youngsters contradict prevailing global discourses of childhood as a period of care-free socialisation in which young bodies are protected from physically demanding, and potentially harmful, manual work while engaging in schooling and play.

Thus children's bodies in sub-Saharan Africa (as elsewhere) are contested by policy-related concerns, particularly debates on eliminating child labour, child abuse (especially rape, but also involvement of children in witchcraft) and child trafficking. Meanwhile, in everyday circumstances, parents and young people themselves argue that for children's bodies to perform work is acceptable, even desirable, so long as the burden is appropriate to the age, ability and strength of the child and does not jeopardise his or her health or education. This chapter explores the complexity of questions of embodiment and children in sub-Saharan Africa, especially for children who work. Issues addressed include those that affect children and young people's physical and emotional well-being as children, as well as the adults they are to become.

By demonstrating how children's bodies undertake work and caring responsibilities in sub-Saharan Africa, this chapter illustrates a little of the importance of embodiment in the processes through which children participate in social life – an area somewhat neglected by the 'new approaches to childhood research' (James et al. 1998: 147). While social and cultural theorists, including geographers, are increasingly giving bodies form, presence and importance, children's geographies have lagged behind (Horton and Kraftl 2006a: 76). Early work on embodiment by geographers focused largely on adult bodies – for example, exploring how bodies and places make each other (Nast and Pile 1998), or considering bodies within geographies of sexualities (Bell and Valentine 1995). Following the lead of other social and cultural theorists concerned with embodiment, and especially the recognition that all geographies are embodied, children's geographers have recently come to assert that embodiments matter (Horton and Kraftl 2006b: 273). Although children's geographers have come belatedly to this position, it should be remembered that, by definition, children are considered a separate category from adults by virtue of corporeal differences thus '"Children's Geographies" – as a tradition of research and writing – has been about bodies all along' (Horton and Kraftl 2006a: 77). This assertion is especially true for those working in Majority world contexts with, for example, their particular concerns for child labour and child health (Ansell 2005). However, with few exceptions, those concerned with the Majority world have not engaged with social and cultural theories of embodiment which remain largely western-focused. Thus, this chapter responds both to the call by children's geographers for a 'closer apprehension of the bodily details of children's lives' (Horton and Kraftl 2006a: 79) and to the need for rebalancing the thus far predominantly western focus of attention to issues of embodiment.

Many years' research with children in different countries of sub-Saharan Africa, including Nigeria, Kenya, Zimbabwe and Malawi, lie behind this chapter. Although the case studies presented here come from Kenya and Zimbabwe respectively, they are typical of the lives of young people across sub-Saharan Africa (and the Majority world generally). In such poor economies school provision is inadequate, attendance is patchy, not possible or desired by many children, especially beyond primary level; and working is simply an accepted, normal and inevitable part of everyday life from a young age. The first case study comes from a poor, remote, semi-arid village in Kenya, which is familiar with inadequate rainfall for food production, ethnic conflict and environmental degradation. In contrast, the second case study focuses on young people in some of Zimbabwe's low-income, high-density urban communities, which are experiencing the ravages of HIV/AIDS, economic decline and political autocracy. The challenging circumstances which contribute to the work burdens placed on children's bodies in these situations share many resonances with working boys and girls across the continent, and indeed the Majority world more widely.

Children's bodies at work in Kenya

This chapter opens by examining compositions, drawings and observations gathered from rural youngsters in Marich village, Pokot district, north-west Kenya,[2] which reveal how their bodies engage in daily work alongside schooling and leisure. Gender and age divisions in children's work and activities are revealed which highlight the social construction of adult/child and societal expectations that children's bodies are working bodies. Even school attendance does not protect children from the work demands placed on them. For example, primary school boarding pupils in Marich village in written compositions[3] demonstrate how they undertake work while at school in term time:

> ... after game we were going to fetch firewood.
>
> (Boniface Kiramwai,[4] 18 years)

> ... after bell ring I'm going to did activities example to fech[5] water and colecting some fire wood from the bush.
>
> (Sarah Pkiyach, 14 years)

> My duties for working at this school as a border student ... we wake up early in the morning and ... we can start by sweeping the rubbish paper or any unwanted durty thing found around the dormetrys, after finish sweeping we know mopping the flour with a duster.
>
> (Thomas Mwetich, 14 years)

Unlike in Minority world schools, there are no caretaking or cleaning staff – a situation common to most government schools in sub-Saharan Africa, especially in rural areas. Hence the pupils are expected to clean their dormitories, classrooms, staffroom, teachers' offices, assembly area and surrounding area (Figure 11.1). Marich primary school has no regular water supply, so it is the responsibility of students to fetch water from the nearby river for all washing, drinking and cooking needs of themselves and their teachers. Water carried in buckets and jerry cans on the head or back is a heavy load that can cause headaches, neck strain, back

Figure 11.1   'Sweeping at boarding school'

and 'waist' pain, especially for young, fragile bodies struggling on the steep uphill climb from the river. Pupils are expected to take care of their own (bodily) needs, e.g. washing themselves and their clothes at the river.

Meals for the boarding pupils' hungry and growing bodies are provided using foodstuffs donated by INGOs and donors, but firewood for the school kitchen has to be collected by students from the surrounding semi-arid/arid scrubland. Accidents can happen with the sharp *pangas* (knives) used and thorns scratch legs, hands and arms. There is little access to healthcare for injured and infected bodies – the nearby village clinic is very under-resourced. There is a resident matron who oversees the cooking and suchlike, though cooking with wood exposes pupils to risks of burns and smoke irritates eyes and throats. Pupils are also expected to undertake domestic labour for teachers who live in corrugated metal huts near the classrooms. There is some evidence of gender discrimination in the physical demands made on pupils, as girls report

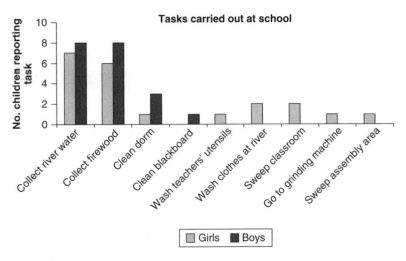

Figure 11.2 Tasks carried out at school

doing more manual work than boys and a wider range of tasks necessary to the reproduction of the school community (see Figure 11.2). This is not surprising and reflects prevailing gender divisions of labour and findings elsewhere.

When not in school – for example, during the school holidays – the children described in their written compositions how they engage in bodily work of social reproduction at home, such as caring for younger siblings and livestock, cooking and cleaning:

> during holiday I would help my mother work like looking after the baby, fetching water, washing clothes and cleaning the house.
>
> (Winifred Chepkamol, 16 years)

> My activities at home is to wash utencils, prepared some food and wash children.
>
> (Norah Cheputo, 15 years)

> At home my duties is to look after our children ... I help my mother to fetch water and firewood and also to look after our goats.
>
> (Rebecca Chepalan, 14 years)

With respect to having responsibility for daily chores of reproduction for themselves and others, the children's school and home lives are not very different. In this respect going to boarding school offers little, or no,

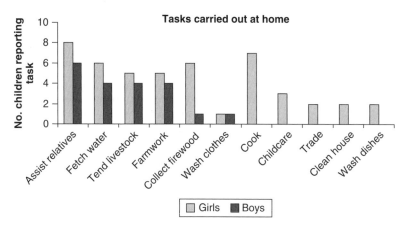

Figure 11.3   Tasks carried out at home

respite from the physical demands placed on young bodies by domestic and other reproductive work. Given prevailing norms of gender discrimination it is not surprising that it is also the case that at home more girls report undertaking domestic tasks than boys (Figure 11.3). In addition, during school holidays both boys and girls report carrying out some productive tasks, including care of livestock and farming (Figure 11.3).

Young Kenyans in Marich are aware that their productive work at home, especially on the family farm, is not just for the benefit of the household as a whole, but also helps them continue their education. Some young people trade vegetables from family plots specifically to earn money for their school fees:

> during the holidays we our school closed I went and do the business with other people. I went to sell vegetable in the market during the holidys. Then I will get my school fees.
>
> (Nancy Lochale, 17 years)

> When the school got closed, I usually go...home to help my dear parents to cultivate more land and plant more crops so that it can be sold to a nearby shopping centre so as to get more income which will satisfies my school-fees.
>
> (David Lapol, 16 years)

Finding that children in Marich village undertake bodily work to support family livelihood activities and to earn their school fees correlates with the census data, which record that in West Pokot 27 per cent[6] children work unpaid on family farms (girls 26 per cent, boys 28 per cent), 2.6 per cent worked unpaid in a family business and 0.1 per cent worked for pay (Government of Kenya 1999). Children working to earn their school fees is also a common phenomenon elsewhere in the Majority world, e.g. in India (Nieuwenhuys 1993).

Observations by the author in and around Marich village provide further evidence for the range of productive and reproductive bodily work carried out by rural children in West Pokot district (Tables 11.1 and 11.2). For example, observations over a single day along the banks of the Morunyi river revealed children engaged in water collection, clothes washing, fishing, watering livestock, collecting wild foods and gold panning (Table 11.1, Figures 11.4 and 11.5). Of course, children also play on the riverbank, swim and sing while they work, thus juxtaposing playful bodies and working bodies.

Children's work in Marich village can be divided by gender and includes a range of activities, some of which are undertaken regularly and some more occasionally (Table 11.2). Gold panning is a seasonal activity reliant on appropriate levels of water flow in the river and can yield good economic returns. But it is arduous work in the hot sun, involving hours of bending and standing in the river which can cause leg ulcers, as well as back pain and headaches. The distribution of tasks between boys and girls does not simply reflect adult gender divisions of labour. Boys, especially younger boys, are sometimes expected to carry out domestic tasks that belong to the domain of girls and women that men would not be expected to do, e.g. collecting water and firewood

Table 11.1   Observations of children at the Morunyi river

Time	Observation
07.27	*Two girls aged about five and six years fill their water containers*
08.04	*A small girl wades out to fill a plastic water container*
12.50	*Two girls are gold panning in the shallows*
13.10	*A boy fishing has two or three fish he has caught on string*
14.36	*A boy brings a group of goats and sheep to drink*
15.01	*Seven girls are panning for gold alongside older women*
15.45	*A girl and her grandmother collecting leaves along the riverbank to cook*
15.55	*A boy fishing with a rod after two hours has no fish, but yesterday got four*
16.10	*Two girls and a boy come with containers for water*
18.40	*Three girls are washing clothes and collecting water as dusk falls*

Source: Extracts from author's field notebook.

Figure 11.4   Girls collecting water from Morunyi river, Kenya

for the household. However, there are strong traces of adult gender divisions of labour being mirrored by children, e.g. only boys hunt birds and small rodents with bows and arrows. Such equipment can injure young bodies, even accidentally in play; but for the youthful carrier they signify a male body and masculine identity.

The data from the pastoralist community in Marich offer plentiful evidence for the ways both boys and girls contribute to social reproduction and production. The data reveal that these young African bodies bear considerable burdens of productive and reproductive work, not least through their daily chores, including water collection, cleaning, care of younger children, cattle herding, and so on. This is not unusual for many children elsewhere in sub-Saharan Africa. The next section considers the risks of emotional and bodily impacts for a particular (but growing, albeit largely hidden) group of working children who care for an adult incapacitated with (presumably) HIV/AIDS-related ill health.

Figure 11.5　Washing clothes in the Morunyi river, Kenya

Table 11.2　Observed work of children out of school

Girls	Boys
Regular work activities	
Collect water	*Collect water*
Collect firewood	*Collect firewood*
Pan for gold	*Water and graze livestock*
Wash clothes in river	*Fish*
Care for younger siblings	*Hunt (with bows and arrows)*
Trade	*Errands for adults*
Errands for adults, e.g. carry maize to grinding machine	
Occasional work activities	
Fish	*Care for younger siblings*
Collect wild foods	*Collect wild foods*
Trade	*Cook*
	Trade
	Pan for gold

Source: Compiled from observations by author, recorded in field notebooks.

Young carers' bodies at risk in Zimbabwe[7]

Given the alarming scale of the HIV/AIDS pandemic across sub-Saharan Africa many youngsters are engaged in caring for chronically sick and dying adult relatives. What little is known about the children in extraordinary circumstances who find themselves caring for someone with HIV/AIDS (Baumann et al. 1996, Robson 2000, 2004a, Robson and Ansell 2000, Robson et al. 2006, Evans and Becker 2007) does not reveal much about the embodied impacts of undertaking caring responsibilities. The number of child carers in sub-Saharan Africa is unknown, but given the escalating scale of the pandemic, can be presumed to be increasing.

Caring is not only emotionally draining and traumatic, but also physically demanding. In Highfields, a high-density suburb of Harare, Thomas[7] (17 years), living with his older brother and ill father since his mother died, had been looking after his father for the last eight months. Thomas became the carer after their father had been discharged from hospital, so his brother could go out to work to support them. Thomas explained his caring work for his father: '[I] do almost everything for him, bath, feed, do all the necessary things, including taking him to the toilet, accompany for treatment quite often.'

Caring makes heavy demands on Thomas's own body: 'it's a very tiring job, this is a very demanding task. It's difficult.' Other young carers like Thomas, interviewed in Zimbabwe, are at risk not only of catching infections from the ill relatives (mostly mothers) they care for at home, but also from problems including back strain from lifting heavy adults in and out of bed for toileting and bathing, supporting them on long journeys to seek healthcare at clinics, etc. At government facilities it is not unknown for patients and their carers to have to wait long hours (even overnight) to be attended to; they may be bullied, pushed around and also verbally abused. Scalds and burns may injure young bodies as they struggle with cooking and heating water for bathing.

Thomas's mental health was also suffering from the impacts of care, as noted by the interviewer: 'already lost mother, the young man was very stressed and is scared of losing his father.' Young carers have not only physical, but also emotional, bodies whose needs may be neglected during the painful experience of caring for and losing a loved one. It can be frightening caring for a parent and not being told why that parent is sick or has died. In African cultural settings children find bereavement hard, but are rarely given support to cope emotionally; they lack time and space to express their fears or feelings and are often told to forget the bad things which have happened. Children may blame themselves when their parents die and lose a sense of self-worth. It is reported by UNICEF that children in Uganda trapped at home all day caring for a dying parent have been known to develop psychosomatic symptoms of HIV infection (Black 1991: 10).

Lack of respite care and inadequate state provision for the chronically and terminally sick are exacerbating the strains for young carers in Zimbabwe. Young carers' own physical growth may be stunted from carrying heavy loads of water, firewood, etc. and their health could be damaged by cooking on fires because exposure to smoke can cause eye, throat and respiratory problems.

Despite the negative emotional and physical impacts of caring work on the young people interviewed, some reported benefits: that it had made them strong, they had matured, learnt to take decisions, found it a privilege to be close to a loved one and found vocational direction to pursue a caring career (e.g. nursing) (Robson et al. 2006: 104).

African children's bodies contested by policy

The bodies of sub-Saharan Africa's children are contested by policy-related debates and well-intentioned efforts to eliminate child labour, child abuse (including rape and children's involvement in witchcraft), child trafficking, and so on. The labour responsibilities of the majority of ordinary African children contradict prevailing global discourses of protected youthful bodies enjoying a care-free childhood of socialisation devoid of responsibility. Such discourses, as enshrined for example in the UN Convention on the Rights of the Child, are heavily informed by western Minority world, white, middle-class norms, which sit uneasily with the cultural values, everyday lives and bodily experiences of children in the Majority world. The media play a significant role in global discourses on children and portraying their imagined bodies, often representing them as victims of (often sexual) violence and exploitation. For example, in Malawi there is much coverage in national newspapers of children's bodies as victims of defilement (rape), child labour on tea, tobacco and other estates (albeit outlawed) and other forms of abuse, including trafficking and involvement in witchcraft. Children's bodies also feature in policy-related concerns – UNICEF in 2007–8 ran a 'Stop Child Abuse' campaign in Malawi to coincide with the child protection law being formulated in the country (Figure 11.6).

Figure 11.6 UNICEF Stop Child Abuse campaign, *Malawi News*, 6-12 October 2007

Acceptable burdens of work?

'Child labour' is often seen in the West as the unacceptable face of Third World poverty, yet in many societies it is considered entirely normal that children work.

(Ansell 2005: 158)

In everyday circumstances in sub-Saharan Africa parents and children argue that for children's bodies to perform work is acceptable, even desirable, so long as the burden of labour is appropriate to the age of the child. Some communities in southern Malawi complain that laws outlawing child labour on tea estates have harmed their livelihoods because those under 18 years can no longer earn money.[8] Those who call for the elimination of child labour often posit school attendance as an alternative to the exploitation of work. However, children also work at school, as explained by the children at Marich primary school, in Kenya. Children in many schools in sub-Saharan Africa also have to undertake hard bodily work at school, including sweeping, mopping floors, hoeing, cutting grass to maintain the classrooms and school surrounds. These unpleasant manual tasks are often assigned as punishments, e.g. after arriving late for classes. Furthermore, children's bodies in many African schools are physically disciplined – corporal punishment, by and large, is uncontested and beatings are considered by children and adults alike as normal, even good, necessary or desirable (Ansell 1999). Children who cannot earn money for their school fees may be denied the opportunity to get a school education. In Zimbabwe there are schools on tea estates where children combine earning and learning (Bourdillon 2000).

Conclusions

This chapter has explored a little of the geographies of bodily experiences of childhood across Africa through case studies and vignettes from fieldwork conducted by the author with communities and children, including young carers and other children in and out of school in Kenya, Zimbabwe and Malawi. It has been shown through the case studies (arguably resonant of embodied children's lives across sub-Saharan Africa) that questions of children who work and embodiment are complex, not least because they contradict western notions of childhood, encapsulated in policy documents like the UN Convention on the Rights of the Child and universally promoted by mainstream media (even in Africa) as a period of life which should be free of manual work. I argue in this chapter that although the vast majority of ordinary children in sub-Saharan Africa do work, working does not always only negatively affect their physical and emotional well-being, but can benefit them by contributing to their daily reproduction and survival of their households; as well as equipping them as future adults with skills and education for securing a livelihood. It is hoped that the examples and case study material presented draw attention to the need to rebalance the (to date) mainly western and adult focus within consideration of issues of embodiment by geographers.

Acknowledgements

Thompson, John Lomaria, the late David Roden and staff at Marich Pass Field Studies centre who supported the fieldwork in Kenya. Abby Mgugu who conducted the interviews with young carers in Zimbabwe. The editors who made helpful suggestions.

Dedication

I would like to dedicate this chapter to the memory of Dr David Roden, late director of the Marich Pass Field Studies Centre, who died early in 2007 after a road accident in Kenya having done much to facilitate improvements to children's lives in the surrounding Pokot communities.

Notes

1. The terms Majority and Minority world are adopted following Punch (2000), who argues for the need to rebalance worldviews which privilege 'Western' and 'Developed' populations and issues. By referring to Majority and Minority worlds instead of Third and First worlds or Developing and Developed worlds, the majority of population, poverty, land area and lifestyles in the former world are foregrounded.
2. Data were collected during almost annual field visits from 1997 to 2004.
3. Children at school were asked to write in English under the title 'My life' and to describe their daily activities.
4. Respondents' real names are not used but have been replaced with pseudonyms of typically similar names in order to protect their true identity.
5. The children's original spellings and grammar are reproduced without corrections to avoid distorting their voices.
6. In reality, this figure may be higher, but household heads interviewed for the census may well have deliberately underestimated the work done by children due to fears of accusations of child labour. Another reason why the figure is less than one third of children is because being predominantly pastoralists, many families in West Pokot district do not have farms.
7. This section draws on semi-structured interviews conducted with young carers and key informants in Harare and Chitungwiza in 1997 by the author and a social worker in a RGS-HSBC-funded project 'Young carers in Zimbabwe'.
8. Malawi's Employment Act 2000 prohibits children under 18 years from employment in agriculture.

References

Ansell, A. (1999) 'Southern African Secondary Schools: Places of Empowerment for Rural Girls?' unpublished PhD thesis (Keele, Staffs: Keele University).

Ansell, A. (2005) *Children, Youth and Development* (London and New York: Routledge).

Baumann, L et al. (1996) 'Children care for their ill parents with HIV/AIDS', *Vulnerable Children and Youth Studies* 1(1): 1–14.

Bell, D. and Valentine, G. (eds) (1995) *Mapping Desire: Geographies of Sexualities* (London: Routledge).

Black, M. (1991) *Report on a Meeting about AIDS and Orphans in Africa*, Florence 14/15 (June) (New York and Geneva: UNICEF).

Bourdillon, M. (2000) 'Children at work on tea and coffee estates', in M. Bourdillon (ed.) *Earning a Life: Working Children in Zimbabwe* (Harare: Weaver Press), pp. 147–71.

Evans, R. and Becker, S. (2007) *Hidden Young Carers: The Experiences, Needs and Resilience of Children Caring for Parents and Relatives with HIV/AIDS in Tanzania and the UK: Stakeholder Report* (Nottingham: School of Sociology and Social Policy, University of Nottingham).

Government of Kenya (1999) *Kenyan National Census* (Nairobi: Government Printer).

Horton, J. and Kraftl, P. (2006a) 'What else? Some more ways of thinking and doing "children's geographies"', *Children's Geographies* 4(1): 69–95.

Horton, J and Kraftl, P (2006b) 'Not just growing up, but going on: materials, spacings, bodies, situations', *Children's Geographies* 4(3): 259–76.

James, A., Jenks, C. and Prout, A. (1998) *Theorizing Childhood* (New York: Teachers College Press).

Katz, C. (2004) *Growing up Global: Economic Restructuring and Children's Everyday Lives* (Minneapolis, MN and London: University of Minnesota Press).

Kayongo-Male, D. and Walji, P. (1984) *Children at Work in Kenya* (Nairobi: Oxford University Press).

Nast, H. and Pile, S. (eds) (1998) *Places Through the Body* (London and New York: Routledge).

Niewenhuys, O. (1993) 'To read and not to eat: South Indian children between secondary school and work', *Childhood* 1: 100–9.

Punch, S. (2000) 'Children's strategies for creating playspaces: negotiating independence in rural Bolivia', in S. L. Holloway and G. Valentine (eds) *Children's Geographies: Living, Playing, Learning & Transforming Everyday Worlds* (London: Routledge), pp. 48–62.

Reynolds, P. (1991) *Dance Civet Cat: Child Labour in the Zambezi Valley* (Athens, OH: Ohio University Press/Harare: Baobab/London: Zed).

Robson, E. (1996) 'Working girls and boys: children's contributions to household survival in West Africa', *Geography* 81(4): 403–7.

Robson, E. (2000) 'Invisible carers: young people in Zimbabwe's home-based health care', *Area* 32(1): 59–69.

Robson, E. (2004a) 'Hidden child workers: young carers in Zimbabwe', *Antipode* 36(2): 227–48.

Robson, E. (2004b) 'Children at work in rural Northern Nigeria: patterns of age, space and gender', *Journal of Rural Studies* 20: 193–210.

Robson, E. and Ansell, N. (2000) 'Young carers in Southern Africa? Exploring stories from Zimbabwean secondary school students', in S. L. Holloway and G. Valentine (eds) *Children's Geographies: Living, Playing, Learning & Transforming Everyday Worlds* (London: Routledge), pp. 174–93.

Robson, E., Ansell, N., Huber, U. S., Gould, W. T. S. and van Blerk, L. (2006) 'Young caregivers in the context of the HIV/AIDS pandemic in Sub-Saharan Africa', *Population, Space & Place* 12(2): 93–111.

Schildkrout, E. (1981) 'The employment of children in Kano (Nigeria)', in G. Rodgers and G. Standing (eds) *Child Work, Poverty and Underdevelopment* (Geneva: ILO), pp. 81–112.

12
Militarised Bodies: The Global Militarisation of Children's Lives

Inbal Solomon and Myriam Denov

Introduction

In her book entitled *Maneuvers: The International Politics of Militarizing Women's Lives*, Cynthia Enloe (2000) challenges her readers to broaden their understanding of the military as a stand-alone institution, and highlights the importance of exploring the military's presence and impact on people's daily lives. Enloe argues that formal militaries *require* and elicit the participation, support and trust of civilians, particularly women, in order to ensure their own and their soldiers' sustainability (Enloe 2000: xiv). Despite being an institution primarily aimed at *men*, Enloe argues that the military *needs* women 'to boost morale, to provide comfort during and after wars, to reproduce the next generation of soldiers, to serve as symbols of the homeland worth risking one's life for, [and] to replace men when the pool of suitable male recruits runs low' (Enloe 2000: 44). According to Enloe, in formulating and promoting feminised and militarised roles for women as military wives, military prostitutes, military mothers, military nurses and female army recruits, militaries essentially 'embrace' a variety of women into a military's fold and each group of women is tasked with a role for supporting the military and its soldiers.

'Militarisation' is regarded as a step-by-step transformative historical process by which a person or a phenomenon gradually comes to be controlled by a military regime or comes to depend for its well-being on militaristic ideas (ibid.: 3). Enloe suggests that the process of militarisation has the capacity to affect all aspects and facets of society, including employment, fashion, toys, faith, local economies and voting. Given the vast reach and breadth of the militarisation process, it is of no surprise that children may be deeply affected and transformed by it. Building on Enloe's conceptualisation, this chapter explores the militarisation of children's lives and realities across the globe. The chapter begins by tracing Enloe's conceptualisation of militarisation and the ways in which militarisation is made possible through the 'manoeuvring' of people into positions which support military ideals. The chapter then turns to the subtle militarisation of children's lives through education, the domestic sphere, play and recreation, alongside more overt ways, such as their direct participation in militarised violence. In the context of armed conflict, children associated with fighting forces have become one of the armed forces' most *valuable* commodities, and simultaneously their most impacted victims. Ultimately, the chapter highlights the ways in which children can be seen as 'militarised bodies' whereby an assortment of global practices, both subtle and overt, contribute to the militarisation of their lives. The chapter concludes with a discussion of the implications of militarising the young.

Understanding militarisation: 'How do they militarise a can of soup?'

> For several years I kept a can of Heinz tomato and noodle soup on the kitchen counter. I had bought it in a London supermarket... The Heinz chefs had added little pasta bits to the condensed tomato soup. But instead of the usual alphabet letters, the soup designers had cut their pastas into the shape of Star Wars satellites... The designers and dietitians sitting around the corporate table probably tried to imagine a typical mealtime in the household of a busy woman. Tomato soup is healthy. But a mother has to get a child to eat the healthy meal she prepared. Sometimes that can be a challenge. Little a, b, and c's might not be sufficiently enticing to a french-friesandcoke-lusting child. But add little space weapons. Maybe that would get the young diner to dig the spoon down deep into the mealtime soup bowl... Militarisation, therefore, affects not just the executives and factory floor workers who make fighter planes, land mines and intercontinental missiles but also the employees of food companies, toy companies, clothing companies, film studios, stock brokerages, and advertising agencies. Any company's employees are militarised insofar as they take their customers fascination with militarised products as natural, as unproblematic.
>
> (Enloe 2000: 1–2)

For Enloe, militarisation is a complex process involving the military's 'subtle manoeuvring' of societies to support or take for granted the military's continuation of the business of 'war-waging'. Militarisation is thus broadened from being confined within the specific realm of militaries and is instead understood to occur at the level in which the societal definitions, attitudes, thoughts and expectations are produced (and reproduced), and the societal organisation towards violence (or the acceptance of violence) becomes normalised. Indeed, Geyer (1989: 79) has defined militarisation as the 'contradictory and tense social process in which civil society organises itself for the production of violence'. This process is facilitated by the obfuscation of the traditional boundaries between combatant and civilian statuses (Enloe 2000, Feldman 2002), wherein the diffusion of boundaries involves both

> a material and an ideological dimension. In the material sense it encompasses the gradual encroachment of the military institution into the civilian arena... [while t]he ideological dimension... is the degree to which such developments are acceptable to the populace, and become seen as 'common-sense' solutions to civil problems.
>
> (Enloe 1983: 9–10)

Accordingly, militarisation seeps into society, to encompass realms not traditionally associated with soldiering, combat, war-waging or even peace-keeping (Enloe 2000). In fact, Enloe (ibid.: 2) argues that 'many people can become militarised in their thinking, in how they live their daily lives, in what they aspire to for their children or their society, without ever wielding a rifle or donning a helmet'. For example, entertainers whose purpose is to raise the morale of military troops and toys that allow children to turn violence into play exemplify forces of militarisation (ibid.: 5). The very subtleties of militarisation permeate the daily lives of individuals, 'nudging' them to be more accepting of and reliant on militaristic ideals, including the importance of military endeavours, the patriotic superiority of those enlisted and their families, and the military's status as representative of the broader state (Enloe 2000).

The politics of manoeuvring

Enloe maintains that the militarisation of individuals and collectivities of people is made possible through their subtle – and sometimes more overt – 'manoeuvring' into positions which support the military ideals (Enloe 2000). 'Manoeuvres' involve the manipulation and exertion of (political) control over those populations not traditionally associated with soldiering. In her work, Enloe (ibid.: xiii) discusses the 'efforts that the military and their civilian supporters have made in order to ensure that ... groups of [militarised] women feel special and separate', persuading them to accept the military. For example, citizens generally regard military wives, particularly those who have become military widows, as having contributed the ultimate sacrifice to the collective nation. Entire societies are encouraged to see soldiers as a collective group of 'our boys', necessitating the (re-)alignment of the definitions of such concepts as 'national security' and 'defence' with those of the military. In this way, the dependence on the military, as well as a reliance on its ideals and values, contributes to the process of militarisation.

In other contexts, Enloe (2000) notes that militaries have exhibited overt control over women, militarising their lives in so far as the latter become dependent on the militaries for employment. For example, the stationing of militaries in foreign countries has facilitated a niche market for 'military prostitutes' to meet the ever-growing demands of male soldiers. Moreover, this employment continuously affects less obvious aspects of these women's lives, particularly as they are obliged by the military to undergo invasive health examinations in order to maintain their 'acceptability' and, therefore, their 'employment' on the base. Accordingly, their dependence on the military 'manoeuvres' women into relying on the military, guiding them through the process of militarisation. However, this manoeuvring need not be of a completely totalitarian nature. Enloe (ibid.: 10) explains that 'a militarizing maneuver can look like a dance, not a struggle, even through the dance may be among unequal partners'.

Militarising the young

While historical evidence suggests that children have long been associated with militaries (Shahar 1990), they have been largely excluded from academic research on militaries and militarisation. In recent years, the proliferation of small arms is said to have increased the 'effectiveness' of children on the front line and has made their recruitment into combat more 'profitable' and 'efficient' for armed groups, who take advantage of children's 'agility' and 'suggestibility', and the overall economic hardships experienced by the society in which these children live (Singer 2005). Not only have millions of children been first-hand witnesses of war and the atrocities that invariably accompany armed aggression, but children also continue to be drawn into conflict as active participants. Between April 2004 and October 2007, children were actively involved in armed conflict in government forces or non-state armed groups in 19 countries or territories (Coalition to Stop the Use of Child Soldiers

2008). Importantly, however, children who are not actively soldiering in an armed conflict may nonetheless be affected by and intimately connected to the process of militarisation. The following section explores the militarisation of children's lives through education, the domestic sphere, play and recreation, followed by a discussion of the more overt ways through direct participation in militarised violence.

The militarisation of children's lives: education, domesticity and recreation

As previously noted, the process of militarisation may infuse a society's social conditions and may be seen in the increasing encroachment of the military on civilian populations. Children are not spared from the military's influence, which may diffuse into formal education, the domestic setting and in their play and recreation through television programmes, toys and games (Reagan 1994). Each of these elements is addressed in greater detail in the following subsections.

Militarising education

Militarisation may infuse the content of children's education, particularly when schools 'socialize children to look upon soldiering [or involvement in militant groups] as an attractive career prospect' (Enloe 2000: 242). Gor (2003: 178) refers to the mobilisation of children's 'thinking and emotional readiness to accept the use of power as answers to political problems' as 'militaristic education'. In assessing Israeli society, Gor argues that given the numerous historical threats to Israel, including the repeated annihilation-threatening wars Israel has fought with its Arab neighbours, the content of children's education is often framed by the discourse of 'preparedness', remaining nationally steadfast and resisting victimisation. With the memory of the collective trauma of the Holocaust still looming in the minds of Israeli educators and administrators, Israeli Independence Day is celebrated by teaching children

> that Arabs wanted to throw us into the sea and that the armies of all seven Arab states surrounding us invaded Israel. The day is celebrated in kindergarten as a military holiday. Kids visit military camps and teachers display flags of various military corps.
>
> (ibid.: 179)

Coupled with the potential and omnipresent threat of annihilation, such education may be understood as manoeuvring children's support for the Israeli military, in so far as it has helped to 'emotionally imprint' the military's necessity for national survival in the minds of Israel's youth (ibid.: 180).

The education provided to children may also contribute to the already-present and socially constructed 'enemy', further fuelling cultural cleavages. Research has shown, for example, 'that children's perception of differences between the communities can be concretised, unwittingly or intentionally by the school's teaching environment' (Brocklehurst 1999). An example can be drawn from the early infusion of Nazi dogma in the teaching afforded to German pupils just prior to the Second World War. The Nazi government systematically changed the content of children's schoolbooks and mandated pledges from teachers, promising to educate children according to Nazi ideology, thereby further perpetuating the already present animosity towards Jews and others considered 'genetically inferior' (Cairns 1996). Similar to other contexts in which militarised education permeates, even children who recognised the oppressive nature of this education may have their attempts at dissent stifled by peer pressure and by their subordinate position within the classroom. Indeed, Brocklehurst (1999) argues that children's 'position as consumers of information, in a hierarchal relationship with...an institution is not conducive to their questioning of received bias'. In this way, children may be socialised into the dominant ideology and therefore manoeuvred into accepting the construction of the 'enemy', so prevalent in militarised societies (Enloe 2000).

Militarisation in the domestic sphere

The militarised education of children extends beyond the realm of state institutions and has entered children's homes. The infusion of militarisation into the domestic sphere continues to shape the conditions in which children live, thereby promoting acceptance of armed resistance (Brocklehurst 1999). In Northern Ireland, the central heroes of children's stories were often political leaders and martyrs who were killed during the struggle for Irish independence (Brocklehurst 1999). Brocklehurst explains that in Northern Ireland, folk stories offer '[v]ivid constructions of heroes, demonisation of the enemy, and polarisation of good and bad, "us" and the "other" ... [These] have been typical of children's stories' told by their parents and communities.

The domestic atmosphere may further solidify the militarised educa-tion of children. Brocklehurst has noted that, in Northern Ireland, 80 per cent of Republican children have fathers and brothers involved in the Republican movement, a phenomenon which, she argues, exempli-fies the transmission of Republicanism as an 'hereditary tradition'.

Yet, the militarisation of children in the domestic sphere may also involve more subtle cues. For example, Cairns (1996: 126) explains the particular potency that exists in the act of naming a child, argu-ing that 'naming the child is a politically symbolic act and may be instrumental in constructing the child's political views from birth'. In fact, 'politically active' families in South Africa often chose to name their children after political leaders in the African National Congress (ibid.). Likewise, in Northern Ireland, the naming of children con-tinued to fuel 'the Troubles' by further demarcating citizens into the two rival factions; children's names were chosen explicitly to indicate whether the child was Protestant or Catholic (ibid.). Such divisions continue to fuel community-wide militarisation, in that children are taught that belonging to and supporting 'our' community requires the negation of and (militarised) domination over the 'other'. Indeed, Brocklehurst (1999) argues that '[t]he "internalizing" of the enemy into civilian life ... contributes to community-wide blame and desire for retaliation and necessarily makes children's homes and families part of the battleground'.

Militarising children's play and recreation

Children's play and recreation have also been militarised throughout history and in various different contexts. For example, Orme (2001: 182) explains that in medieval Europe, hunting became an acceptable and encouraged pastime for children. Moreover, a '1512 statue of Henry VIII ... laid down that all men with boys in their houses, aged between seven and seventeen, should provide them with a bow and two arrows, and bring them up to shoot ... [as] a kind of military training' (ibid.: 183, 182). Additionally, Reagan argues that 'war toys', defined as 'toys evok[ing] images of the military, battle situations or war in general', and films 'with patriotic or war themes ... are part of the process of militari-sation' (1994: 49, 52). These games and toys introduce the notion of violence to children, enabling them to incorporate militarisation into their play. Indeed, Marten (2004) highlights that in the US revolution-ary war, children's play and literature centred on supporting their 'side' of the conflict, with many engaging in role-play as soldiers.

Brocklehurst (1999) explains that in Northern Ireland, children's 'popular songs and games clearly express[ed] violent animosity'. Children also joined their parents in Nationalist parades, wherein they participated in 'pseudo-military displays'. In attempting to militarise and gain public support for the war in Sri Lanka, the Tamil Tigers of Tamil Eelam (LTTE) spearheaded '[p]ublic displays of war paraphernalia, posters of heroes, speeches, videos and heroic songs... to invoke patriotic feelings in children and create a cult of martyrdom' (Hogg 2006: 9).

Hesse and Mack (1991: 148, cited in Reagan 1994: 47) suggest that, historically, 'television cartoons have some impact on the child's identification of an enemy, and that "most of the cartoon shows... implicitly introduce[d] children to the superpower struggle between virtuous and righteous Americans and godless, evil communists"'. Therefore, children's recreation may further their acceptance of broader societal discourses, allowing them to become more accepting of militarisation and normalising the political violence within their society. Therefore, children's play that is shaped by military ideologies and strategies ultimately works to normalise militarised violence.

The act of militarising children: overt practices

Alongside some of the more subtle and indirect forms of militarisation noted earlier, children may also become directly associated with (government or insurgency) fighting forces as active combatants, or as medical, technical and/or domestic support. It is important to note that 'overt' and 'subtle' forms of militarisation are not mutually exclusive, making the militarisation of children's lives fluid, often encompassing both forms of participation (Maçhel 2001). Nonetheless, overt and direct acts of child militarisation tend to be labelled more often as part of the phenomenon of 'child soldiers' or 'children associated with fighting forces' which is defined as:

> any person below 18 years of age who is or who has been recruited or used by an armed force or armed group in any capacity, including but not limited to children, boys and girls, used as fighters, cooks, porters, messengers, spies or for sexual purposes. It does not only refer to a child who is taking or has taken a direct part in hostilities.
>
> (Paris Principles 2007: 7)

The next subsection explores examples of the overt militarisation of children. It begins with a general overview of children's direct participation in hostilities, as well as the recruitment and socialisation of children into armed groups.

An overview of children associated with fighting forces

Worldwide, the phenomenon of children's association with fighting forces has reached estimates of 250,000 (Coalition to Stop the Use of Child Soldiers 2004). Despite international condemnation of the involvement of children under 18 in fighting forces, children *under 15* have been participating in armed conflicts, spanning geographically Mexico to Papua New Guinea (Brett and McCallin 1998). While a large number of these youths have been subject to abduction and forced conscription (Maçhel 2001), some have become involved in fighting forces out of frustration with and disenfranchisement from their current social situations, which in many cases have been plagued by extreme poverty, high unemployment and severely limited educational opportunities (ibid.). Indeed, for many children worldwide, '[s]oldiering is often attractive...because it provides meaning, identity, and options civilian life does not afford' (Wessells 2006: 4). At times, the recruitment or enlistment of children into fighting forces receives community approval and '[c]hildren mobilised and militarised are narrated as sacrificial victims to a variety of just causes' (Feldman 2002: 291).

However, the extent of children's militarisation includes more than their participation in combat. In fact, 'depending on the context, child soldiers may serve as sentries, bodyguards, porters, domestic labourers, medics, guards, sex slaves, spies cooks, mine sweepers, or recruiters' (Wessells 2006: 8). For example, in the Iran/Iraq war, children as young as 13 were forced to join the militaries in order to stroll minefields and assist soldiers in detecting unexploded sites (Cairns 1996: 131), while paramilitary groups in Colombia often 'use children called "little bells" as an early warning system, deploying them to front lines to draw fire and identify traps' (Wessells 2006: 17). Children's greatest 'assets' to military and insurgency groups centre on their 'small size', 'agility' and 'greater suggestibility', as 'the greater suggestibility of children and the degree to which they can be normalised into violence means that child soldiers are more likely to commit atrocities than adults' (Brett and McCollin 1998: 20).

Children's direct involvement with armed forces is not a new phenomenon. The earliest data on the overt militarisation of children's actions can be traced back to the children's crusade of 1212, when hundreds of young boys and girls joined French and German armies on a crusade to recapture the Holy Land (Shahar 1990). During the American Civil War, 'drummer boys' often followed armies and assisted the forces by signalling troop movements, delivered mail between troops, assisted military medics and dug ditches to assist the combating battalions (Marten 2004: 128). Although these boys were not supposed to come to harm, some were injured by shrapnel or were even killed in the armed confrontations (ibid.: 137). Despite these historical examples, the recent proliferation of small arms has arguably amplified the roles of children as active combatants, facilitating their participating in front-line combat (Maçhel 2001).

Recruitment and socialisation into the military

In the contemporary context, children who have been conscripted into fighting forces, particularly those involved in civil wars, have often been press-ganged into participation or have been abducted from their families (Denov and Maclure 2007). Press-ganging involves 'a group abduction wherein soldiers sweep through marketplaces or streets, rounding up youths like fish in nets, or raid[ing] institutions such as orphanages or schools' (Wessells 2006: 40–1). Often, armed groups, such as the Revolutionary United Front (RUF) in Sierra Leone, and the Lord's Resistance Army (LRA) in northern Uganda, abduct 'any children who happen to be in their path' (ibid.: 38). Others have been recruited through their religious educational institutions. Wessells (ibid.: 15, 38) notes that the Taliban in Afghanistan often recruit students in madrassas, a process that has been coupled with 'house-to-house' recruitment programmes, wherein parents are either threatened or made to feel a 'sense of duty' to volunteer a child to the greater cause. The Tamil Tigers too promoted a 'one family, one child formula', persuading families to volunteer a child for combat by exempting this family from LTTE-imposed taxation (Hogg 2006: 10).

Other children are manoeuvred into their militarised positions with armed groups through the 'promise' of social and material benefits (Rosen 2006). Wessells (2006: 46) terms such incentives the 'pull' factors of military recruitment, as they offer 'positive rewards or incentives for joining armed groups', explaining that children may be lured into joining armed forces, who may offer them benefits that would have otherwise been denied to them. For example, children may gain prestige and a sense of empowerment (Denov and Maclure 2006), they may experience a sense of belonging to a broader community and they may receive material rewards, such as education and wealth (Wessells 2006).

Joining a fighting force may also be their sole means of survival if their family members have been murdered (Rosen 2006) as the armed group may be their 'only hope of [obtaining] food, medical support or protection from further attack' (Wessells 2006: 47). In this way, the armed groups may offer their child recruits immediate benefits, which may entice them to join the group and later remain within its ranks.

Additionally, the manoeuvring of children into overtly militarised roles is a process which involves training and initiation. Maclure and Denov (2006: 125) highlight that in the Sierra Leonean conflict, children were provided with 'methodical' training about 'engage[ment] in armed conflict...and the perpetuat[ion] of mayhem and terror on behalf of the rebel movement'. For the youth involved with the RUF, violence became 'a feature of daily interaction that inculcated deep-seated fear and unquestioning compliance among the young recruits' (ibid.: 126). Yet, for many of these youth, the years spent with the fighting forces, accompanied by their complete disconnection from their families and communities, led them to be reliant on the rebel group for their survival, and eventually to view 'their captors as sources of succour and guidance' (Maclure and Denov 2006: 125). Cut off from their families, under continuous threat of punishment and often impaired by the forced consumption of hallucinogenic drugs, the child soldiers in Sierra Leone's rebel movement 'gradually acquiesced to the rebel movement's system of warlord clientelism...[and] came to regard the RUF as a surrogate family and themselves as *bona fide* RUF fighters' (ibid.: 128).

For some children, the combat training they receive mirrors the merging of violence and play. For example, in her study of girl soldiers in Sri Lanka, Keairns (2003: 8) found that recruits to the LTTE were given 'dummy guns' in order to normalise their interactions with firearms, allowing them to 'graduate' to actual weaponry only when they have displayed a lack of fear. Moreover, in this context, the girls were given cyanide capsule necklaces to wear prior to engaging in battle; should they be captured by opposing forces, the girls were supposed to take the poison to spare themselves the horror of torture in captivity (Keairns 2003). Interestingly, the ability to control their own fate, albeit only in these rare instances, made the girls 'feel safe because it was a guarantee that the enemy could not capture them alive and abuse or harass them' (ibid.: 8).

Children's overt militarisation often contributes to the 'efficiency' and 'effectiveness' of the groups with which they are associated. The children's multiple roles provide armed groups with the resources necessary for armed combat. Moreover, children's roles within armed forces are often 'highly fluid and contextual, as children ... perform multiple roles in the same day' (Wessells 2006: 72). Paradoxically, children become one of the armed forces' most *valuable* commodities and their most impacted victims. In this way, children's overt militarisation, as well as their roles within these fighting forces, support the overall production of violence and foster the continuation of the armed conflict.

Importantly, one of the emblematic features of children's association with fighting forces is the ways in which sexual violence has been militarised. In some fighting forces, sexual access to girls is a privilege bestowed on successful male soldiers (McKay and Mazurana 2004, Denov 2006). As this former child soldier noted:

> As a commander, you got to choose the girl that you liked and wanted to be with. Girls were used as gifts. I had three wives.
>
> (Denov in press 2010)

Research has underscored that sexual violence may be a universal experience among girls associated with fighting forces in Africa (McKay and Mazurana 2004). Many girl conscripts have been forced to 'marry' and become the 'sexual property' of individual commanders of rebel forces (Denov 2006).

Although children's militarisation is most obvious through their armed participation as child soldiers, militarisation also includes their participation (violently or otherwise) in a highly visible form of public disobedience. In South Africa, children actively resisted the imposition of apartheid policies by

> barricad[ing] streets, set[ting] up roadblocks of burning tyres, and ston[ing] police and other vehicles manned by whites that attempted to enter these [youth-imposed] no-go areas ... [They organised] their own initiation rites by which youth attained a kind of political adulthood.
>
> (Feldman 2002: 297)

Many belonged to the political activist organisation Young Lions of South Africa (Feldman 2002). In yet another context, during the first *Intifada* in the Palestinian territories, children organised bouts of stone-throwing against Israeli army forces and civilian vehicles, with different roles (e.g. distracting soldiers by setting fire to tyres or warning the youth when soldiers were approaching) being self-imposed according to the child's age (Kuttab 1988). The distinguishing feature making these forms of participation militaristically overt is that the youth in such contexts are 'at the forefront... rather than the followers' of the political violence (Cairns 1996: 112). It is important to note that 'as children get older... overt action gives way to more clandestine activities often involving highly organised guerrilla movements' (ibid.: 117). In this way, such militarised activities often paved the way for more violent means of resistance later in life.

Conclusion: the implications of militarising the young

The militarisation of children's lives has a powerful impact on traditional conceptualisations of warfare, particularly as it can no longer be understood as conflict waged solely between sovereign armies or armed groups and where the boundaries between soldiers and civilians are clearly distinguished. Children appear to be an integral part of warfare, both indirectly and directly.

The analysis has underscored the ways in which societies may 'nudge' (Enloe 2000) children's participation in militarised activities. As we have seen, there is a myriad of social realms, including children's education, familial environments, play and recreation, which may contribute to the militarisation of children's lives. Providing attention to these forces enhances the understanding of children's wartime experiences and broadens the conceptualisation of children's involvement in armed conflict. Moreover, exploring these militarised 'grey areas' of armed conflict provides a more complex picture of the experiences of children, both those on the front line and those on the sidelines. We can also begin to understand how children have been exploited in combat as well as how their participation 'fertilises' (Enloe 2000) militarisation.

The fluidity and subtlety of the militarisation process makes it extremely difficult to oppose or uproot. Indeed, various demobilisation programming efforts for children formerly associated with fighting forces have been instituted in contexts of armed conflict and in the post-conflict period. However, when children's militarisation is understood to encompass more subtle manifestations, such programming may indeed fail to address or include the broader population of children and youth affected by militarised violence. Moreover, understanding the subtleties of children's militarisation also draws attention to the fact that militarisation is often socially entrenched and may require more than demobilisation programming for its eradication.

The militarisation of children's lives has taken diverse forms, both subtle and overt. In many countries around the world, children have been first-hand victims and witnesses of war and the atrocities that invariably accompany armed aggression. In addition, children continue to be drawn into conflict as active participants. However, as this chapter has demonstrated, subtle and more indirect forms of militarisation continue to shape and alter the everyday lives of children worldwide. As profoundly militarised bodies, children are shaped by and in turn shape the militarisation of their society.

References

Brett, R. and McCollin, M. (1998) *Children: The Invisible Soldiers* (Sweden: Radda Barren).

Brocklehurst, H. (1999) 'The nationalisation and militarisation of children in Northern Ireland', *Conflict Archive on the Internet (CAIN)*, available at http://cain.ulst.ac.uk/issues/children/brocklehurst/brocklehurst99.htm, accessed 8 November 2007.

Cairns, E. (1996) *Children and Political Violence* (Cambridge, MA: Blackwell).

Coalition to Stop the Use of Child Soldiers (2004) *Global Report* (London).

Coalition to Stop the Use of Child Soldiers (2008) *Global Report* (London).

Denov, M. (2006) 'Wartime sexual violence: assessing a human security response to war-affected girls in Sierra Leone', *Security Dialogue* 37(3): 319–42.

Denov, M. (in press, 2010) *The Making and Unmaking of Child Soldiers in Sierra Leone* (Cambridge: Cambridge University Press).

Denov, M. and Maclure, R. (2006) 'Engaging the voices of girls in the aftermath of Sierra Leone's conflict: experiences and perspectives in a culture of violence', *Anthropologica* 48(1): 73–85.

Denov, M. and Maclure, R. (2007) 'Turnings and epiphanies: militarisation, life histories, and the making and unmaking of two child soldiers in Sierra Leone', *Journal of Youth Studies* 10(2): 243–61.

Enloe, C. (1983) *Does Khaki Become You? The Militarization of Women's Lives* (Boston, MA: South End Press).

Enloe, C. (2000) *Maneuvers: The International Politics of Militarizing Women's Lives* (Berkeley, CA: University of California Press).

Feldman, A. (2002) 'X-children and the militarisation of everyday life: comparative comments on the politics of youth, victimage and violence in transitional societies', *International Journal of Social Welfare* 11: 286–99.

Geyer, M. (1989) 'The militarisation of Europe: 1914–1945', in J. R. Gillis (ed.) *The Militarisation of the Western World* (New Brunswick, NJ: Rutgers University Press), pp. 65–102.

Gor, H. (2003) 'Education for war in Israel: preparing children to accept war as a natural factor of life', in K. J. Saltman, and D. A. Gabbard (eds) *Education as Enforcement: The Militarisation and Corporatization of Schools* (New York: Routledge Falmer), pp. 177–88.

Hogg, C. L. (2006) 'Child recruitment in South Asian conflicts: a comparative analysis of Sri Lanka, Nepal and Bangladesh', *Chatham House* and *Coalition to Stop the Use of Child Soldiers*, available at www.childsoldiers.org/document_get.php?id=1162, accessed 11 October 2007.

Keairns, Y. E. (2003) 'The voices of girl child soldiers: Sri Lanka', *UNICEF*, available at www.quno.org/newyork/Resources/girlSoldiersSriLanka.pdf#search=%22 child%2 0soldiers%20-%20sri%20lanka%22, accessed 24 August 2006.

Kuttab, D. (1988) 'A profile of stonethrowers', *Journal of Palestine Studies* 17(3): 14–23.

Maçhel, G. (2001) *The Impact of War on Children: A Review of Progress Since the 1996 United Nations Report on the Impact of Armed Conflict on Children* (New York: Palgrave).

Maclure, R. and Denov, M. (2006) '"I didn't want to die so I joined them": structuration and the process of becoming boy soldiers in Sierra Leone', *Terrorism and Political Violence* 18(1): 119–35.

Marten, J. (2004) *Children for the Union: The War Spirit on the Northern Home Front* (Chicago, IL: Ivan R. Dee Publishing).

McKay, S. and Mazurana, D. (2004) *Where Are the Girls? Girls in Fighting Forces in Northern Uganda, Sierra Leone and Mozambique: Their Lives during and after War* (Montreal: International Centre for Human Rights and Democratic Development).

Orme, N. (2001) *Medieval Children* (New Haven, CT: Yale University Press).

Paris Principles (2007) *United Nations: Office of the Special Representative of the Secretary-General for Children and Armed Conflict*, available at www.un.org/children/conflict/english/paris-principles.html, accessed 4 April 2008.

Reagan, P. M. (1994) 'War toys, war movies and the militarisation of the United States, 1900–1985', *Journal of Peace Research* 31(1): 45–58.

Rosen, D. M. (2005) *Armies of the Young: Child Soldiers in War and Terrorism* (New Brunswick, NJ: Rutgers University Press).

Shahar, S. (1990) *Childhood in the Middle Ages* (New York: Routledge).

Singer, P. W. (2005) *Children at War* (New York: Pantheon Books).

Usher, G. (1991) 'Children of Palestine', *Race and Class* 32(4): 1–18.

Wessells, M. (2006) *Child Soldiers: From Violence to Protection* (Cambridge, MA: Harvard University Press).

13
Commentary: Disciplining Bodies

Elizabeth A. Gagen

I recently gave birth to my first child. Immediately after he was born, the midwives conducted the usual examination – counting toes, checking vital signs, etc. They mumbled a few comments under their breath and made a few minor observations, but nothing seemed to cause undue concern. I looked at the paperwork after they left, and my eyes scanned down to the section titled 'Abnormalities'. To my surprise, there was an affirmative tick in a section I was expecting to be blank. The offending feature was listed as 'webbing between third and fourth toes'. My surprise was not that my child had webbing between his toes – I had already noticed that and considered it to be entirely unremarkable. Rather, I was taken aback by the naming of this as an abnormality. Everyone at some point in their lives is made aware of their position on the normal curve (some, unluckily, feel this more often and more acutely than others), but I had never experienced the modern clinical state so squarely classifying my own flesh and blood. Over the next few months, my child's body was measured and weighed and his progress plotted along a curve of normality that immediately imposed an expected standard of physical development. In a little red book, I conspired with health visitors and GPs to record minute changes to my child's body as part of the Pre-school Surveillance Programme. To some, this is comforting: it provides a sense of watchful concern by professionals and experts who are trained to notice problems and intervene with solutions. To others, it imposes unrealistic standards of development and instils anxiety that their child is not developing 'normally'. Either way, it reminds us unmistakably that the disciplining of bodies begins not during childhood but at, and indeed prior to, birth.

For Foucault (1973, 1977), the act of imposing a language of normal health and development which emerged during the late eighteenth and

178

nineteenth centuries brought bodies within the gaze of medical science from which they have never escaped. Since the nineteenth century, medicine has provided a systematic way of monitoring and classifying physical health, operating an increasingly bureaucratic system of surveillance to render bodies visible and knowable. That infant bodies are brought immediately and abruptly within this field of knowledge should come as no surprise. Although children feature only anecdotally in Foucault's work, they do so frequently to illustrate the high stakes placed on children's education as governable and self-governing individuals. Combining the disciplinary techniques of the modern state and the biopolitical ordering of populations through, among other things, modern medicine, Foucault's concept of governmentality is particularly useful for explaining the importance placed on children's health and later their education. As Margo Huxley, citing Foucault, explains, governmentality is

> a generalized power that seeks to fashion and guide the bodily comportments and inward states of others and of the self; a form of action on the actions and capacities of the self and of others. In this sense, government is the form of power 'by which, in our culture, human beings are made subjects'.
>
> (2007: 18)

Governmentality includes all those practices which aim to shape subjectivity and encourage subjects to govern one another's behaviour; the calculations and measurements necessary to know, and therefore control, a population; and the forms of 'truth' which authorise people – 'experts' – to intervene in the process (Huxley 2007). It is understandable, therefore, that children and young people would be central to this project. Indeed, Foucault states, with regard to children as a privileged point of power, that 'it was childhood which was at stake for the parents, the educational institutions, for the public health authorities; it was childhood as the breeding ground for the generations to come' (in Stoler 1995: 144). If the purpose of governmentality is to create governable, self-regulating individuals, then the most efficacious route is through institutions of childhood, including the family. Many of Foucault's cases are drawn from late eighteenth- and nineteenth-century contexts in which rank-and-file militarism and the strict ordering of space pervaded schools, hospitals and prisons. However, the more disseminated and networked spaces of twenty-first-century societies are no less committed to disciplinary and biopolitical strategies of governmentality.

Indeed, the goal of self-government is entirely compatible with, and indeed presupposed by, neoliberal democracies. With regard to childhood, the goal of harmonising the desires of the subject with the desires of the state remains the business of governmentality; and young bodies are persistently normalised, tutored in self-regulation and policed in old-fashioned techniques of imposed order.

Of relevance to this volume, then, is the question of modern childhood and youth. How does the modern neoliberal state continue the project of governmentality, and how are children being mobilised within it? Perhaps because of the emphasis on children's independence as competent social actors, the subfield of children's geographies has been cautious about studying the disciplinary technologies of modern governmentality. It has tended to focus on empirical studies of children's active involvement in shaping social life, on giving young people voice and pursuing child-centred research methodologies. While this has produced some necessary and important work, it has also created a false opposition between children's competence as active agents, on the one hand, and disciplinary structures, on the other. In Foucault's work, the production of governable subjects is dependent on a sense of personal freedom. Liberal democratic government requires people to be complicit in their own governing. Indeed, the self-government of individuals through autonomy, enterprise and freedom is the cornerstone of the internalised disciplinary project (Rose 1996). Children, as well as adults, regulate themselves and each other, and, while children are pulled into this project from infancy and earlier, adults are no more or less exempt. Both are disciplined and both are competent, but to avoid studying disciplinary technologies for fear of negating children's active role in social life would be to misunderstand the operation of discipline society.

This section on disciplining young bodies is therefore a useful addition to the literature. Soloman and Denov illustrate the far-reaching strategies of neoliberal disciplinary technologies by claiming that children's lives, globally, are being systematically militarised through overt and covert disciplinary strategies. Their claims rest on existing research which many of us will be familiar with: that there has been an increase in the number of child soldiers in war zones across the world and that children's play, education and home life are increasingly militarised (although they discuss a more general trend among children rather than the differential socialisation of boys and girls). However, by connecting all these literatures Solomon and Denov argue that there is a discernible and collective trend towards the militarisation of all childhoods the world over. How, then, do we intervene in this trend? As they rightly note, it will require more than demobilisation to solve the problem since the socialisation of children is so entrenched and, I would argue, reliant on self-regulation. Any parent who has tried to dissuade a young child from playing with toy guns or attempted to discourage a teenager from violent computer games will have collided head on with the force of peer pressure, or, in Foucauldian terms, devolved surveillance. We are confronting not simply school curricula, marketing companies and media images, but the interiorised gaze of collective youth. For boys – and I would argue that much of what Solomon and Denov discuss is targeted disproportionately at boys – punishment for nonconformity is sometimes severe. Boys' bodies are invested with immense political capital and, as men's studies has been at pains to point out, there is a steep hierarchy within masculinity that ranks physicality and militarism over intellectualism and emotions in many mainstream settings (Connell 1995). This can certainly be applied to childhood and youth; indeed, the hierarchies are perhaps more acute in childhood than they are in adult life. The result is a powerful system of rewards and punishments which make it difficult and sometimes painful to resist. But if we are to resist the militarisation of childhood, it will surely require both painful decisions and hurtful experiences for our children.

The hierarchisation of young bodies is also the subject of Hopkins and Hill's chapter on unaccompanied asylum-seeking children and young people, where the material effects of disciplinary processes which rank bodies are made apparent. Part of this research involved understanding how local communities categorised and ranked asylum-seeking young people, concluding that their relative experiences of abuse and their access to services and resources differed according to their placing on a racial and age-related hierarchy. Clearly, the indexing of race was active in shaping the institutional and everyday experiences of asylum-seeking children. Hopkins and Hill focus on both the state-centred attempts to categorise and therefore make governable the bodies of foreign-born youth and the way local communities enforce their own system of categories to make sense of, and discipline, young asylum-seeking bodies. While many have questioned Foucault's relative silence on race (Young 1995), others have drawn from his writing to theorise the histories of racial discourse and colonial relations (Stoler 1995, 2002). Stoler's claim that the indexing of race which took place during the colonial era was not the result of white colonialism but constitutive of it has implications for reading the racialised body politics of the present. In the context of

Hopkins and Hill, this means understanding racial hierarchies not as a consequence of white rankings, but as embedded in the regulation of whiteness itself. More specifically, Stoler also argues for the examination of discourses of race and sexuality as an interface, particularly in childhood where sexual and racial dangers are often marked together. What struck me in the discussions of racial hierarchies in Hopkins and Hill's chapter was the discourse of exoticism which draws precisely on this interface. At the centre of this is young African masculinity which is serially exoticised by local communities and immigration workers. My concern here is that by focusing on the ranking of marginalisation (i.e. that African masculinity was less marginalised than Asian masculinity), we are missing the work that exoticism does in constructing raced and sexualised African youth. While the discourse of black male sexuality may work in young asylum-seekers' favour in some situations, such as those documented in the chapter, in other contexts it might represent a more dangerous and transgressive threat to whiteness. My point is that the racial ordering of bodies is a flexible and context-driven process and we must be wary of reifying the categorical politics in operation at any one time.

A second category in operation in this chapter is age. Unaccompanied asylum-seeking children and young people, often without formal documentation, are frequently assigned an age by the authorities. This raises questions about the boundaries of childhood and adulthood and the kinds of assumptions the state makes about what constitutes a child's body and childlike experience. A child who has experienced responsibility, work and hardship may be judged to be older than a child who has not, simply because our western understanding of childhood assumes it to be a period of relative ease, education and freedom of leisure. As Elspeth Robson explores in her chapter, childhood in the global South is not always subject to the same governing principles. In sub-Saharan Africa there is profound conflict between the impulse to discipline children through formal institutional mechanisms of education, supported by the UN Convention on the Rights of the Child and most western liberal democracies, and the impulse to discipline children's bodies through working and caring roles. In a context where the governability of citizens is dependent on a degree of both, the result is a hard-working childhood where education and labour combine with backbreaking force.

The other two chapters in Part II turn to the issues of health and health visitors with which I opened. This is the subject of Pamela Dale's chapter in which she explores health visitors in early twentieth-century

Halifax and argues against a straightforward analysis of infant health checks as part of the disciplinary mechanism of the modern state. Instead, she suggests that visits were neither wholly unwelcome nor unhelpful. That benevolent outcomes might emerge from a system of surveillance, classification and regulation, however, does not contradict the disciplinary thesis. Indeed, few would contest the fact that modern health care has had enormous material benefits while simultaneously exercising undeniable control over the bodies it treats. This is certainly true of the infant bodies born into modern health care to be routinely categorised, charted and pathologised. Their parents may invite intervention, a child might benefit from the care given, but the child is also rendered into normality or abnormality according to an inescapable medical and developmental language. Indeed, to categorise this process as good or bad, useful or harmful, misses Foucault's point. The intentions of individuals are secondary to their collective effect. Moreover, that disciplinary practices might be entered into voluntarily and willingly is the inevitable outcome of a system of self-regulation whereby authority is decentred and diffuse, owned and administered, however unevenly, by all subjects.

This is not to say that it is not useful to examine local practices to determine how strategies are operationalised. However, with reference to the operation of strategies, Foucault (1977: 27) reminds us that 'none of its localized episodes may be inscribed in history except by the effects that it induces on the entire network in which it is caught up'. The surveillance of my child's health and growth is not imposed on us: I am a good, governable subject and I engage willingly in it. But the effects are infinite. It protects him against disease; it establishes the parameters of acceptable weight gain, no doubt setting up a lifelong relationship between body image and social expectation; it alerts me to sensory abnormalities; it tells me of desirable rates of mental and physical development, projecting what kind of child he will be should he be ahead of the curve and what he might be should he fall behind; It contains within it the seeds of future embodiments that are just beginning to insinuate themselves into his infancy.

Such future embodiments are evident too in Jo Pike's chapter on the social management of childhood obesity. Here, Pike examines a Europe-wide health promotion programme aimed at reducing childhood obesity. While outwardly the programme aimed to tackle the structural determinants of obesity, promoting positive environmental changes, it is critiqued for falling back on individual behaviour modifications, which ultimately locate the cause and resolution of obesity within children's bodies. Again, this is commensurate with Foucault's diagnosis of the operation of governmentality. It is precisely because subjects need to be governable that they must also be taught to assume responsibility for their embodied selves. Self-regulation and individual responsibility are pervasive elements of disciplinarity and, as Pike demonstrates, children increasingly come to govern themselves and each other through public health discourses on body size.

By way of conclusion, I turn briefly to the issue of infancy which began this discussion. Perhaps unsurprisingly, we have been neglectful of infants in children's geographies. Our attention to giving children and young people voice and conducting participatory research which relies on a certain degree of verbal, physical or imaginative skill obviously precludes the very young. But within the domain of governmentality and disciplinary technologies, the study of infants would yield fascinating new insights. Newborn babies require almost everything doing for them, so are subject to the vicissitudes of expert advice. Once their young bodies begin to exert control, they are forever and necessarily being tutored and coached in fine and gross motor skills and social behaviour. Moreover, the reach of the medical gaze has never been longer. The point at which medical technologies can see life now begins long before a child is born. With ultrasound and intrauterine diagnostics, medics can observe, classify, regulate and treat the foetal body. As technologies impose themselves on younger and younger life, it raises uncomfortable questions about the point at which children's geographies become relevant. While there is a rich sociological and anthropological literature which critiques discourses of parenting (e.g. Hardyment 1995, Furedi 2001), and a growing field of science and technology studies which has critically engaged with the reproductive science (e.g. Clarke 1998), few in childhood studies have engaged with geographies of infant bodies themselves, and fewer still have grappled with the issue of foetal 'life'. Both life-stages, however, offer us ways to understand how young bodies are disciplined and regulated and how those bodies act and live.

References

Clarke, A. E. (1998) *Disciplining Reproduction: Modernity, American Life Sciences and 'the Problem of Sex'* (Berkeley, CA: University of California Press).
Connell, R. W. (1995) *Masculinities* (Cambridge: Polity Press).
Foucault, M. (1977) *Discipline and Punish: The Birth of the Prison* (New York: Vintage).
Foucault, M. (1973) *The Birth of the Clinic* (London: Routledge).

Furedi, F. (2001) *Paranoid Parenting: Why Ignoring the Experts may be Best for Your Child* (London: Penguin).

Hardyment, C. (1995) *Perfect Parents: Baby-care Advice Past and Present* (Oxford: Oxford University Press).

Huxley, M. (2007) 'Geographies of governmenality', in J. W. Crampton and S. Elden (eds) *Space, Knowledge and Power: Foucault and Geography* (Aldershot: Ashgate).

Rose, N. (1996) *Inventing Our Selves: Psychology, Power and Personhood* (Cambridge: University of Cambridge Press).

Stoler, A. L. (1995) *Race and the Education of Desire: Foucault's History of Sexuality and the Colonial Order of Things* (Durham, NC: Duke University Press).

Stoler, A. L. (2002) *Carnal Knowledge: Race and the Intimate in Colonial Rule* (Berkeley, CA: University of California Press).

Young, R. J. C. (1995) 'Foucault on race and colonialism', *New Formations*, 25: 57–65.

Part III
Performing Bodies

14
Stigma, Health Attitudes and the Embodiment of Youth(ful) Identities: Understandings of Self and Other

Natalie Beale

Introduction

The impact of peer pressure on young people's health attitudes and behaviour has been explored extensively in academic and popular discourses. However, there has been less discussion of how stereotypes and stigma influence young people's health attitudes and the ways these relate to bodies and youth(ful) identities. Media and popular discourses frequently stigmatise young people from working-class or underprivileged backgrounds, emphasising deviance, youth subcultures and fear of crime. In contrast, this chapter explores processes of stigmatisation within youth cultures and the role of bodies and place within this.

Drawing on research undertaken with young people in County Durham, in north-east England, this chapter aims to explore relationships between bodies and stigma in respect to two key issues: the development and maintenance of young people's identities, self-concept and health attitudes; and the relatedness of stigmatised people, bodies and places. Bodies played a key role in shaping young people's identities and helped enable both the expression of identity and the enactment of health attitudes. Furthermore, bodies were of central importance in the outworking of local cultures of bullying and victimisation and in the (re)productions of prejudices and stigma. The stigmatisation of people, bodies and places I discuss appeared to be mediated by both local peer group and school dynamics and wider social and cultural influences.

The fieldwork discussed was undertaken through three organisations[1] in a small city within County Durham. Blakely Comprehensive School serves a mixed catchment area in the suburbs of the city. Highview

High School is an independent selective school which draws its intake predominantly from wealthier families across a larger geographic area. The Netherton Youth Project works with young people in the wider Netherton area, serving peripheral council estates in the Netherton and Northgate areas of the city (including the highly deprived Northgate Hill estate) and a number of outlying ex-mining villages. The young people involved in the research were in school years 8 (aged 12–13) or 10 (aged 14–15).

In all three organisations, I undertook work with small groups in sessions consisting of a mixture of discussion work[2] and participatory diagramming. Approaches to the diagramming varied, with one group rejecting the method outright, but typically used a two-stage diagram similar to Figure 14.1. The base layer shows what participants thought 'health' means and the second layer used Post-it notes to identify risks and barriers to health for people their age. These diagrams were used to help focus discussions around the issues participants considered important.

Figure 14.1   An example of a two-stage diagram
Source: (Year 10 females, Highview).

This chapter is in three main sections. The first introduces ideas relating to gender, bodies, stigma and ontological security and the second discusses the role of the body in young people's performances of gender and identity. Building on these ideas, the third section discusses stereotypes and stigma as they relate to people, bodies and places, and ways in which various people, bodies and places were constructed as 'other'.

Gender, bodies, stigma and ontological security: some key ideas

A significant amount of attention has been given elsewhere to ways of theorising masculinities and femininities (McRobbie 1991, Mac an Ghaill 1994, Connell 1995, MacInnes 1998, O'Donnell and Sharpe 2000, Frosh et al. 2002, Haywood and Mac an Ghaill 2003), and it is not necessary to revisit the debate here. I am viewing masculinities and femininities as socially constructed identities which relate to and reinscribe material bodies without determining them. Empirical work I have undertaken suggests that both embodied aspects of gender and identity and an individual's physique/appearance and its reception are integral components in young people's perceptions of health. Embodiment involves not only the physical appearances associated with different masculinities and femininities, but also their corporeality and performance.

This chapter recognises that health and well-being are experienced in and through the body; as Howson notes, '"Health" is not an abstract concept...but refers to specific *bodily* experiences that are shaped by material circumstances' (2005: 50; emphasis in original). Whilst geographers have tended to draw a distinction between discursive bodies and material bodies, emphasising the former (see Longhurst 2001, for fuller discussion), I view bodies as both discursive and material. Discourses and knowledges are deployed on and over bodies, thus establishing certain knowledges and representations of truth regarding the lives and behaviour of individuals and particular bodies (Foucault 1975). Such discursive practices are related to the performativity of gender, which should be understood as the reiterative and citational practice by which discourse produces the effects that it names (Butler 1993). Butler goes on to argue that the body, its contours and movements are material, but that materiality needs to be reconceptualised as the effect of power. This chapter acknowledges that bodies are physical, fleshy, corporeal entities which take on different shapes and appearances and, whilst bodies and embodiment may be influenced and sculpted by power and discourse, bodies are also material entities in their own right. Like other authors (e.g. Bordo 1993, Grosz 1994, Gatens 1996, Howson 2005), I reject the idea of a Cartesian mind/body dualism and consider a person's mind and body to be inextricably linked, with physical, mental and emotional health and well-being directly influencing each other.

It is widely accepted that stigma may be attached to people or places seen to differ in an undesirable way from social norms or expectations. Goffman (1963) identifies three categories of stigmatisation: blemishes of the body such as physical deformities; blemishes of character or behaviour such as alcoholism; and tribal stigma associated with membership of a particular social group. He also argues that stigma may be either enacted or felt. Enacted stigma is experienced through the ways other people act towards or around the stigmatised person, whereas felt stigma is where the stigmatised person internalises their fear of stigma being enacted and does so in a manner which limits their behaviour or opportunities. Enacted stigma is based on a perceived distinction between 'self' and 'other' in which the self is seen as normal and the other as abnormal or defective. As Aitken (2001) notes, the othering of young people is common. However, most literature focuses on the ways young people are othered by society at large and ignores processes operating within their peer group. This chapter argues that the processes of stigmatisation and othering are multidirectional. In many instances, young people who stigmatised or othered sections of their peer group were simultaneously themselves stigmatised by others.

Experiences of stigma or othering can have a significant impact on an individual's ontological security. Put simply, ontological security refers to an individual's sense of being in, or belonging to, the world and underlies their ability to engage in the activities of day-to-day life. Laing states that an ontologically secure individual

> may have a sense of his [*sic*] presence in the world as a real, alive, whole, and, in a temporal sense, continuous person. As such, he can live out into the world and meet others... Such a basically *onto-logically* secure person will encounter all the hazards of life, social, ethical, spiritual, biological, from a centrally firm sense of his own and other people's reality and identity.
>
> (Laing 1960: 40; emphasis in original)[3]

Felt stigmas and experiences of being 'othered' can challenge an individual's ontological security through undermining their self-esteem, confidence and sense of self-worth and identity. As the next section discusses, performances of gender and identity frequently help maintain young people's ontological security but also, in some instances, provide a mechanism for undermining this through processes of bullying, victimisation and stigmatisation.

Performing gender and identity: the impact of local cultures and upbringing

The idea that gender identities are asserted through performance is well documented (Butler 1990, 1996). This was most obvious with the year 10 males whom I worked with at the Netherton Youth Project. They displayed a marked enactment of white working-class masculinities, similar to the 'Geordie'[4] masculinities discussed by Nayak (2003a, 2003b). For this group, the maintenance of a 'macho' or 'hard' image was an essential survival strategy in an environment where physical and emotional bullying was commonplace and this gave the young people a 'status' in the eyes of peers. Elements of macho behaviour were observed among male participants in several sessions, especially in relation to risk-taking behaviours, and there was a certain kudos associated with domestic problems. These participants promoted their status by contrasting themselves with 'softies' or 'swots' (see Box 14.1).

Box 14.1

Steve   The way you're brought up. 'Cos if you've like been brought up like... like as a softy or someone that can stand up for themself.

NHB   So you think that, you think that's people's upbringing not their character?

Steve   It's just like the way you've been brought up.

Ben   It's just the way that you are and that.

Chris   If people think you can't stand up for yourself that's... like the people you've use to peer pressure.

[*This was followed by discussion of fighting as main method participants use for standing up to peer pressure.*]

Steve   Exactly. Most of them fight in gangs though 'cos they can't fight by themselves 'cos they're softy shites.

Jake   Yeah, but when people fight in gangs they normally get everyone else against the person that they're against. 'Cos everyone else is scared of going against them, aren't they?

(Year 8 males, Netherton)

The idea that sport can play an important role in the construction and maintenance of masculine identities is well documented (O'Donnell and Sharpe 2000, Frosh et al. 2002, Gorely et al. 2003, Swain 2003). For many male participants, physical prowess and a sturdy appearance were an important aspect of their identity. These attributes were associated with 'hardness' and macho behaviour, helped foster a sense of belonging to the 'gang'[5] and, as in Swain's (2003) study, promoted status and popularity. Like the 'softies' and 'swots', males who were less good at, or less interested in, sport and physical activities were marginalised and derided by many of the young males I worked with. Box 14.2 is particularly revealing in this respect. Here, the comments relate to a number of interwoven issues which Steven and Chris use to place Edward in an inferior category to themselves. First, the comment relates to a perceived lack of skill on Edward's part, second, to the culture of bullying and victimisation at Netherton (of which Steven was both a perpetrator and victim), third, to Edward's smaller build and less muscular appearance and, fourth, to Edward's chosen sport. In their culture, as in many other areas of North-East England, football is the most esteemed sport and rugby is seen as a southern and middle-class activity.

Box 14.2

Steven   'E just stands there, you know ... Do you know what position Edward plays in rugby? Left back in the changing rooms!

Chris   There's no such thing as left back in rugby is there?

Steven   Left back in the changing rooms.

(Year 8 males, Netherton)

The performances of femininity during fieldwork sessions appeared less marked, but may have been obscured by my femaleness. However, when discussing health, the female participants generally placed more emphasis on environmental cleanliness and hygiene, possibly reflecting the gendering of domesticity. At Highview this was used as a means of promoting their superiority compared to people in less affluent areas which they considered to be dirty and full of people smoking, drinking, taking drugs and racing cars. In addition, many Highview participants emphasised personal appearance and hygiene. For example, Victoria placed considerable value on her immaculate appearance and promoted her status by setting this off against supposed deficiencies in other students' appearances. This was apparent from the way she looked at Louise and Shannon when talking about appearance and good teeth, and from points that Louise and Shannon made on their diagram (Figure 14.2). Social identity and appearance are often intertwined in the creation of young women's embodied identities, and perceived deficiencies in appearance can lead to stigma, shame and low self-esteem (Frost 2005). Whilst, from my perspective, neither Louise nor Shannon seemed unattractive in terms of their appearance, it was apparent that they felt the stigma which other group members enacted – a theme which I return to later.

At Netherton, and to some extent Blakely, female participants frequently emphasised the importance of being seen as 'cool' or 'hard'.

Figure 14.2   Diagram extract about the impact of appearance on health
Source: (Louise and Shannon, Year 10, Highview).

In line with other studies (e.g. Plumridge et al. 2002, Rugkasa et al. 2003), smoking was complexly intertwined with a 'coolness' that was integral to the maintenance of their identity, especially in a culture where educational achievement carried little prestige. At Netherton, the girls gave graphic descriptions of the impact smoking was having on their bodies but, whilst a number of them had tried to quit, they had been unable to manage the bodily and emotional ramifications of nicotine withdrawal. Many of the participants had started smoking when they encountered stresses or problems, such as family break-ups, which challenged their existing self-image and security. Several Netherton girls mentioned being dropped by existing friendship groups when their parents separated and the need to (re)form their identity and image with new groups. The protective function of their new friendship groups was highlighted by Lorri, who stated that 'all of us we talk to Hayley and Sarah because our parents have split up and so we just find people and go ah "have your parents split up?" and we make sure they don't get no hassle' (Lorri, Year 8, Netherton).

In most instances, the performances discussed in this section were not single, calculated or deliberate acts. Rather, they were a repetition and reiteration of practices which structured the individual peer group and local cultures and their place in wider society. Beliefs and discourses surrounding how bodies should look or behave were embodied by the young people I worked with in a variety of ways as they sought to negotiate and establish their emergent identities. This process was complexly interwoven with both local social and cultural norms and the ensuing networks of prejudice and stigmatisation. It was clear that many of the young people I worked with had carved out their identities along social class and gender lines, associating primarily with other young people from a similar background to themselves. This led to the enactment of stigmas by the different groups based on the social or friendship groups individuals belonged to, or where the lived, in a similar manner to the tribal stigma discussed by Goffman (1963). Enactments of tribal stigma were an important means by which many of the young people maintained their ontological security through constructing themselves as 'normal' and the beliefs, behaviours or appearances of different groups as 'other'. This in turn served to reinforce, both positively and negatively, the different identities which the young people were developing. As the next section discusses, young people's identities and ontological security are further enhanced, or restricted, by the relatedness of people, bodies and places and associated issues of stigma.

Stigma: the relatedness of people, bodies and places

Academic literature has generally focused on specific groups or types of people who are stigmatised by wider society; even when authors are seeking to unpick or challenge such stigmatisation. Notable examples include homeless people (Cloke et al. 2000, May 2000, Johnsen et al. 2005), prostitutes and homosexuals (Vescio and Biernat 2003, Scambler 2007), HIV/AIDS sufferers (Cullinane 2007, Robertson 2007, Tempalski et al. 2007) and 'deviant' youth (Jones 2002, Kraack and Kenway 2002). In my research it appeared there was also a more complex process of stigmatisation operating at the local level, through which different sections of the peer group were othered. Furthermore, stigmatised places and stigmatised people were related in the eyes of the young people I worked with, and were often discussed interchangeably. In Box 14.3 participants immediately mentioned cities they knew as examples of unhealthy places when asked whether they thought some places were healthier than others. The reasons given centred partly on the people they associated with these places and partly on perceived deficiencies in the material environments.

Box 14.3

Lorri	Birmingham.
Fred	Birmingham. So why is that not a good place to be?
Lorri	'Cos it's like scruffy. There's loads of like tramps on the street.
Ruth	Aye it's like 'cos I go like – places like Sunderland like that 'cos you out for anything and it's just like sitting in a circle and drinking and that.
Lorri	I think cities have spoilt it.
Fred	So do you think it is scary?
Jemma	Not scary.
Lorri	Not scary, just minging.
Anna	So what's minging about it?
Hayley	Tramps and that.
Ruth	It's embarrassing 'cos like say someone comes to visit you and they like see loads of people
Lorri	sitting on the street.

(Year 8 females, Netherton)

In their discussion of air pollution and neighbourhood stigma in Teesside, Bush et al. (2001) identify a hierarchy of stigma in which residents frequently differentiated between their own neighbourhoods and other areas which they considered to be more polluted, thereby distancing themselves from the perceived stigma. Alongside environmental stigma associated with place, the authors identify social stigmas associated with residents due, for example, to high crime levels and unemployment. They argue that the interweaving of these different stigmas is used to discredit both Teesside as a place and the people who live there (see also Howel et al. 2002, Phillimore and Moffatt 2004). Like Wakefield and McMullan (2005), I found that some places were simultaneously stigmatised by some and viewed more favourably by others. There appeared to be a hierarchy of stigma in which Highview and Blakely participants stigmatised the general Netherton area, those living in Netherton and the surrounding villages stigmatised the Northgate Hill estate and a number of participants from Northgate identified other places as being worse.

The relatedness of stigmatised places and stigmatised people was particularly apparent in discussions about Northgate. Whilst Northgate was, in general, viewed as a stigmatised area by all the groups I worked with, the views of individual participants who either lived in Northgate or had close connections with the area varied. Sam and Tom, who lived on the Northgate Hill estate, believed it was healthy because of the local sports facilities and swimming pool, and contrasted the area to 'dirty' countryside. Jemma was quick to defend Northgate and made it clear through her body language and tone that she disagreed with, and was offended by, what the other participants were saying. Here, whilst the stigma associated with Northgate was enacted by many participants, the stigma was not felt by Jemma, Sam and Tom. In contrast, Shannon, whom I mentioned in the previous section, clearly felt the stigma associated with living in Northgate and was extremely uncomfortable mentioning where she lived in front of the other group members. It was apparent from (non-)interactions between other group members and Shannon that they had marked her as 'other' on a number of fronts, and she was frequently looked at when they made comparisons between their virtues or advantages and perceived deficiencies in other types of people. Louise, who also lived in an area the Highview participants stigmatised, encountered similar problems.

Both Louise and Shannon were subjected to stigmatisation on the basis of interrelated hierarchies of bodies and place. These hierarchies were shaped by processes of power operating within the peer group and by the dominant discourses embedded in the local cultures. Through these processes the young people involved were, with the exceptions of Louise and Shannon, able to assert the normality of their lives and identities and thereby promote their sense of self-worth and ontological security. The hierarchies of bodies and place varied between different groups, and whilst participants from middle-class areas, such as those attending Highview (and in some instances Blakely), frequently stigmatised young people from working-class areas like Netherton and Northgate, they were in turn stigmatised by the young people in these areas who labelled them as 'softies' and 'swots'.

Conclusion

In contrast to media and popular discourses surrounding young people, bodies and stigma, this chapter has not focused on issues like anti-social behaviour which are commonly used to construct specific groups of young people as deviant or 'other'. Instead, it has explored the ways young people themselves stigmatise people, bodies and places. As discussed, young people's embodiment was intrinsically related to their performed identities and played a significant role in the stigmatisation of both people and places. The young people's beliefs, attitudes and behaviours were sculpted by the environments in which they lived or socialised and by dominant local social and cultural norms and expectations. These varied between different social groupings, primarily along social-class and gender lines. Many participants living in areas stigmatised by others, or who might stereotypically be stigmatised by factors such as school exclusion, had adopted strategies through which they were (superficially at least) able to maintain their ontological security by promoting the normality of their identities and marking alternative sections of their peer group as 'other'. For example, with the exception of Shannon, those living in Netherton and Northgate Hill asserted the normality of their neighbourhoods; stigmatising other places and the bodies associated with these. Nevertheless, the exceptions to this, such as Louise and Shannon, clearly struggled to deal with the stigma they felt and the ways in which enactments of stigma were targeted at both their embodied identities and appearance and at their places of residence.

Young people's health attitudes, and behaviours such as smoking, were frequently related to their emergent identities and self-concept and thus to their embodiment. Furthermore, the low self-esteem and confidence exhibited by Edward, Louise and Shannon suggest that processes of stigmatisation enacted within youth peer groups can impact on emotional health and well-being. As noted earlier, emotional, mental and physical aspects of health are interrelated. Challenges to a young person's ontological security can directly affect their emotional and mental health and well-being and, as illustrated by the female smokers at Netherton, can also have direct implications for physical health. Therefore, understanding the different ways in which young people construct 'self' and 'other', and the ensuing stigmatisation of people, bodies and places, can have wider implications. It is relevant not just to discussions about contested bodies of childhood and youth, but also to ways in which young people's emotional and health needs are supported.

Notes

1. The names of all places, organisations and people have been changed to protect the confidentiality of those involved. The pseudonyms used in this chapter are not meant to reflect any places or persons known to the author or hold any intrinsic meaning.
2. Not all the sessions were recorded because some groups were uncomfortable with this. Therefore, this chapter uses direct quotations from a limited number of groups only. In these quotations, the researcher's initials and names of staff members have been printed in capital letters, in order to distinguish their contributions from those of the young people involved. All of the recordings were transcribed verbatim and the language used by the young people involved has not been sanitised or modified.
3. Although Laing's initial discussion of ontological security focused on people with schizophrenia, the concept has since been widely used to apply to other contexts.
4. The term 'Geordie' refers to people from the Tyneside area of North-East England, particularly the city of Newcastle-upon-Tyne, and to their culture. This area is adjacent to County Durham and, whilst County Durham was formerly a coal-mining area and Tyneside combined this with shipbuilding, the two areas have similar cultures and histories.
5. 'Gangs' were an important aspect of the youth cultures at Netherton. These were friendship groupings rather than the media stereotype of a criminal or inner city-style gang. Nevertheless, it was clear from the ways they were described and mentioned by the young people that such gangs held an important protective function.

References

Aitken, S. (2001) *Geographies of Young People: The Morally Contested Spaces of Identity* (London: Routledge).

Bordo, S. (1993) *Unbearable Weight: Feminism, Western Culture and the Body* (Berkeley, CA: University of California Press).

Bush, J., Moffatt, S. and Dunn, C. (2001) ' "Even the birds round here cough": stigma, air pollution and health in Teesside', *Health and Place* 7 (1): 47–56.

Butler, J. (1990) *Gender Trouble: Feminism and the Subversion of Identity* (London: Routledge).

Butler, J. (1993) *Bodies that Matter: On the Discursive Limits of 'Sex'* (London: Routledge).

Butler, J. (1996) 'Gender trouble, feminist theory and psychoanalytical discourse', in L. Nicholson (ed.) *Feminism/Postmodernism* (London: Routledge).

Cloke, P., Milbourne, P. and Widdowfield, R. (2000) 'Homelessness and rurality: "out-of-place" in purified space?' *Environment and Planning D: Society and Space* 18(6): 715–35.

Connell, R. (1995) *Masculinities* (Cambridge: Polity Press).

Cullinane, J. (2007) 'The domestication of AIDS: stigma, gender, and the body politic in Japan', *Medical Anthropology* 26(3): 255–92.

Foucault, M. (1975) *Discipline and Punish* (London: Penguin).

Frosh, S., Phoenix, A. and Pattman, R. (2002) *Young Masculinities: Understanding Boys in Contemporary Society* (Basingstoke: Palgrave).

Frost, L. (2005) 'Theorizing the young woman in the body', *Body and Society* 11(1): 63–85.

Gatens, M. (1996) *Imaginary Bodies: Ethics, Power and Corporeality* (London: Routledge).

Goffman, E. (1963) *Stigma: Notes on the Management of Spoiled Identity* (Harmondsworth: Penguin).

Gorely, T., Holroyd, R. and Kirk, D. (2003) 'Muscularity, the habitus and the social construction of gender: towards a gender-relevant physical education', *British Journal of Sociology of Education* 24(4): 429–48.

Grosz, E. (1994) *Volatile Bodies: Toward a Corporeal Feminism* (Bloomington and Indianapolis, IN: Indiana University Press).

Haywood, C. and Mac an Ghaill, M. (2003) *Men and Masculinities: Theory, Research and Social Practice* (Buckingham: Open University Press).

Howel, D., Moffatt, S., Prince, H., Bush, J. and Dunn, C. (2002) 'Urban air quality in north-east England: exploring the influences on local views and perceptions', *Risk Analysis* 22(1): 121–30.

Howson, A. (2005) *Embodying Gender* (London: Sage).

Johnsen, S, Cloke, P. and May, J. (2005) 'Transitory spaces of care: serving homeless people on the street', *Health and Place* 11(4): 323–36.

Jones, J. (2002) 'The cultural symbolism of disordered and deviant behaviour: young people's experiences in a Welsh rural market town', *Journal of Rural Studies* 18(2): 213–17.

Kraack, A. and Kenway, J. (2002) 'Place, time and stigmatised youthful identities: bad boys in paradise', *Journal of Rural Studies* 18(2): 145–55.

Laing, R. D. (1960) *The Divided Self: An Existential Study in Sanity and Madness* (London: Tavistock).

Longhurst, R. (2001) *Bodies: Exploring Fluid Boundaries* (London: Routledge).

Mac an Ghaill, M. (1994) *The Making of Men: Masculinities, Sexualities and Schooling* (Buckingham: Open University Press).

MacInnes, J. (1998) *The End of Masculinity* (Buckingham: Open University Press).

May, J. (2000) 'Of nomads and vagrants: single homelessness and narratives of home as place', *Environment and Planning D: Society and Space* 18(6): 737–59.

McRobbie, A. (1991) *Feminism and Youth Culture: From Jackie to Just Seventeen* (Basingstoke: Macmillan).

Nayak, A. (2003a) '"Boyz to men": masculinities, schooling and labour transitions in de-industrial times', *Educational Review* 55(2): 147–59.

Nayak, A. (2003b) '"Last of the 'real Geordies'"? White masculinities and the subcultural response to deindustrialisation', *Environment and Planning D: Society and Space* 21(1): 7–25.

O'Donnell, M. and Sharpe, S. (2000) *Uncertain Masculinities: Youth, Ethnicity and Class in Contemporary Britain* (London: Routledge).

Phillimore, P. and Moffatt, S. (2004) '"If we have wrong perceptions of our area, we cannot be surprised if others do as well." Representing risk in Teesside's environmental politics', *Journal of Risk Research* 7(2): 171–84.

Plumridge, E., Fitzgerald, L. and Abel, G. (2002) 'Performing coolness: smoking refusal and adolescent identities', *Health Education Research* 17(2): 167–79.

Robertson, L. (2007) 'Taming space: drug use, HIV, and homemaking in Downtown Eastside Vancouver', *Gender, Place and Culture* 14 (5): 527–49.

Rugkasa, J., Stewart-Knox, B., Sittlington, J., Santos Abaunza, P. and Treacy, M. (2003) 'Hard boys, attractive girls: expressions of gender in young people's conversations on smoking in Northern Ireland', *Health Promotion International* 18(4): 307–14.

Scambler, G. (2007) 'Sex work stigma: opportunist migrants in London', *Sociology* 41 (6): 1079–96.

Swain, J. (2003) 'How young schoolboys become somebody: the role of the body in the construction of masculinity', *British Journal of Sociology of Education* 24(3): 299–314.

Tempalski, B., Friedman, R., Keem, M., Cooper, H. and Friedman, S. (2007) 'NIMBY localism and national inequitable exclusion alliances: the case of syringe exchange programs in the United States', *Geoforum* 38(6): 1250–63.

Vescio, T. and Biernat, M. (2003) 'Family values and antipathy toward gay men', *Journal of Applied Social Psychology* 33(4): 833–47.

Wakefield, S. and McMullan, C. (2005) 'Healing in places of decline: (re)imagining everyday landscapes in Hamilton, Ontario', *Health and Place* 11(4): 299–312.

15
Embodying and Destabilising (Dis)ability and Childhood

Louise Holt

Introduction

This chapter explores the embodied, interconnected corporeal and sociocultural experiences of young people with mind–body–emotional differences. By illuminating some varying responses to difference, which does not always denote otherness, the chapter begins to illuminate the emancipatory potential of theorising identities as dynamic, interconnected social and corporeal becomings. The research presented is contextualised within changing institutional geographies of disabled children's education in the UK, where increasingly young people with a range of mind–body–emotional characteristics are co-located within mainstream schools[1] (Holt 2003a, 2003b, 2004a, 2004b, 2007). However, the shift from segregated special to mainstream education for disabled children has occurred across much of the globalised world, albeit interpreted variously in different national and subnational contexts (Ballard 1999).

The aim of this chapter is to illuminate how the process of subjection/subjectification (Butler 1997) into dominant identity categories is equivocal and open to disruption, enabling young people to transform disability as a negative identity positioning. I have elsewhere focused more explicitly on some of the myriad practices that serve to reproduce young people as disabled (Holt 2007, 2008).

The findings presented emphasise that children can construct relationships based on recognition (Benjamin 1988, cited in Butler 2004) and empathy (Bondi 2003), along with those that reproduce difference negatively. Such social interactions can construct mind–body–emotional differences, which would be understood as disability under dominant discourses, such that they are not enacted as *different* among young people. However, empathetic, affirmative relationships can be established when children are recognised as being different, or labelled disabled. The meaning of disability can be resignified among young people, and difference is not always presented as otherness.

Unravelling moments of social relations that transform disability is pertinent to the changing institutional geography of disabled children's education. A key motivation of 'inclusive' education is the opportunity it presents for transforming dominant, negative, social and cultural relations of (dis)ability by children, in both their everyday lives and adult futures (Alderson and Goodey 1998).

The chapter draws on ethnographic research in two primary (elementary) schools in one large urban centre in the UK. The broader research involved participant observation with approximately 100 children, semi-structured interviews and a semi-projective exercise with 44 children (age 7–10) with a range of mind–body–emotional characteristics, half of whom were diagnosed with 'Special Educational Needs' (SEN). In this chapter I focus on the experiences of two children, 'Alfie' and 'Sharon'.[2] Sharon has body differences: achondroplasia; Alfie has socio-emotional differences, with a specific diagnosis of Asperger's syndrome, which is one of the many autistic spectrum disorders. He also has a visual impairment.

Focusing in depth on just two individuals' experiences facilitates a fuller understanding of their embodied lived experiences. Rather than leave the young people's bodies (which I take here to incorporate interconnected bodies, minds and emotions) as untheorised matter, and in keeping with the theme of this book, I want, as much as the data allow, to explicitly draw out and consider the corporeality of the children's lived experience; the messy reality of the young people's complex embodied experience, emphasising the interplay between the materiality and signification of bodies to the subjection of children.

Context: disembodied geographies of disability, children and young people?

The terrains of geographies and social studies of disability and childhood have adopted relatively disembodied conceptions of the social construction of identity. This has been part of a deliberate political attempt to illustrate that the ways in which disability/childhood are performed in contemporary societies are not natural givens. In such accounts, bodies are sidelined as signifiers around which otherness is constructed.

In addition to a body/society (impairment/disability) dualism, geographies and social studies of disability have frequently drawn on a Cartesian mind/body split (Parr and Butler 1999). The adoption of these dichotomies is problematic. Mind/body dualism serves to render the knowledge of many individuals constructed as too immersed in their bodies as invalid, including disabled people (Shakespeare 1996). Equally, the tendency to emphasise the fully functioning mind of many disabled people has led to the marginalisation of individuals with mind differences, particularly those with learning disabilities (although see Hall and Kearns 2001, Holt 2003a, 2003b, 2004a, 2004b, 2007, Hall 2005, Philo and Metzel 2005). The dualism between impairment and non-impairment has sidelined the experiences of individuals whose experiences of mind–body–emotional differences are contested, either by themselves or others, but who may be the subject of disablements. Individuals with emotional differences, who often lack specific diagnoses, have been almost completely absent within the critical disability field (Holt under review). In this chapter I begin to address some of these gaps by focusing on Sharon, whose bodily difference contests the dualistic representation of (dis)ability, and Alfie, who has socio-emotional differences, along with a visual impairment.

Exceptions to the general tendency towards disembodied social constructivism within critical accounts of disability (Moss and Dyck 1996, Butler and Bowlby 1997, Hughes and Peterson 1997, Parr 1999, Moss 2002) and childhood (James et al. 1998: 146–68, Prout 2000, Aitken 2001) point to ways of incorporating more fully bodies as both simultaneously corporeal and symbolic. Indeed, as Moss and Dyck emphasise:

> our experience of discourse is not one of disembodied, free floating, signified-less, intangible words and ideas. Rather, our experiences are grounded in practices that produce and reproduce very specific meanings.
>
> (1999: 377)

Discourses and corporeal bodily materiality intertwine within everyday practices to construct particular identity positionings (Moss and Dyck 1996). It is through everyday practices that dominant, normative identity relations are reproduced. It is also via these quotidian practices that alternative identity performances can be forged which contest hegemonic social relations.

Challenging dominant practices and representations of disability: the need for an embodied approach

Dominant representations posit disability as an 'other' identity positioning, as ontologically distinct and inferior to non-disability (Dear et al. 1997). Such representations are intertwined with, and serve to (re)produce, the marginalisation of disabled people within interconnected social, cultural, economic and political arenas – marginalisations which often have spatial expressions.

Significant challenges have been mounted to the marginalisation of disabled people. However, while the legal position of disabled people has changed with the introduction of a variety of anti-discrimination measures (e.g. the Disability Discrimination Act 2004), enduring sociocultural representations prove more complex to transform. The meanings attached to different identity locators are often subconsciously reproduced. Understandings of others and ourselves become embodied as part of a habitus (Bourdieu 1984, see Holt 2008). Although it is possible to transform embodied discourses of disability, such change is rendered complex by the embodiment and hence apparent 'naturalness' of such meanings.

Butler's (1997) theories of subjection and her conceptualisation of recognition (2004) provide useful tools to begin to unravel how discourses that situate bodies hierarchically become embodied, via the subconscious, intertwined with corporeal bodies, and reproduced as seemingly 'natural'. This process is so insidious that individuals often reproduce as 'natural' aspects of their identities that lead to their relative marginalisation. Butler (2004) explores the importance of 'recognition' to subjection. Individuals have an emotional need to be 'recognised' within acceptable frames of reference for personhood. Thus, subjection, which enables an individual to become a subject/agent who can act, simultaneously constrains the possibilities of personhood (see Holt 2007).

Although these processes of subjection display a resistance to change, they can be transformed. The concept of 'recognition' opens up possibilities for the transformation of socio-psychic relations (Butler 2004). Butler's discussion of Jessica Benjamin's reworking of 'recognition' is particularly insightful. Benjamin views psychic relations to others as a constant tension between the competing desires for mutual recognition, and to conceive of the other as outside and distinctive to the self. Recognition 'takes place through communication, primarily, but not exclusively verbal, in which subjects are transformed by virtue of the communicative practice in which they are engaged' (Butler 2004: 132). Thus, recognition involves intersubjective dialogue that can transform all/both engaging subjects. Benjamin views psychic life as 'vacillat[ing] between "relating to the object and recognizing the outside [O]ther"' (Benjamin 1999, cited in Butler 2004: 133). Failure to recognise the outside as other and distinctive from the self risks the psychic destruction of (both/all) subjects through dissolution.

The concept of socio-psychic relations as hovering between recognition and disavowal opens up potential for transforming the same/other. Recognition provides spaces for appreciation that the other is different, but that this difference can be valued. Consequently, difference is not always 'otherness' (see also Bondi 2003, 2005). The importance placed on communication highlights that transformations are constrained when groups, identified as 'discrete' through essentialising their differences, are segregated.

In the following sections, I draw on the experiences of Alfie and Sharon to unravel explicitly how the contextual, relational, embodied practices of themselves and their peers can challenge/transform dominant representations of (dis)ability. The vignettes presented are open to multiple interpretations. The two children attended the same primary (elementary) school, 'Church Street', which was viewed as 'inclusive', particularly for those with learning or socio-emotional differences.

Alfie

Alfie is eight years old and is white and working-class. Alfie has been diagnosed with Asperger's syndrome;[3] he also has a visual impairment and holds a statement of Special Educational Needs (SEN). The resources attached to this statement provide a Special Needs Assistant (SNA) and an enlarging machine. This machine is kept in a storeroom attached to the side of his classroom. Thus he spends some time in a space which is both marginal and privileged. The storeroom is separate from the classroom, and is the place for storing books and stationery. However, the other children cannot enter this room without the teacher's consent, and it also contains the teacher's personal possessions and a coffee machine.

Even when in the classroom with his peers, Alfie generally works with his SNA rather than with other children. This could be represented as reproducing Alfie as both 'different' in a negative sense from his peers and as dependent. However, in interview, Alfie stated a preference for working with his SNA rather than his classmates.

Alfie generally does not play with other children, and I often observed him alone, sitting or standing at the edge of the playground next to the classroom door. Unlike the other children, who appeared extremely unhappy when alone, Alfie seemed contented. There were exceptions to this general trend and during wet playtimes Alfie often played on the computer with two other boys. Despite his social isolation, in interview Alfie named many of his classmates as friends, and this friendship was reciprocated, with many children counting Alfie among their friends. Alfie was not stigmatised by the other children.

Alfie's body–mind–emotional differences must be considered in his preference for playing alone and sitting with his SNA. It is a defining characteristic of Asperger's syndrome to form social relationships and express sociality differently. I am, however, cognisant of reproducing dominant, individual tragedy representations of disability by situating Alfie's limited socialisation with peers entirely within *his individual* mind–body–emotional state. This is particularly salient given the contested nature of autism spectrum conditions, which brings into focus the powerful construction of some mind–body–emotional characteristics as 'different' (Molloy and Vasil 2002).

Although Alfie was often isolated from his peers, the other children in his class were relatively accepting of his behaviour patterns, which often conflicted with expected practices in classroom and playground spaces. The following extract (Box 15.1) demonstrates a positive moment wherein Alfie is constructed as different, without this difference being viewed as otherness.

Box 15.1   Extract from research diary: a geography lesson

The children are sitting on the carpeted area of the floor and the teacher is discussing the lesson with the children. The atmosphere is calm, but fairly lively. The teacher invites involvement from the children and asks many questions.

About five minutes into the lesson, Alfie and his SNA emerge from the cupboard. Alfie sits on the floor with, but a little apart from, the other children. He crouches over, with his head almost on his crossed legs, and starts to count in quite a loud voice. He then rolls up into a ball and puts his hand over his head. After a few moments, he sits up and fiddles with his eyes. Then he puts his head on his crossed legs again, and rocks with his bottom in the air. When he stops this, he starts clapping.

> *(Meanwhile, the teacher continues to ask questions and the children answer them. Although to me Alfie's behaviour seems rather out of keeping with normative classroom practices – such behaviour would usually lead to some kind of sanction – the classroom business continues as normal and no-one is distracted by Alfie.)*
>
> Alfie sits still for about a minute before he starts rocking again. Then he sits very close, almost touching, another boy. The boy doesn't react in any way.
>
> ...
>
> *The other children just don't react to Alfie. They ignore him, as though this is just part of their classroom setting.*
>
> Alfie continues to do as above, as the other children continue getting ready.
>
> The teacher makes a joke, and all the children laugh. After a pause, Alfie laughs really loudly.

Rather than representing a negative attempt to 'ignore' Alfie, it appears that his behaviour is naturalised and accepted within this classroom setting, and his embodied practices are not construed as 'out of place' within this context. This is further supported by the number of children who identify Alfie as a friend. The relative inclusion and acceptance of Alfie's difference is particularly insightful given young people with socio-emotional differences experience a high level of exclusion from mainstream schools relative to other groups of children with SEN (Cooper 2003). The acceptance of Alfie's difference might point to the potential for more fully including children with socio-emotional differences within mainstream school contexts.

Sharon

Sharon is in the same year as Alfie, but in a different class. She is white, working-class and has achondroplasia. Many people with body differences are likely to be the only member of their family with such differences. However, all of Sharon's immediate family have achondroplasia and identify as Dwarfs. Achondroplasia, or being a Dwarf, has many parallels to d/Deafness (Skelton and Valentine 2003). There is not usually anything inherently problematic about this body difference.

Equally, there is a strong positive 'collective' identification, with events such as the Dwarf Games.

Sharon's body 'differences' serve to question dichotomous representations of 'disabled' and 'non-disabled'. She is unusually small. However, there is clearly a height continuum, and the line drawn around when someone is abnormally small is contestable. Sharon could be viewed as the archetypal disabled person, as understood through social models. Her body difference itself is neutral and does not usually cause pain. However, many of the spaces that she occupied are designed for taller people. At the time of the research, Sharon had a statement of SEN. This emphasises the myriad diagnoses that young people are subjected to within education institutions, given she did not have any more educational needs than the majority of her peers. According to staff, the resources attached to her statement facilitated physical modifications in her classroom, such as having a lower coat peg.

Box 15.2 points to some of the processes of identifying Sharon as different, along with some empathetic relationships of recognition forged with her peers.

Box 15.2   Extract from research diary: in the classroom

The class is preparing to go on a short geography fieldtrip to the local shopping centre. The teacher specifically requested that I attend this fieldtrip in order to ensure that there was a suitable adult to child ratio.

The teacher talks to the class about what is going to happen during the afternoon. Then she organises the groups to go on the local field trip. She puts me in charge of Sharon's group....

Walking along the street on the field trip

Janie asked Sharon to be her partner. They were partners, but for much of the time, Sharon wanted to hold my hand and to walk with me.

When I was walking with the teacher, she said, quite loudly, and in front of the other children, that I need to watch out for Sharon as she gets tired, because 'her little legs just can't move as fast as ours'. When I went back, Sharon said 'I heard that!...I can walk as well as anyone else.' She looked quite annoyed, and spoke in an angry tone of voice.

We were walking along and Sharon insisted on holding my hand. She was chatting to me, and she told me that she gets pains in her legs. I asked her why that was, and she said 'it's my bones'.

Janie laughed and said: 'It's growing pains.'

Sharon replied, in a serious tone of voice; 'I don't know!'

As we walked to the shopping centre, every time the teacher walked past, she asked, 'Are you all right, Sharon?' She used a rather over-concerned tone, which was out of keeping with how she usually talked to the children.

Sharon would reply 'yes', and the teacher said something like 'good girl'. The teacher did not ask any other children if they were all right.

On the way back, Sharon and Janie talked to each other a lot, about many topics. They spent most of the time discussing the older work-experience boys from the secondary school, who were helping out in their classroom. They were teasing each other, suggesting that they had crushes on the boys.

Sharon had many (dis)abling experiences, and her teacher and the other children sometimes emphasised her differences. However, these practices, especially her teacher's,[4] did not generally lead to negative stigmatisation by her peers. Her body difference is interesting to the other children, and sometimes worthy of note. Indeed, Sharon often emphasises her difference from her peers. Arguably, the interest that young people display in each others' different bodies does not always identify difference negatively. The comment about Sharon's legs is quickly followed by discussion of a topic of mutual interest; the work experience boys – demonstrating that Sharon both expects, and is expected by her friends, to develop her 'sexuality' along the lines of her peers. This contrasts with dominant understandings of disability, which posit disabled people as a-sexual (Butler 1999, Anderson and Kitchin 2000). Sharon had many friends with whom she had relatively equal power relations. Although her peers sometimes commented on her body differences, this did not lead to the reproduction of other aspects of negative interpretations of disability, such as dependency (cf. Holt 2004).

Conclusion

In this chapter I have focused on the experience of two children to begin to consider how individuals are subjected as disabled or non-disabled.

In particular, the focus has been on unravelling moments that present embodied experiences of recognition and/or positive identification of Alfie or Sharon by their peers; moments when their body–mind–emotional states are not enacted as negatively different. Within some time-spaces, the bodily differences of these young people, which are reproduced by their peers in other contexts, are suspended, with the effect that these children are not performed as disabled. More often, these children are still presented as being different/disabled. However, this difference does not negate the possibility of being recognised as a relatively equal other, with empathetic relationships forged.

These processes of resignification and/or inter-subjective relations of recognition have proved difficult to retrieve and unravel; especially in comparison to (dis)abling practices. Clearly othering and recognition are often intertwined. The mundane performances presented in this chapter have a multitude of affects and motivations; both consciously intended and subconscious/unintended. Further, few relationships are typified solely by empathetic intersubjective exchange. Rather, most social relations are simultaneously conflictual, serving to position people hierarchically, and empathetic. In seeking to unravel more affirmative social relationships between young people with various mind–body–emotional characteristics, perhaps it is necessary to attempt to discover those that are no more unequal and conflictual than those between their peers. Relations of empathy and recognition are fragile, shifting and interspersed with events that serve to subjectify children, often negatively, as disabled.

Notes

1. This policy is currently being contested nationally and internationally (see Holt 2007).
2. All names, including those of teachers, children and schools, are pseudonyms.
3. Asperger's syndrome is an autistic spectrum disorder and can be defined as a specific socio-emotional difference given its diagnosis is based on non-normative behavioural patterns. There has been a bourgeoning of young people diagnosed with autistic spectrum disorders in recent decades (Molloy and Vasil 2002).
4. It is important to emphasise that Sharon's teacher was extremely kind and well intentioned, and her negative reproduction of disability was clearly not conscious or deliberate. Indeed, dominant discourses and practices of disability (gender, race, sexuality, class, and so on) are often reproduced subconsciously by individuals who would consciously endeavour to promote equality within a variety of arena; similar practices could no doubt be witnessed in whichever context was the focus of study, including the academic arena.

References

Aitken, S. C. (2001) *Geographies of Young People* (London: Routledge).

Alderson, P. and Goodey, C. (1998) *Enabling Education: Experiences in Special and Ordinary Schools* (London: Tufnell Press).

Anderson, P. and Kitchin, R. (2000) 'Disability, space and sexuality: access to family planning services', *Social Science and Medicine* 51: 1163–73.

Ballard, K. (1999) 'International voices: an introduction', in K. Ballard (ed.) *Inclusive Education: International Voices on Disability and Justice* (London and New York: Routledge), pp. 1–9.

Bondi, L. (2003) 'Empathy and identification: conceptual resources for feminist fieldwork', *ACME* 2: 65–76.

Bondi, L. (2005) 'Making connections and thinking through emotions; between geography and psychotherapy', *Transactions of the Institute of British Geographers* 30: 433–48.

Bourdieu, P. (1984) *Distinction: A Social Critique of the Judgement of Taste* (London and New York: Routledge).

Butler, J. (1990) *Gender Trouble: Feminism and the Subversion of Identity* (New York: Routledge).

Butler, J. (1993) *Bodies That Matter: On the Discursive Limits of 'Sex'* (New York: Routledge).

Butler, J. (1997) *The Psychic Life of Power: Theories in Subjection* (Stanford, CA: Stanford University Press).

Butler, J. (2004) *Undoing Gender* (London: Routledge).

Butler, R. (1999) 'Double the trouble or twice the fun? Disabled bodies in the gay community', in R. Butler and H. Parr (eds) *Mind and Body Spaces: Geographies of Illness, Impairment and Disability* (London: Routledge), pp. 203–20.

Butler, R. and Bowlby, S. (1997) 'Bodies and spaces: an exploration of disabled people's experiences of public space', *Environment and Planning D: Society and Space* 15: 411–33.

Cooper, P. (2003) 'Editorial: including students with social, emotional and behavioural difficulties in mainstream secondary schools', *Emotional and Behavioural Difficulties* 8: 5–6.

Dear, M., Wilton, R., Gaber, S. and Takahashi, L. (1997) 'Seeing people differently: the socio spatial construction of disability', *Environment and Planning D: Society and Space* 5: 455–80.

Disability Discrimination Act (2004) (London: The Stationery Office).

Hall, E. (2005) 'The entangled geographies of social exclusion/inclusion for people with learning disabilities', *Health and Place* 11: 107–15.

Hall, E. and Kearns, R. (2001) 'Making space for the "intellectual" in geographies of disability', *Health and Place* 7: 237–46.

Holt, L. (2003a) 'Disabling Children in Primary School Spaces', PhD thesis (Loughborough: Department of Geography, Loughborough University).

Holt, L (2003b) '(Dis)abling children in primary school micro-spaces: geographies of inclusion and exclusion', *Health and Place* 9: 119–28.

Holt, L (2004a) 'The "voices" of children: de-centring empowering research relations', *Children's Geographies* 2: 13–27.

Holt, L (2004b) 'Childhood disability and ability: (dis)ableist geographies of mainstream primary schools', *Disability Studies Quarterly* 24(3): n.p.

Holt, L. (2004c) 'Children with mind–body differences: performing (dis)ability in classroom micro-spaces', *Children's Geographies* 2: 219–36.

Holt, L. (2007) 'Children's socio-spatial (re)production of disability in primary school playgrounds', *Environment and Planning D: Society and Space* 25: 783–802.

Holt, L. (2008) 'Embodied social capital and geographic perspectives', *Progress in Human Geography* 32 (2): 227–46.

Holt, L (under review) 'Young people with socio-emotional differences: theorising disability and destabilising socio-emotional norms', *Disability and Society*.

Hughes, B. and Peterson K. (1997) 'The social model of disability and the disappearing body: towards a sociology of impairment', *Disability & Society* 12: 325–40.

James, A., Jenks, C. and Prout, A. (1998) *Theorising Childhood* (Cambridge: Polity Press).

Molloy, H. and Vasil, L. (2002) 'The social construction of Asperger's syndrome: the pathologising of difference?' *Disability and Society* 17: 659–69.

Moss, P. (2002) *Women, Body, Illness: Space and Identity in the Everyday Lives of Women with Chronic Illness* (Lanham, MD, Boulder, CO, New York and Oxford: Rowman & Littlefield).

Moss, P. and Dyck, I. (1996) 'Inquiry into environment and body: women, work and chronic illness', *Environment & Planning D* 14: 737–57.

Moss, P. and Dyck, I. (1999) 'Body, corporeal space and legitimising women with chronic illness: women diagnosed with M.E.', *Antipode* 31(4): 372–97.

Parr, H. (1999) 'Delusional geographies: the experiential worlds of people during madness/illness', *Environment and Planning D* 17: 673–90.

Parr, H. and Butler, R. (1999) 'New geographies of illness, impairment and disability', in R. Butler and H. Parr (eds) *Mind and Body Spaces Geographies of Illness, Impairment and Disability* (London: Routledge), pp. 1–24.

Philo, P. and Metzel, D. (2005) 'Introduction to theme section on geographies of intellectual disability: outside the participatory mainstream?' *Health and Place* 11: 77–85.

Prout, A. (2000) 'Childhood bodies: construction, agency and hybridity', in A. Prout (ed.) *The Body, Childhood and Society* (London: Macmillan), pp. 1–18.

Shakespeare, T. (1996) 'Disability, identity and difference', in C. Barnes and G. Mercer (eds) *Exploring the Divide* (Leeds: The Disability Press), pp. 94–113.

Skelton, T. and Valentine, G. (2003) ' "It feels like being Deaf is normal": an exploration into the complexities of defining D/deafness and young D/deaf people's identities', *The Canadian Geographer* 47: 451–67.

16
Time for Bed! Children's Bedtime Practices, Routines and Affects

John Horton and Peter Kraftl

Introduction

> Sleep tends to be considered as a time of quiescence and tranquillity,
> a time when the body and the mind relax...a time when relatively
> little happens. These assumptions are partly incorrect since sleep is,
> in fact, an active process.
>
> (Sloan and Shapiro 1997: 7)

On average, a third of every person's life is spent 'asleep'.[1] Moreover, we each spend considerable periods of time, be it 'awake', or 'awake-ish', concerned with issues, practices, routines and spaces related to sleep. Whether furnishing a bedroom, attempting to achieve the *right* ambient bedroom temperature, finding *that* position where we habitually find slumber or waking from a nightmare, sleeping is an important and – as our opening quotation reminds us – *active, embodied* preoccupation.

However, sleep and especially embodied practices of/around sleep, have conventionally received minimal attention from sociologists, geographers and historians,[2] even in domains of enquiry (e.g. concerning bodies, subjectivities, selfhood) wherein sleep might reasonably be considered relevant and thought-provoking. Reasons for this omission – which is, in our view, both significant and deeply problematic – may be manifold: perhaps sleep ostensibly 'goes without saying'; perhaps sleep is such an assumed part of daily/nightly existence; perhaps sleep has historically been viewed as economically, morally and socially unproductive; or perhaps sleep is both so intimate and so ungraspable for traditional social-scientific modes of inquiry that it escapes methodological and ethical frames of reference.

In this chapter, we seek to develop nascent work on sleep by sociologists (Taylor 1993, Williams 2002, 2005), geographers (Kraftl and Horton 2008) and historians (Ekirch 2005) via reflection on bodily rituals, practices and spaces of younger (0–8 year-old) children's sleep. We focus on 'bedtime': the peculiar, domestic, night-after-night construction of the moments preceding children's sleep in contemporary Minority global north contexts.

We draw on examples from mass-mediated discourses and interview-based research with children and families to suggest how children's bodily habits are regulated, negotiated and contested in specific bedtime space-times. In so doing, we pose three kinds of question in the context of a book on 'contested bodies of childhood and youth'. First, what forms of intimate, intergenerational or intra-familial relationality, contestation and negotiation are part-and-parcel of every-night routines and rituals surrounding sleep? Second and relatedly, what are some of the (em-)bodily, practical, material characteristics of such relationships? Third, what are the implications of these often overlooked kinds of intimacy and (em-)bodily practices for conceptions of childhood, youth and embodiment more generally?

We develop these questions in the following way. First, we present four vignettes: extracts from websites dedicated to younger children's sleep. We use these examples to introduce the intricacies of bodily techniques, strategies and geographies in the regulation of children's bedtimes (and thereby sleep). Second, we present in-depth qualitative research with one group of UK-domiciled families regarding children's bedtime routines. In conclusion, we contend that the myriad emotional, bodily and practical issues raised in such intimate moments are evocative of a range of contemporary societal issues, and should prompt further critical reflection.

Getting children to sleep: 'expert' knowledge online

The social/cultural history of western 'expert' knowledge regarding children's sleep has, in many respects, been well chronicled, albeit often obliquely via analyses of historical childcare advice and manuals (e.g. Stearns 2003, Hardyment 2007). Such accounts typically chart the proliferation of Anglophone, mass-mediated 'expert' advice about childhood sleep, from the latter decades of the eighteenth century onwards. At particular historical moments, the characteristic form of such advice is thus recognised as constituted from contemporary forms of mass mediation and contemporary idea(l)s regarding children's psychosocial development, parenting practices and domesticity (Stearns et al. 1996).

More recent mass-mediated representations of, and prescriptions for, childhood sleep should be understood as similarly constituted.

Recent sociological research on sleep suggests that – as in many other aspects of contemporary (western) societies – individuals' lifestyles are becoming increasingly commercialised (Williams and Boden 2004) and medicalised (Hislop and Arber 2003). At intersections of these processes there exist manifold forms of internet resources and guidance dedicated to sleep in general[3] and to children's bedtime in particular. From an extensive survey of the latter, we identify in such online material three broad, intersecting and widely recurring motifs: attentiveness to 'rituals', 'bodily techniques' and 'environmental techniques'. The following vignettes illustrate these motifs.

'Consistency and predictability': rituals-*bodies*-*environments*

The sooner you establish a bedtime routine, the better. When your baby is as young as 6 or 8 weeks old, start following a set pattern every night; she'll quickly come to appreciate the consistency and predictability. 'Your baby will be more relaxed if she knows what's coming next,' says BabyCenter sleep expert Jodi Mindell, author of *Sleeping Through the Night.* 'The more relaxed she is, the more likely she'll go to bed easily and fall asleep quickly'. Stick to your routine as best you can even when you're not home – it can make it easier for your baby to settle down in unfamiliar surroundings.[4]

One of the most popular parts of many bedtime rituals is a bath. Sitting in warm water is a soothing experience, and getting your baby warm and clean and dry is a great way to ease her into bedtime. A bath is also a wonderful way for your partner to spend some special time with the baby, especially if you're breastfeeding and he can't help as much with meals.[5]

Although there are distinct, profound differences of opinion about how (and how rigidly) bedtime routines should be achieved, the importance of some sort of routine goes more or less uncontested in online advice. Very often – as in the reference to bathing above – discourses about routines are couched in highly specific bodily techniques and broader, normative assertions about 'what's good' for younger children. Here, consistency, predictability, relaxation and even adaptability are more immediate goals of the bedtime routine and socialisation of a baby. The capacity for such simple, bodily routines to promote and foster the involvement of a father – for that is assumed here – is implicitly related to broader (western) ideals surrounding the nuclear family and the importance of family cohesion and bonding *around* children (Jenks 1996).

At this juncture, it is appropriate to highlight how sociologies of sleep provide three distinct lenses through which to interpret the preceding vignettes. First, sociologists have sought to explore gender imbalances in sleeping, especially relationships between sleeping and women's professional and domestic roles, and the social patterning and disruption of sleep in respect of emotional labour women invest in the well-being of their family (Hislop and Arber 2003). Ever present here is an attentiveness to contemporary normative constructions of 'motherhood' (and 'childhood'), which are overwhelmingly inequitable and (socially and spatially) limiting (Oakley 1979, Phoenix et al. 1991). Second, as Williams and Boden (2004) suggest, sleep is increasingly subject to the reach of (global) consumer capitalism. Citing inventories of multifarious products – alarm clocks, self-help books, herbal remedies, etc. – Williams and Boden highlight how burgeoning sleep industries increasingly colonise 'every-night life'. Third, Williams (2005: 155) indicates that 'more porous forms of knowledge and rhetorical forms of authority' are increasingly appearing, not just on the internet but in the form of self-help guides and sleep clinics. Not only is sleep subject to increasing professional intervention ('medicalisation'), but numerous 'expert' – and perhaps not-so-expert – voices vie for attention in newly constituted discursive communities. Hence, to reflect on websites dedicated to children's sleep is to approach these processes. We begin to understand, then, that the seemingly intimate, familial, micro-geographical routines of children's bedtimes are enmeshed in, and productive of, trends and discourses operating at much broader socio-spatial scales.

Of blankets and circulation: rituals-bodies-environments

Question: What is 'swaddling'? What are the pros and cons?

Answer: Swaddling is an age-old technique for keeping an infant warm and secure. To swaddle your baby, spread a receiving blanket out flat, with one corner folded over. Lay your baby face-up on the blanket, with his [sic] head resting on the folded corner. Wrap the left corner over his body and tuck it beneath him. Bring the bottom corner up over his feet, and then wrap the right corner around him, leaving only his head and neck exposed. Don't cover your baby's face with the blanket, since that could overheat or suffocate him. And make sure you don't wrap your baby too tightly, or his circulation could be cut off.[6]

In the past two decades, social scientists have become particularly attuned to the body's role as a fleshy, material locus of socio-spatial rhythms and relations (as this volume's assumptions demonstrate). Drawing on diverse literatures which unpick the politicised and contested nature(s) of embodied practice, human geographers have sought to demonstrate how 'micro'-geographical relations between moving, socialising, practising bodies may implicate a range of more or less banal meanings (Teather 1999, Laurier and Philo 2006). What, then, of relationships between these seemingly banal, inter-bodily practices and broader political relations (Phelan 1993, Evans 2006) as they are manifest in childhood sleep? We suggest that the very intimate, overtly embodied practices implicated by the process of 'swaddling', and the intricate details of the bedtime routine heralded by such attentiveness, are significant in two related senses. First, that, as much as such banal details matter in themselves, when it comes to *learning* about, *worrying* about, *fussing* about a newborn baby for example, the explicitly embodied, affective details may be heightened, perhaps all-consuming: the stakes are just so high. These details matter perhaps most to 'new' parents – in the emotive, practical and discursive process of what we might term 'becoming'-parents. Second, as Paul Harrison (2008) demonstrates, since the (dis-)embodiment of sleep is associated with loss or giving-over of intentional, auto-affective activity, it invokes a broader sense of vulnerability, which in turn entails specific forms of responsibility to others. There is not space here to explore this observation further; we merely highlight the very particular understandings of *responsibility* which are always implicated in the facilitation of another's sleep – particularly where the relative corporeal fragility of a young baby heightens parental responsibility in terms of safety, health, development, etc. This responsibility is symptomatic of more multifarious foldings of moral-political-social norms into the intimate embodiment of bedtime – as the vignettes throughout this chapter show – and processes of identification that even permeate sleeping practices (Meadows 2005).

Of walls and moods: rituals-bodies-environments

Let the rule be: creating peaceful, calm moods and soft gentle impressions at these most precious times of day and night. This rules out television and radios! Children are especially sensitive and more open to impressions when going to sleep and upon waking. Therefore a great responsibility rests on parents and teachers to create calm moods and meaningful rituals with our children at these times of day.

Children and adults alike are enriched and nourished by such time spent together. Make sure the walls of the room are calming. Do take down any loud images or pictures. Find beautiful ways to decorate the room, hanging silk cloths from the ceiling, and a lovely mobile with angels or golden stars. Children can find this very comforting.[7]

Geographers and environmental psychologists have attended to relationships between children's bodies and emotions, and various built environments (see Gagen 2000, Gallacher 2005, Spencer and Blades 2006, Kraftl et al. 2007). Such work demonstrates, in diverse ways, relationships between built environments 'for' children and the many conflicting idea(l)s that are implicated in notions of 'childhood'. Increasingly, though, childhood professionals and the mass media have articulated a 'crisis' in modern childhood and the environments inhabited by younger children, populated by fast food, computer games, illegal substances, 'anti-social behaviour', etc. (Wyness 2000). In this light, the preceding vignette performs three functions. First, it stresses the key role of *spaces*, moods and material details in/of bedtime, so that the embodiment of bedtime becomes situated (in an 'ideal' sense) – in this case in a calm, soothing atmosphere at school and at home. Second, it ensures that sleep and bedtime are enrolled in the implicit environmental determinism of the 'crisis in childhood' debate – where, for instance, criticism of a range of environmental problems accompanies familiar fears of social breakdown.[8] And third, very explicitly, it highlights once again that it is *parents'* (and teachers') 'responsibility' to resolve certain elements of this crisis via the sensitive design of sleeping spaces, in conjunction with 'meaningful rituals'.

Thus far, we have argued that in 'expert' online discourses, the rituals and bodily/environmental techniques which constitute children's bedtimes are mutually implicated and part-and-parcel of broader moral, political and social discourses which permeate intimate spaces for and around sleep. However, we also seek to understand how such normative bedtime rituals and embodiments are negotiated and contested in practice. In the rest of this chapter, then, we explore parents' and children's experiences of 'bedtime', highlighting some issues which both speak of and evade discourses introduced above.

Getting to sleep; not getting to sleep: *doing* 'bedtime'

This section reports qualitative data from research conducted in 2000–4.[9] The project concerned children's everyday practices of play, fun and consumption. Part of the project entailed interviews with 21 families, with children aged 5–8, in the West Midlands. When these children and parents/carers discussed the everyday spaces/practices of their domestic lives, 'bedtime' repeatedly emerged as a fundamentally important practice/moment.

In the following subsections, vignettes[10] suggest the nature and particularities of 'bedtime' in a small number of homes, there and then. As we elaborate thereafter, three always related characteristics of bedtime recur – gently but manifestly – in each vignette: first, the embodied, practical nature of *doing* bedtime; second, the work and routine-making which fundamentally constitute bedtime; and third, the affective state(s) and importance of bedtime.

Of toes and toothbrushes: *bodies*-routines-affects

Paul's bedtime (part 1)

> Paul   At bedtime, what happens is, I put my pyjamas on, and I get all tucked up in bed, like I put my toes right, right down to the end of the bed, and then I choose a teddy and my dad gets that, and then I'm all ready, and that's when my dad reads a story to me.
>
> Mr. I   I sort of perch on the side of the bed, and read out aloud, and well, I suppose it depends on the book. With something a bit difficult, it's a case of me being in charge of holding the book and reading the story out, but if it's something with more pictures, it's more a case of the two of us holding the book together, and we turn the pages together and we do a lot of pointing and talking about things on the page. We do that for about half an hour, or until we get to the end of a chapter, and then it's lights out.
>
> Paul   Then my mum comes and gives me a night-night kiss.
>
> Mr. I   That's our little routine.

Daisy's bedtime

> Daisy   When it's time to go to bed, I get ready, like brush my teeth and everything, and I get snuggly in bed and I have a goodnight cuddle off my mum and then she goes, and then my dad reads me a story, and then I have a goodnight cuddle off my dad, and then dad turns the lamp off and I go to bed properly.
>
> Mr. A   She's normally out like a light, before I'm out the door.
>
> Daisy   And my Dad always leaves the light on for me.
>
> Mr. A   That's right – she always has to have the landing light left on.

Surely, we all have 'little routines' to get us 'ready' for sleep. Perhaps, too, we recall such routines from childhood; indeed, perhaps we can recognise their echoes, decades later, in the routines that comfort and becalm us now. Paul's and Daisy's accounts were, at once, very similar, broadly typical of children's accounts of bedtime there and then, and yet in their details – in the specific arrangements of lights, limbs and bedclothes, for example – entirely idiosyncratic. They remind us that, at the intersection of the trends and techniques described in the first half of this chapter, and the contemporary societal norms, histories and geographies underlying them, there exist individual children's bodies 'readying' themselves and/or being made 'ready' for bed.

Simply, then, reflection on Paul's and Daisy's bedtimes – or recalling bodily, domestic minutiae and preferences of our own bedtimes, past or present – makes plain the embodied, practical nature of sleep. Sociological accounts of sleep have tended (after Taylor 1993: 464) to interrogate and represent this embodied practice in terms of two, mutually implicated problematics: on the one hand, investigating the (largely wakeful, mindful, agentic) bodily techniques involved in, and surrounding, *'doing'* sleep; and, on the other, reflecting on the (largely unconscious) physiological state and sensation of *'being'* asleep. The following subsections consider each of these conceptualisations in turn via glimpses of the bodily, gestural and domestic minutiae of bedtime routines and affects.

Orders and tantrums: bodies-*routines*-affects

Lee's bedtime

> Mrs Y   For ages, we used to have big arguments about bedtime. We could never get Lee to bed, when we told him to…It was just no go…But we've tried and tried and insisted and, touch wood, we've got a routine now. I've really drilled it into him that at eight [o'clock] we have telly off, a brush of the teeth, a wash of the face, pyjamas on, de-de-de-de-de-de. And then dad *will* read a story, and yes, you *will* listen, while I make the sandwiches, then it's *straight* to bed by nine [o'clock], no ifs and buts, no 'oww mum' this or 'oww mum' that…But it took a while to that – like getting him into a habit, get into to find a middle ground, like an arrangement it's like trying that suits us all. There's been a few tantrums along the way, and not just from Lee! They're as bad as each other! Either Lee'll be like 'oww do I have to?' or [Mr. Y]'ll be like 'oww can't you do it tonight?'…And I'm like 'yes, that is an *order*!'…

JH   Why is it so important to have a routine, like that?

Mrs Y   Because if you see that state of him if he stays up late – he gets so bloody grumpy when he's tired. And they say having a good routine [for sleeping] helps with school, and that . . . It's not right for them to stay up [late].

David's bedtime

David   [One night] I got into bed like normal, and had a goodnight kiss and got right under the covers, but what my mum didn't know was I'd got a little light – like a little key-ring one – and I was shining it under the covers, so I stayed awake for *ages* that way.

As Williams (2007: 314) notes, questions about sleep, whether in research or in other contexts, almost invariably elicit responses which articulate the practical 'doing' of sleep. What, then, can be said about the nature of this 'doing'? Lee's and David's bedtimes prompt three realisations about the habitual bodily praxes of bedtime.

First, in Lee's home, preparing for sleep is manifestly and to an important extent an active, contrived, *doing*, with clear rules, routines and parameters: 'dad *will* read a story . . . you *will* listen . . . *straight* to bed by nine'; you *shouldn't* hide under the bedcovers with a torch. The particular details and preferences of these bedtimes may be unique, but their essentially routinised, rule-bound character – and the forms of bodily work, repetitions and discipline that constitute them – are surely in common with many, post-war, 'western', nuclear family childhoods. As with diverse other forms of domestic routine (e.g. Valentine 1999a on meal-time, Valentine 1999b on spatial boundaries) such bodily disciplining can occasion dismay ('oww do I have to?', 'oww can't you do it tonight?'); while subverting such routines can occasion glee ('I stayed awake for *ages*').

Second, the various 'orders', 'tantrums' and kisses which structure Lee's and David's bedtimes – and, likewise, Paul's and Daisy's carefully choreographed book-holding and cuddling routines – bespeak the inherent *sociality* of these children's bedtime practices. This is perhaps counterintuitive: for, as Williams and Bendelow (1998: 172) note, sleep is often and easily imagined as a 'highly personal, privatised . . . "a-social", "in-active" form of corporeal "activity"'. However, in the vignettes represented in this chapter, bedtime is revealed as always socio-cultural, always interactional, always negotiated. For, whether in the sharing of a 'night-night kiss', in the passing of a teddy bear from father to son – these bedtimes are never solitary happenings.[11] Rather, these preparations for sleep always entail and affect others besides the sleeper; these bedtimes are fundamentally constituted by, and constitutive of, these families' relationships[12] and domestic spaces. Indeed, reading these slight vignettes, we may feel that we have learnt a great deal about the protagonists, their lives, homes and interrelationships.

Third, consider the statements 'it's not right for them to stay up' and 'they say having a good routine [for sleeping] helps with school'. Statements such as these alert us to the complex array of meanings and 'moral'/cultural *norms* which are attached to (childhood) sleep. Thus, through the notions of 'it's not right for them to stay up', 'having a good routine', the bodily praxes of bedtime are constituted by a taken-for-granted sense of 'what's good for children' and thus – we might infer – by broader contemporary idea(l)s regarding 'childhood', child development, 'parenthood', 'family' and 'home'. Although norms of this kind are taken for granted, and can thus feel or appear universal *in situ*, there is abundant evidence that sensibilities, conventions and taboos regarding children's sleep vary considerably over space and time.[13]

That bedtime routines are so taken for granted and yet so culturally specific raises the question of how and when they are learnt and (re)produced. Indeed, such is the effort invested in producing and delimiting the sleeping patterns of human beings in the first days, weeks and months of their life – as manifest in the techniques and technologies described in the first half of this chapter – should we not regard bedtime as amongst the earliest and most fundamental forms of socialisation and spatial-temporal orientation?

Not going to sleep: bodies-routines-*affects*

Paul's bedtime (part 2)

> JH   And do you go straight to sleep?
>
> Paul   Yes.
>
> Mr. I   As long as he gets his goodnight kiss and his story he drops off pretty well. On the odd occasion when I have to work late, it can be difficult. He can get a bit tearful because it's different to normal, so often he'll be lying in bed awake when I get in [from work].

Christmas Eve 1

> Rose   I was really excited, the night before Christmas. It's always exciting.
>
> JH   Did you go straight to sleep?

Rose   I really, really tried. Like I was closing my eyes really, really tight and I was really tired, but I was too excited – like, you know when you can feel your heart really beating, and you just can't wait? I just kept thinking about [Christmas day] and wondering what [presents] I was going to get, and every time there was a noise I was looking around to see what it was.

Christmas Eve 2

Simon   On Christmas eve, my mum was like 'you will go to sleep now, or Father Christmas won't come', so I got into bed, and shut my eyes and pretended to go to sleep, but as soon as my mum went out of my bedroom, I got out and sat on top of the bed, and I can see out of the window.

As previously noted, the practical 'doing' of bedtime encompasses many of the most readily *articulable* aspects of sleep. However, as the vignettes featuring Paul, Rose and Simon suggest, there is more to bedtime than its *doing*: there is more at stake than simply getting to sleep; indeed, almost certainly, there is more to bedtime than can be adequately represented. Paul's tears, Rose's rapidly beating heart and Simon's expectant sky-gazing prompt three observations about the emotional/affective import and state of bedtime, which gesture towards broader questions which are elaborated more fully in this chapter's conclusion.

First, simply, it is clear that bedtime *matters* a great deal to these children and their parents/carers. As anyone who has lain awake (whether tearfully or excitedly) at night must know, bedtime is an emotive, sometimes delightful, sometimes fraught, affair. Meadows attempts to map the emotional nature of sleep in terms of four combinant 'modes of embodiment', namely:

- 'Normative embodiment' ('what I am told about healthy sleep' [and how this makes me feel in relation to my every-night practices]).
- 'Pragmatic embodiment' ('what I have to do in practice [to sleep]' [and how this makes me feel in relation to my every-night practices]).
- 'Visceral embodiment' ('what I feel my body needs' [and how this makes me feel in relation to my every-night practices]).
- 'Experiential embodiment' ('how this [given situation] makes me feel').

(2005: 247; parentheses added)

We wonder, though, whether the emotive nature of sleep is satisfactorily represented by a (certainly useful) typology of this kind. For, second, the preceding vignettes prompt reflection on the affective bodily conditions or states of sleep (and sleeping and sleepiness): after all, what does it mean (most immediately for contemporary understandings of embodiment) to *be* asleep, to *fall* asleep or to *get ready* for sleep? Likewise, in a bodily/affective sense, what is the difference between '*going straight to sleep*' and '*pretending to go to sleep*'? Or, to give one example, how could something like 'snug'-ness be adequately represented? As we elaborate in the conclusion, we suggest that the bodily/affective happenings of these children's bedtimes – '*getting a bit tearful*', '*feeling your heart really beating*' – pose some broader, challenging questions for contemporary social scientific accounts of embodiment, childhood and youth.

More specifically, third, we note again the amount and variety of preparation required to ready the material/textural, bodily, sensate and affective aspects of/spaces for these children's bedtimes. Again, this preparatory effort echoes the bodily routines and techniques described earlier in this chapter; again, these small stories may tug at our heartstrings, appealing, as they do, to contemporary idea(l)s of childhood and familial love and care.[14]

Thus, fourth, an event such as Christmas Eve sleeplessness is suggestive of the problem of adequately accounting for affective/bodily happenings. To wonder how an (entirely socially constructed, culturally specific) event such as Christmas eve can affect an individual child, emotionally, viscerally and embodily (racing heart, butterflies in the stomach, inability to sleep despite great tiredness) is (after Williams 2001: 39–55) to encounter the 'irreducibility' of bodily/affective states such as sleep to neat (e.g. physiological or cultural) representations or explanations. Thus, an ostensibly simple moment of bedtime is comprised of manifold factors occurring at once: a combination of 'the experience (i.e. phenomenological) as well as the representational (i.e. discursive/symbolic), the material as well as the cultural, the institutional (i.e. macro-) as well as the individual (i.e. micro-) aspects of sleep' (Williams and Bendelow 1998: 186).

On bedtime, childhood and embodiment

Several key realisations regarding the nature of bedtime recur throughout the preceding reflections: that sleeping is always already an embodied practice; that sleeping is typically and intricately structured by rules and routines, co-constituted by relationships, environments, communities and domestic/familial arrangements and structured by broader contemporary norms; that 'sleep' encompasses a spectrum of affective/somatic states (see Bissell 2008), which themselves are constructed/articulated as *mattering*. This being the case we now briefly consider the implications of sleep for contemporary understandings of embodiment, and especially the bodily/affective condition of 'childhood'. We suggest that at least four substantial problematics emerge, even from the (very small, particular and culturally specific) instances described in this chapter.

First, and most simply, the vignettes should heighten awareness of some typically overlooked characteristics of sleeping and other forms of bodily repose. For, ironically, a consideration of these bedtimes directs attention to their inherent *sociality*, inherent *vitality* and the *work* needed to constitute and sustain (preparedness for) each child's sleep, night after night. Thus, perhaps contrary to perceptions, sleep is never entirely solitary, never entirely self-centred and certainly never entirely passive; rather, sleep is constitutive, in so many ways, of practices/routines, affects, relationships and geographies (sleeping environments); moreover, sleep is always part and parcel of wider contemporary relations and social formations ('childhood', 'parenthood', 'home').

Second, an apprehension of sleep might suggest some significant lacunae in many contemporary scholarly accounts of embodiment. We might simply ask: Where are the accounts foregrounding the embodiment of that third of most humans' lives which is spent asleep? And likewise, what of the bodily, affective and neurological states of being sleepy or awake; or the conditions of being 'snuggled', 'grumpy', 'excited', 'tucked in' or afraid of the dark? Furthermore, such questions might prompt critical reflection on the nature and notion of 'the body' and 'embodiment' as it appears in chief social scientific accounts. For:

> central to much recent [social scientific] work on embodiment ... has been a focus upon the *body-in-action*, on the body apprehended as practically and constitutively engaged in the disclosure of the world and in the creation and maintenance of meaning and signification ... [W]ithin the current growth of work on and concerned with embodiment there has been a general lack of thought and reflection upon corporeal existence in its susceptibility and its passivity.
>
> (Harrison 2008: 423)

Third, in particular, we suggest that this overlooking of 'susceptible' and 'passive' embodiment constitutes a significant lacuna in contemporary (e.g. social scientific) accounts of 'childhood' and 'youth'. Thus, if embodiment is fundamental to the 'going on and on and on' of life (Horton and Kraftl 2006: 274), we should ask: How do sleeping and sleepiness matter in geographies and sociologies of 'childhood' and 'youth'? How are bodily practices/routines/rules of sleep constitutive of 'childhood', and vice versa? How do patterns, rhythms and habits of sleep relate to 'growing up'? Alternatively, we might wonder: to what extent are our current (adult) sleepy rituals a continuation, and nightly repetition, of childhood routines and rituals?

Finally, the sleepy examples in this chapter might give us pause for thought, to consider the difficulty of adequately knowing or representing ourselves, our habits and our everyday lives, experiences, contexts and geographies. For sleep is an example *par excellence* of a bodily practice/experience wherein 'nothing (clearly) happens but something (obscurely) is and has been afoot' (Seigworth and Gardiner 2004: 140). Whatever goes on with/in our bodies during hours spent asleep – our mood may be deeply affected by a bad (or good) night's sleep; we may be plagued by bizarre dreams and thrash around, dislodging the bedcovers; we may sleepwalk in the night – it is quite likely that we will be unable to articulate, or even remember, exactly what has gone on after the event. It is this characteristic of sleep that prompts Williams and Bendelow (1998: 176) to speak of a troubling, unfathomable, existential 'inner darkness' occasioned by attempts to recall/represent one's own sleep. Likewise, this quality led de Certeau (1984: 190–3) to position sleep (alongside laziness, indolence and, especially in de Certeau's account, dying) as a kind of being/practice which is ultimately unthinkable, non-signifiable, 'unnameable' and 'unbearable' for the way in which it makes manifest the limits of available representational/discursive practices. At the very least, a consideration of sleep should prompt us to take seriously claims that bodily practices, emotions and affects are 'never easy to define or demarcate', or to observe, name, express, represent or map (Bondi et al. 2005: 1). More than this, though, we suggest that a consideration of sleep ought to begin a more difficult round of critical (self-)reflection – regarding sleep's implications for (understandings of) consciousness, agency, subjectivity, witnessing, becoming and positionality, for example. Thus, we suggest that the 'unbearable' 'unnameability' of sleep – of more or less a third of our whole lives and, therefore, ourselves – poses questions which might trouble and haunt us, long after bedtime, long into the night ...

Notes

1. Throughout this chapter we use the terms 'sleep' and 'asleep' (and indeed 'awake') as convenient, though by no means unproblematic, shorthand terms to denote a wide range of bodily, somatic, affective states.
2. This omission is especially problematic considering the substantial extant bodies of work regarding sleep in cognate disciplines such as psychology, psychoanalysis and neuroscience.
3. More general websites which discuss sleep include those of the British Sleep Society (www.sleeping.org.uk) and the US National Sleep Foundation (www.sleepfoundation.org).
4. www.babycenter.com/general/baby/babysleep, accessed 31 October 2007. 'babycenter.com' is an advice website, with expert tips, discussion forums, question and answer pages, and links to commercial sites. It is designed for new parents, principally mothers, and covers a wide range of issues including sleep.
5. www.babycenter.com/general/baby/babysleep, accessed 31 October 2007.
6. www.babycenter.com/general/baby/babysleep, accessed 31 October 2007.
7. www.wellnessgoods.com/sleepchildrensleep.asp, accessed 31 October 2007.
8. See, for example, a recent article in the *Daily Telegraph* (UK) which linked usage of electronic media, the loss of bedtime routine and sleep deprivation amongst children: www.telegraph.co.uk/news/main.jhtml?xml=/news/2004/03/26/ndoze26.xml, accessed 30 October 2007.
9. See Horton (2004) for contextual and methodological details of this doctoral project.
10. Throughout this chapter, the identities of children and parents/carers are protected via pseudonyms.
11. Although relationships with family members are emphasised in the present analysis, it is of course the case – as with any bodily practice – that bedtime is done with and via a host of nonhuman, material 'others', too: witness the centrality of teddy bears, duvet covers, torches, toothbrushes, pyjamas, story-books in the vignettes. In the bedtimes represented here, practically all of these material objects took the form of mass-produced consumer goods. As we have written elsewhere (Kraftl and Horton 2008), the mass-produced, mass-mediated objects and texts which increasingly surround sleeping bodies warrant further research.
12. Moreover, it can be argued that sleep is a 'functional prerequisite' for social activity *per se* and as such is 'fundamental to any given society and group ... permeating its institutions as well as its embodied agents, its beliefs as well as its practices, its rituals as well as its mythologies, its spatio-temporal arrangements as well as its discursive and culturally-constituted boundaries' (Williams and Bendelow 1998: 172).
13. Thus, Williams and Bendelow cite diverse anthropological evidence regarding cultural differences in sleeping positions: '[I]ndeed, all sorts of different ways of sleeping are practised throughout the world ... There are ... people with pillows and those without; people with mats and those without; populations who lie very close together in a ring, with or without a fire ... and those ... who can sleep on their feet ... Members of certain societies ... take

their rest in what, through Western eyes, seem very "peculiar positions" [after Mauss (1973[1938]: 81)]' (1998: 174–5).
14. The fact that affective/bodily conditions such as 'trust', 'love', 'snug'-ness, 'care', etc. are underlying principles of the bedtimes described in this chapter betrays their very particular, relatively fortunate, social-historical position. Of course, very different preparations for children's sleep – and very different affective/bodily conditions and coping strategies – characterise contexts affected by, for example, domestic violence (Lowe et al. 2007), conflict/terror (McIntyre 2002) or natural disasters (Harada 2000).

References

Bissell, D. (2008) 'Comfortable bodies: sedentary affects', *Environment and Planning A* 40 (7): 1697–712.

Bondi, L., Davidson, J. and Smith, M. (2005) 'Introduction: geography's "emotional turn" ', in L. Bondi, J. Davidson and M. Smith (eds) *Emotional Geographies* (Aldershot: Ashgate), pp. 1–16.

de Certeau, M. (1984) *The Practice of Everyday Life* (Berkeley, CA: University of California Press).

Ekirch, R. (2005) *At Day's Close: Night in Times Past* (London: Weidenfeld and Nicolson).

Evans, B. (2006) 'Gluttony or sloth: critical geographies of bodies and morality in (anti)obesity policy', *Area* 38: 259–67.

Gagen, E. (2000) ' "An example to us all": child development and identity construction in early 20th century playgrounds', *Environment and Planning A: Society and Space* 32: 599–616.

Gallacher, L. (2005) ' "The terrible twos": gaining control in the nursery?' *Children's Geographies* 3: 243–64.

Harada, T. (2000) 'Space, materials, and the "social": in the aftermath of a disaster', *Environment and Planning D: Society and Space* 18: 205–12.

Hardyment, C. (2007) *Dream Babies: Childcare Advice from John Locke to Gina Ford* (London: Frances Lincoln).

Harrison, P. (2008) 'Corporeal remains: vulnerability, proximity, and living on after the end of the world', *Environment and Planning A* 40: 423–45.

Hislop, J. and Arber, S. (2003) 'Sleepers wake! The gendered nature of sleep disruption among mid-life women', *Sociology* 37: 695–711.

Horton, J. (2004) 'Children's Everyday Popular Cultural Consumption: Things, Practices, Spacings, Times', PhD thesis (Bristol: University of Bristol).

Horton, J. and Kraftl, P. (2006) 'Not just growing up, but *going on*: children's geographies as becomings; materials, spacings, bodies, situations', *Children's Geographies* 4: 259–76.

Jenks, C. (1996) *Childhood* (London: Routledge).

Kraftl, P. and Horton, J. (2008) 'Spaces of every-night life: for geographies of sleep, sleeping and sleepiness', *Progress in Human Geography* 32: 509–24.

Kraftl, P., Horton, J. and Tucker, F. (2007) 'Children, young people and built environments', Special issue of *Built Environment*, 33.

Laurier, E. and Philo, C. (2006) 'Cold shoulders and napkins handed: gestures of responsibility', *Transactions of the Institute of British Geographers* 31: 193–207.

Lowe, P, Humphreys, C. and Williams, S. (2007) 'Night terrors: women's experiences of (not) sleeping where there is domestic violence', *Violence Against Women* 13: 549–61.

Mauss, M. (1938/1973) 'Techniques of the body', *Economy and Society* 2: 70–88.

McIntyre, A. (2002) 'Women researching their lives: exploring violence and identity in Belfast', *Qualitative Research* 2: 387–409.

Meadows, R. (2005) 'The "negotiated night": an embodied conceptual framework for the sociological study of sleep', *The Sociological Review* 53: 240–54.

Oakley, A. (1979) *Becoming a Mother* (Oxford: Martin Robertson).

Phelan, P. (1993) *Unmarked: the Politics of Performance* (London: Routledge).

Phoenix, A, Woollett, A. and Lloyd, E. (eds) (1991) *Motherhood: Meanings, Practices and Ideologies* (London: Sage).

Seigworth, G. and Gardiner, M. (2004) 'Rethinking everyday life: and then nothing turns itself inside out', *Cultural Studies* 18: 139–59.

Sloan, E. and Shapiro, C. (1997) 'An overview of sleep physiology and sleep disorders', in C. Shapiro and A. McCall-Smith (eds) *Forensic Aspects of Sleep* (London: John Wiley), pp. 7–28.

Spencer, C. and Blades, M. (eds) (2006) *Children and Their Environments: Learning, Using and Designing Spaces* (Cambridge: Cambridge University Press).

Stearns, P. (2003) *Anxious Parents: A History of Modern Childrearing in America* (New York: New York University Press).

Stearns, P., Rowland, P. and Giarnella, L. (1996) 'Children's sleep: sketching historical change', *Journal of Social History* 30: 345–67.

Taylor, B. (1993) 'Unconsciousness and society: the sociology of sleep', *International Journal of Politics, Culture and Society* 6: 463–71.

Teather, E. (1999) *Embodied Geographies: Spaces, Bodies and Rites of Passage* (London: Routledge).

Valentine, G. (1999a) 'Corporeal geographies of consumption', *Environment & Planning D: Society and Space* 17: 329–51.

Valentine, G. (1999b) ' "Oh please mum", "oh please dad": negotiating children's spatial boundaries', in L. McKie, S. Gregory and S. Bowlby (eds) *Gender, Power and the Household* (London: Macmillan), pp. 137–54.

Williams, S. (2001) *Emotion and Social Theory: Corporeal Reflections on the (Ir)rational* (London: Sage).

Williams, S. (2002) 'Sleep and health: sociological reflections on the dormant society', *Health* 6: 173–200.

Williams, S. (2005) *Sleep and Society: Sociological Ventures Into the (Un)known* (London: Routledge).

Williams, S. (2007) 'The social etiquette of sleep: some sociological reflections and observations', *Sociology* 41: 313–28.

Williams, S. and Bendelow, G. (1998) *The Lived Body: Sociological Themes, Embodied Issues* (London: Routledge).

Williams, S. and Boden, S. (2004) 'Consumed with sleep? Dormant bodies in consumer culture', *Sociological Research Online* 9, available at www.socresonline.org.uk, accessed 27 June 2006.

Wyness, M. (2000) *Contesting Childhood* (London: Falmer Press).

17
AIDS, Mobility and Commercial Sex in Ethiopia: Implications for Policy

Lorraine van Blerk[1]

Introduction

Since the emergence of the HIV/AIDS pandemic across sub-Saharan Africa, research has emphasised sex work as one aspect of risky sexual behaviour through which the epidemic escalates (Kishindo 1995, Walden et al. 1999, Gysels et al. 2001, Varga 2001). Male mobility has been highlighted as one of the key vehicles for transmission, with men employing the services of sex workers while away from home. In particular, the literature has concentrated on employment-related migration between urban and rural areas, truck drivers travelling along trading routes between major ports and cities and soldiers engaging with sex workers while stationed away from home (Omara-Otunnu 1987, Wood 1988, Cohen 1999, Larson 1990, Gysels et al. 2001). This focus on mobility and AIDS has, however, largely ignored female mobility. One exception is Zuma et al. (2003), who found that migrant women in South Africa were more likely than non-migrant women to engage in risky sexual behaviour, have lower condom use and higher HIV rates.

Similarly, the literature has rarely focused on sex workers' mobility, viewing them as separate from mobility processes and positioning them either as locally resident women or simply noting that they may congregate in towns along trading routes or near to male employment (Campbell 2000). Despite this, mobility processes[2] have characterised the lives of commercial sex workers for generations. Sex work both enables mobility, sometimes over long distances, and restricts movement as girls are tied into contractual arrangements with brothels and middlemen/women (Okonofua et al. 2004). Across continents there is evidence of women and girls moving, often temporarily, into urban areas or other sites of demand to engage in sex work (Manopaiboon et al. 2003) and of women being trafficked across international borders (Day and Ward 2004). More recently, sex workers' mobility has received some acknowledgement as an important consideration in AIDS research and policy agendas, with the Southern African Migration Project (SAMP)/International Organisation for Migration (IOM) (2005) highlighting that sex workers' mobility creates risk to themselves and to other mobile and sedentary groups. The research presented here takes this further, suggesting that mobility needs to be a key consideration in policy and programmes addressing commercial sex workers' needs, particularly in the light of the AIDS pandemic.

Within Ethiopia, sex work has historically involved processes of mobility. In the Middle Ages, respectable women offering sexual services travelled with the emperor's camp.[3] In the nineteenth century, women were found to travel to the coastal towns where there was a demand for sex workers from sailors, later returning to their villages with the money they had made (Pankhurst 1974). Pankhurst further notes that sex workers were also subject to constraints on their mobility. During the Italian occupation in the 1930s, Ethiopian women travelled to the military camps. Once there, those free from disease were obliged to remain in specified houses (brothels) where they were given regular medical inspections.

Although sex work and its association with the spread of disease has a long history in Ethiopia, it is only since the 1980s that HIV/AIDS has been prevalent and an issue for policy agendas (Ministry of Health 1998). Initially, the disease was contained in urban areas but, more recently, HIV infection has become widespread. UNAIDS (2005) notes that although Ethiopia's HIV prevalence, estimated at 4.4 per cent, is low compared to southern African countries, it is now rapidly spreading to rural areas, where approximately 85 per cent of the population live. This is of concern as Alene et al. (2004) reveal that rural youth, although sexually active, are not sufficiently engaging in prevention strategies. They note that condom use is low and almost all the males in their study who had contracted STDs, a known vehicle for HIV transmission, had visited a commercial sex worker. Furthermore, Cherkosie (2000) points out that the majority of young commercial sex workers are rural migrants, highlighting the importance of reaching sex workers in AIDS prevention strategies and taking their mobility into account.

Betemariam (2002) points out that some, albeit only a few, services are currently available to sex workers in the major Ethiopian towns. Non-governmental organisations (NGOs) have implemented skills training programmes for sex workers to enable them to exit the commercial sex industry. Others, particularly those working with young sex workers, have set up drop-in centres where a range of services, including education, recreation, washing facilities, rights advocacy, preventive and curative health services, is provided (Cherkosie 2000, FHI 2002). In addition, one NGO has established a programme for the introduction of female condoms to provide sex workers with greater control in the negotiation of condom use with clients (Betemariam 2002). Such services are usually found in local communities where large numbers of sex workers operate. However, these services generally rely on repeated contact over time and, sometimes, formal registration with an organisation. This does not account for the high levels of mobility (and enforced) immobility of sex workers, which renders their sustained access to projects difficult, if not impossible. As van der Helm points out, this makes it difficult to provide comprehensive health services:

> Ignorance of local services, insecurity about work and the fact that many women are constantly being moved from place to place make it difficult to prioritise health in general and sexually transmitted disease prevention in particular.
>
> (2004: 116–17)

The following sections explore the difficulties young Ethiopian commercial sex workers encounter in their ability to access AIDS prevention and protection services. By focusing explicitly on processes of mobility, the chapter makes recommendations as to how these problems might be overcome.

Methods

This chapter is drawn from a research project exploring the socio-spatial lives of young commercial sex workers[4] in Ethiopia. The research took place in two cities in Ethiopia with relatively large transient populations; Addis Ababa, the capital city, and Nazareth, the regional capital of Oromia district and a major entertainment centre located on the trade route between the capital and the port at Djibouti. Commercial sex work is a diverse and complex industry with girls accessing clients in different ways – as bar girls, red-light district workers and streetwalkers[5] – and at different levels within society. The level of engagement in sex work depends on the type of work participated in, with red-light area workers having the most clients, commanding the least money and being least mobile.

Streetwalkers and bar girls tend to have one client a night between three and seven times a week, although occasionally more, depending on the services requested by their clients. The latter two groups also have more freedom to engage in mobility processes and tend to move over greater distances and for longer periods of time.

Sixty girls, who were currently engaged in commercial sex[6] as part of their work, participated in this research. All were deeply affected by poverty. They commanded little money from clients and generally worked in poor neighbourhoods and in the small local bars and Tella/Tej[7] houses. The girls were aged between 14 and 19 years (mean age 17 years). The length of time they had been engaged in sex work varied from a few months to several years, although none had begun their employment below the age of 13. Approximately 22 per cent (13 participants) were drawn from red-light areas, 37 per cent (22 participants) worked as streetwalkers and 41 per cent (25 participants) worked in bars.[8] The girls were mainly accessed through NGO drop-in centres, although a snowballing technique was also employed to reach those who did not attend a project. Although the girls were not asked their HIV status, approximately a third disclosed that they were either HIV-positive or suspected that they might be. The majority, however, were too afraid to be tested.

A number of methods were employed for this research, with assistance from a local translator. Eight groups of girls participated in a series of three focus group discussions on sex work, space and mobility and semi-structured health interviews, including a section on AIDS. They also drew their own mobility maps, where they represented and discussed the places they moved between as part of their employment strategies (see Young and Barrett 2001 for a discussion of the use of maps as a research method). The research was supplemented with participant observation ad informal discussions with some of the research participants, and six key informant interviews were undertaken with staff from organisations working with young sex workers. This was principally to explore their programmes and methods of working with young commercial sex workers as well as to provide supporting information regarding the nature and extent of the situation.

Given the difficulties inherent in collecting data on sensitive topics and from marginalised groups, this research involved the triangulation of methods, where different methods were used to cross-check the information gathered. In particular, information gained from participant observation/informal discussions, health interviews and mobility maps was compared to the focus group discussion transcripts to check for anomalies in the data. This approach has been commended for research on AIDS (Ackroyd 1997) and also for research with young people in difficult circumstances (Lucchini 1996). In addition, the project was subject to independent ethical scrutiny by Brunel University's ethics committee and issues such as confidentiality and informed consent were a research priority. As many of the girls had little or no contact with their families, parental consent was not sought. However, consent was gained from a number of organisations working with young commercial sex workers. Following this, the nature of the research was explained to the girls at every stage in the process and they were given the opportunity to opt in to the research. It was explained that they could leave the research at any point and a few chose to exercise this right for a variety of reasons, mainly time commitments.

Dissemination of the research among the girls and their comments on the findings and recommendations was also considered important. Therefore, at the end of the research process, workshops were held with the girls to discuss the findings and to think through potential policy recommendations.

Mobility processes

This section outlines the results of the research by considering the factors influencing young sex workers' mobility and the consequences of this, before exploring the reasons for restrictions on girls' mobility and their associated consequences. Following this, current service provision is reviewed and strategies for addressing mobility issues are presented.

In Ethiopia, young commercial sex workers engage in mobility for a number of reasons, although these reasons are not necessarily mutually exclusive. In particular, the girls identified moving between places of work, both within and between towns, in order to improve their working conditions, to access a wider or different client base, to look for new adventures/excitement and to avoid stigmatisation and losing clients if they become sick. The girls mentioned moving between bars/streets/red-light area houses if they felt they were being badly treated by the bar owners or clients. Fights with other girls and owners were the main reason for such moves. Kalkidan[9] (aged 18, bar girl) states that she has moved several times to different bars because of 'the owner's behaviour and other things [fights]'.

Similarly, street workers mention moving between areas to avoid fights and access better clients. The following two extracts illustrate this:

I was doing business[10] in 'stadium' [the area around the sports stadium], but since the street boys started to cause trouble I moved to other places.

(Alem, aged 16, streetwalker)

I moved from working in autobusterra [bus station area] to piazza because better money can be earned there and there are also better clients.

(Shewa, aged 15, streetwalker)

The development (or avoidance) of new personal relationships is another reason why girls will change the area or town in which they work. The stigma associated with sex work means that girls try to separate their work from their private lives. As Yetimwerk points out, girls who develop relationships with their clients, whose status changes from client to boyfriend over time, will move their work to a different location to avoid stigmatisation, thereby accessing a different client base. In addition, some girls, such as Alemework, highlighted that engaging AIDS, mobility and commercial sex in Ethiopia in mobility was directly to avoid having regular clients who might try to establish relationships with them:

I move often so that I don't have regular clients. If I work in one particular place for a long time the problem I have is that clients want to be friends. If you have more attachment with clients they try to have sex without paying.

(Alemework, aged 17, streetwalker)

I had a regular client who became my boyfriend, so I moved here [a different part of Addis Ababa] to do business.

(Yetimwerk, aged 17, streetwalker)

Furthermore, girls chose to move to different places when business would be especially lucrative there or because they are looking for new adventures/challenges. They do this in order to access a wider client base or because they have become bored with their current location. Burtuchan stresses that girls often travel during the coffee and onion seasons as the towns are bustling with migrant farmers and traders:

When coffee and onions grow the farmers sell them and come to the towns to entertain themselves and look for girls...Jimma is the well-known place for coffee production so at coffee season a lot of girls go to Jimma to do business.

(Burtuchan, aged 15, bar girl)

Finally, the girls alluded to the fact that some move because they are sick. When it is known that a girl has an STD or is HIV-positive (because she has been tested) or when it is suspected that she has AIDS (because of opportunistic infections or a change in bodily appearance, usually weight loss and skin problems), she may be forced to move to access clients.[11] Abeba had been ill for a while and unable to do business. Her friends had been supporting her but were no longer able to. She applied to an NGO for money to purchase a bus ticket to her home village where she would live with her aunt. Informal discussions with her friends however revealed that Abeba used the money to travel to another town, where she was not known, so that she could again engage in business.

The consequences of this mobility are three-fold: increasing the risk of infection among girls, positioning them as a risk factor for the spread of AIDS and limiting their access to services. First, these mobility processes place the girls at risk from contracting HIV, not only because of the larger client base accessed but also because of the nature of their interactions, particularly when they move to different trade or entertainment centres. Condom use in rural areas is low (Alene et al. 2004) and the entertaining that takes place, when cash is accrued through trading, usually involves alcohol consumption. The girls are encouraged to accompany their clients in drinking, but this places them at greater risk of infection:

You know to be drunk means to be dead [contract HIV]. We can't control ourselves and clients can have sex without condoms.

(Genet, aged 16, bar girl)

In addition, girls stated that they were less likely to use condoms with their boyfriends despite the fact that relationships had sometimes developed from a sex work context and also that clients may refuse to use condoms or will cut condoms without the girls' knowledge. The girls often did not see the need to protect themselves or their partners beyond the context of their work and therefore did not use condoms in sexual encounters with their boyfriends (see also Manopaiboon et al. 2003). As Frewit explains, she does not use condoms with her boyfriend despite being 'worried' that her clients will ask her to engage in unprotected sex:

I do not use condoms with my boyfriend but with clients I use condoms... But with clients I am not free thinking and he may ask me to have more sex. When I go out with clients I am worried and pray that he will not ask me to have sex without a condom, but when I am with my boyfriend I am happy to have sex or to sleep with him.

(Frewit, aged 15, streetwalker)

Second, mobility processes also identify the girls as a risk factor for infection spread. The account of Abeba's mobility to conceal her HIV status illustrates that girls also place their clients at risk. In addition, girls will often give in when clients refuse to use condoms, particularly if they offer to pay more for this service. As Alem points out, refusal to use condoms no longer worries her as she knows she is HIV-positive, however it positions her as a risk to her clients:

There are clients who ask us not to use condoms but I am not worried because I already know that I am HIV-positive.

(Alem, aged 16, streetwalker)

Third, the mobile lives of the young commercial sex workers discussed here not only increases AIDS risk but also limits their sustained contact with NGOs and their ability to participate in programmes. The following extract highlights that moving to places without NGO facilities can restrict girls' access to support:

Changing places can lead to problems... many places don't have NGOs.

(Frewit, aged 15, streetwalker)

Restricted mobility

The AIDS-associated risks of engaging in sex work can be exacerbated by restrictions placed on girls' mobility. This was mainly a problem for girls working in bars and in the red-light areas but less so for streetwalkers, who tended to have more control over their time during the day.

Bar girls' mobility was restricted through being indebted to the bar owners. These girls are required to work in the bars in return for access to customers and for space in the women's room.[12] This involves serving drinks and entertaining customers at night, usually until early in the morning, as well as cleaning the bar and washing glasses during the day. When the girls are ill or unable to attract clients, the bar owners will provide them with food and medicine, pushing them further into debt. Bar work restricts girls' access to services on days when they have to work in the bars and because they must use the day to catch up on lost sleep. Additionally, when the girls are unable to pay their debts the bar owners will prevent them from leaving the bar, either to work elsewhere or to attend programmes, by taking their belongings:

> The owner controls us when we don't do our work on time and properly. If it is my turn to be at the bar, I should be there.
>
> (Aberash, aged 18, bar girl)

> When we don't get any money we eat on credit from the bar. When we can't pay our debts we can't leave as the owner takes our clothes and shoes.
>
> (Salam, aged 15, bar girl)

The girls who work in the red-light areas tend to be the poorest group of commercial sex workers, having the most clients and earning the least money. As Zenash points out, they are also highly controlled by the room owners (madams) who take half of their earnings as rent and force them to work both day and night:

> Every evening from 6 until 3 am we have to stand outside and wait for clients … Also in the morning and daytime we wait for clients … The owners of the houses wake us up and tell us to do business.
>
> (Zenash, aged 17, red-light worker)

The consequences of restrictions placed on sex workers' mobility are important in the context of the AIDS pandemic. First, these girls have reduced access to services. In particular, the red-light area workers have the least potential to access services as they have to remain in their rooms in case a client arrives. Furthermore, the madams are often highly suspicious of NGO programmes, believing that they will take the girls out of sex work:

> Even to get training or something from the centre [NGO drop-in centre] we have to stay here so that they [NGO social workers] can see our [good] behaviour first but the owners don't allow us to come here … They think that we get something here so they expect us to pay them … Also, if we stay out of the house for a long time, then they ask us to pay them money.
>
> (Senait, aged 18, red-light worker)

Second, girls with restricted mobility report that their inability to access prevention information or free contraception puts them and their partners at greater risk of HIV. As the next extracts demonstrate, the girls continue to engage in sex work even when they suspect or know that they are HIV-positive, yet are unable to take further precautions because restricted mobility makes accessing services difficult:

> I think I am HIV-positive because we do business all the time and because I have no free time I am not able to seek medical treatment.
> (Meberet, aged 17, red-light worker)

> I am HIV-positive but I still do business. I tried to stop but there is no one to help me.
> (Tibiliz, aged 18, bar girl)

Policy implications

The findings from this research demonstrate that the inclusion of commercial sex workers as a high-risk group in Ethiopian AIDS policies needs to be refocused to account for the impact of mobility processes on their lives. The research has demonstrated that many of the difficulties associated with encouraging sex workers to participate in prevention and protection services could be overcome if their needs were more accurately identified and their mobility taken into account. Currently, services are static, operating at the community level in just a few locations. At the time of this research only three NGOs in Addis Ababa and one in Nazareth were providing services for sex workers below the age of 18. All required sustained participation in their projects. Programmes were designed as long-term AIDS, mobility and commercial sex in Ethiopia processes, where participation occurs on a regular basis, rather than information points where girls could drop in to access healthcare advice and counselling. As Frewit explains, services are often only provided after a period of time:

> If we have stayed here for some months, then in September they [NGO] have promised they will send us to school.
> (Frewit, aged 15, streetwalker)

This final section draws on discussions from end-of-research workshops to explore strategies for dealing with these difficulties. The workshops revealed that policy approaches need to consider the implications of mobility in three ways: exploring methods for integrating services; building the capacity of sex workers to take greater control over decision-making in their day-to-day lives; and creating outreach strategies that take services into the girls' workplaces.

For those girls who engage in mobility between towns, access to services is intermittent, resulting in sometimes patchy knowledge of HIV and appropriate prevention strategies. Policies that support such mobility could include a nationally directed service network where information is shared between service providers. This could include sharing or rotating basic AIDS education packages and providing take-away information, such as picture-based leaflets to help ensure that mobile sex workers do not miss out on important information. Alternatively, temporary/mobile services set up in popular seasonal sex work locations may encourage sustained access to the same healthcare services in different towns.

Betemariam (2002) notes that, while mobile services, particularly those focusing on behaviour change and condom use, now exist for truck drivers in Ethiopia, such services have yet to extend to their sexual partners, the majority of whom are commercial sex workers:

> If we go away to another place, we should try to find out information but if there are no NGOs this can cause us problems.
>
> (Burtuchan, aged 15, bar girl)

The limited opportunity some girls have to exercise choice over whether they attend projects needs to be addressed. Policies should seek ways of making services available to those whose daily mobility is restricted. Cherkoise (2000) notes that it is the low socio-economic status and earning capacity of women in Ethiopian society which encourages them to engage in commercial sex work and some projects are already trying to address this, either through skills training or promotion of the female condom.

However, this research revealed that bar girls and red-light area workers are often tied to their place of work, either because of the hours they work or debt. Financial training, including the development of savings and credit schemes, has worked well as a strategy for poverty reduction among other AIDS-affected groups, particularly in the context of reducing burial costs or income-generation (Ansell and Young 2004). Such schemes could be utilised in this context by enabling bar girls to save for days when they have reduced earnings in order to mitigate against debt. As Genet points out:

We could practise saving money. Once we pay our debt we shouldn't have to get into debt again. No one teaches us about money. If we get 100 birr we just spend it. So if we have orientation about saving money from NGOs it would help.

(Genet, aged 18, bar girl)

Finally, policy could support innovative ways of providing outreach services to fit around girls' working conditions. For example, mobile services that take health and social care into the girls' workplaces would reduce the time needed to participate in projects and result in larger numbers of girls accessing initiatives. This would help to dispel the idea that projects are giving handouts thereby reducing the tension between red-light district madams and NGOs:

When we try to come to the centre (NGO) they (madams) won't allow us … social workers should come to us but they only come to register us.

(Meberet, aged 17, red-light worker)

Conclusion

This research has revealed that the concept of mobility is important in the lives of young commercial sex workers. The girls identify that they engage in complex processes of mobility, moving between work locations both within and between towns. Additionally, they highlight that in some instances their work restricts their mobility, tying them to particular locations. The research shows that this might influence sex workers' behaviours, placing them and their partners at increased risk of HIV infection. The research further identifies that in the Ethiopian context young commercial sex workers' mobility is an important consideration in AIDS policy. The girls' reported that it restricts their access to healthcare services and their ability to participate in AIDS prevention and care programmes.

Despite this, policy and programmes currently do not adequately account for mobility-related problems. In conclusion, this chapter calls for mobility process to be considered within AIDS policies that are channelled towards commercial sex workers. In order for girls to gain access to projects that can provide them with greater information and choice in their work, service provision needs to become flexible, with providers developing innovative ways of reaching out to those unable to participate fully in standard programmes.

On a cautionary note, it is necessary to consider the study limitations. Although this in-depth qualitative study has provided very detailed information regarding the mobile lives of young Ethiopian commercial sex workers, this was a small-scale research project and therefore the findings cannot be generalised to wider sex worker populations. Despite this, the research has identified important implications for policy and a much larger project is now called for in order that these suggestions can be translated to other contexts and their potentially far-reaching impact realised.

Acknowledgements

This research was funded by a Nuffield Foundation Social Science Small Grant, however, the views and opinions are entirely my own. I gratefully acknowledge the institutional support of the Institute of Ethiopian Studies, Addis Ababa University and Goal Ethiopia. I would also like to thank Abeba Amare for her work as a research assistant on the project and acknowledge my indebtedness to the girls who participated in the project.

Notes

1. Based on a paper first published in *AIDS Care* 19(1) (January 2007): 79–86.
2. Mobility processes refer to the movements engaged in by commercial sex workers, including movements between work locations as well as between different towns. In addition, restricted mobility is also considered part of these processes.
3. The emperor's camp was a large establishment which moved around the country under the direction of the current ruler.
4. For this chapter, the age of the participants is not significant, although teenage girls may be more mobile than older commercial sex workers if they do not have children or other household obligations.
5. Within these three categorisations there is a diverse range of experiences. It is the poorest groups that were principally the focus of this research.
6. Although it is acknowledged that sex work definitions can be complex, particularly in poor communities where sex may be exchanged for income or other needs at times of hardship, this chapter focuses specifically on girls who exchange sex for cash with a variety of (mainly unknown) men as their main source of livelihood.
7. Tella and Tej are locally produced traditional drinks which are sold in small bars, often the size of one room.
8. As shown below, it was more difficult for red-light workers to participate in the research due to constraints on their mobility, hence the relatively smaller number of participants engaging in this type of sex work.
9. Pseudonyms are used to maintain confidentiality.

10. 'Business' is the term used by the girls when referring to sex work.
11. Not all girls who know or suspect they are HIV-positive are able to stop doing business.
12. The women's room is at the back of the bar where the girls are allowed to keep their belongings and sleep.

References

Ackroyd, A. V. (1997) 'Sociocultural aspects of AIDS in Africa: occupational and gender issues', in G. C. Bond, J. Kreniske, I. Susser and J. Vincent (eds) *AIDS in Africa and the Caribbean* (Oxford: Westview Press).
Alene, G. D., Wheeler, J. G. and Grosskurth, H. (2004) 'Adolescent reproductive health and awareness of HIV among rural high school students, North Western Ethiopia', *AIDS Care* 16: 57–68.
Ansell, N. and Young, L. (2004) 'Enabling households to support successful migration of AIDS orphans in southern Africa', *AIDS Care* 16: 3–10.
Betemariam, W. (2002) 'Gender and HIV in Ethiopia'. Unpublished report (Addis Ababa: Ministry of Health Technical Working Group on HIV/AIDS).
Campbell, C. (2000) 'Selling sex in the time of AIDS: the psycho-social context of condom use by sex workers on a southern African mine', *Social Science and Medicine* 50: 479–94.
Cherkosie, A. (2000) *Situation Analysis. Report on Commercial Sexual Exploitation of Children in East Africa* (Addis Ababa: ECPAT International).
Cohen, D. (1999) *Socio-Economic Causes and Consequences of the HIV Epidemic in Southern Africa: A Case Study of Namibia*, Issue Paper 31, UNDP HIV and Development Programme.
Day, S. and Ward, H. (2004) *Sex Work, Mobility and Health in Europe* (London: Kegan Paul).
FHI (2002) *Mapping and Census of Female Sex Workers in Addis Ababa. Ethiopia* (Addis Ababa: FHI/AACAHB).
Gysels, M., Pool, R. and Bwanika, K. (2001) 'Truck drivers, middlemen and commercial sex workers: AIDS and the mediation of sex in south west Uganda', *AIDS Care* 13: 373–85.
Kishindo, P. (1995) 'Sexual behaviour in the face of risk: The case of bar girls in Malawi's major cities', *Health Transition Review* 5 (Suppl.): S153–S160.
Larson, A. (1990) 'The social epidemiology of Africa's AIDS epidemic', *African Affairs* 89: 5–25.
Lucchini, R. (1996) 'Theory, method and triangulation in the study of street children', *Childhood: A Global Journal of Child Research* (Children out of place: special issue on working and street children) 3: 167–70.
Manopaiboon, C., Bunnell, R. E., Kilmarx, P. H. et al. (2003) 'Leaving sex work: barriers, facilitating factors and consequences for female sex workers in northern Thailand', *AIDS Care* 15: 39–52.
Ministry of Health (1998) *Policy on HIV/AIDS of the Federal Democratic Republic of Ethiopia* (Addis Ababa: Ministry of Health).
Okonofua, F. E., Ogbomwan, S. M., Alutu, A. N., Kufre, O. and Eghosa, A. (2004) 'Knowledge, attitudes and experiences of sex trafficking by young women in Benin City, South-South Nigeria', *Social Science and Medicine* 59: 1315–27.

Omara-Otunnu, A. (1987) *Politics and the Military in Uganda* (London: Macmillan).

Pankhurst, R. (1974) 'The history of prostitution in Ethiopia', *Journal of Ethiopian Studies* 12: 159–78.

SAMP/IOM (2005) *HIV/AIDS, Population Mobility and Migration in Southern Africa: Defining a Research and Policy Agenda* (Geneva: International Organisation for Migration).

UNAIDS (2005) *AIDS Epidemic Update* (Geneva: UNAIDS/WHO).

van der Helm, T. (2004) 'Mobility, policy and health in the Netherlands', in S. Day and H. Ward (eds) *Sex Work, Mobility and Health in Europe* (London: Kegan Paul).

Varga, C. (2001) 'Coping with HIV/AIDS in Durban's commercial sex industry', *AIDS Care* 13: 351–65.

Walden, V., Mwangulube, K. and Makhumula-Nkhoma, P. (1999) 'Measuring the impact of a behaviour change intervention for commercial sex workers and their potential clients in Malawi', *Health Education Research* 14: 545–54.

Wood, W. (1988) 'AIDS north and south: diffusion patters of a global epidemic and a research agenda for geographers', *Professional Geographer* 40: 266–9.

Young, L. and Barrett, H. (2001) 'Adapting visual methods: action research with Kampala street children', *Area* 33: 141–52.

Zuma, K., Gouws, E., Williams, B. and Lurie, M. (2003) 'Risk factors for HIV infection among women in Carletonville, South Africa: migration, demography and sexually transmitted diseases', *International Journal of STD & AIDS* 14: 814–17.

18
Commentary: Performing Bodies and Contestation

Ruth Panelli

Young people like Alfie (ch. 14), Victoria (ch. 15), Simon (ch. 16) and Alem and Shewa (ch. 17) highlight the vitality of their embodied lives, and the dynamics of childhood and youth. Young bodies and 'what they do' remind us of the corporeality of human lives, as well as the interfaces and relations between those bodies/lives and the other adult lives and nonhuman contexts that surround them. Together, the chapters in Part III emphasise the diversity of these issues, and the following commentary reflects some of the more generic strengths of this collection and raises some of the wider ramifications we might consider in performing further research on contested bodies of childhood and youth.

Performing bodies as:

... being/becoming and belonging within socio-spatial worlds

The use of performativity as a conceptualisation of (gender and other) identities has informed our understanding of the discursively constructed nature of being a child or young person, and the associated discourses of childhood and youth (Skelton and Valentine 1998, Holloway and Valentine 2000, Jones 2007). But the chapters in this volume reinforce the significance of embodied becoming and belonging. Holt (ch. 15) reminds us how young people's identities demonstrate their 'corporeal becomings' within wider socio-spatial settings and expectations (at school, and amongst peers), while Beale (ch. 14) shows how both discursive and material embodiment (and performative reiterations) are central to young people's sense of being and belonging via both immediate peer contexts and wider social and cultural expectations in and beyond Country Durham. Individually, these authors are concerned about (dis)ability, health and gender, yet their contentions resonate with broader human geography interests in the dynamics and repeated performances of human becoming and connection (e.g. Crouch 2003, Anderson 2006) that involve people's embodied reiterations of being, becoming and navigation within the social relations and spatialities that touch their bodies and contextualise their associated worlds.

In measure, these contexts and relations echo Butler's (2004: 21) claim that 'my body relates me . . . to others', including other things and spaces. Thus navigating being or belonging involves young people in entanglements, where bodies (their own and others'), other materialities and social relations intersect, bond and/or repel. For instance, van Blerk demonstrates how Ethiopian young women effectively mobilise their bodies in reiterative manifestations both as sex workers interacting with (or avoiding) clients and as workers marshalling their spatial agency to occupy, use or evade different sites. In contrast, Holt explains how Alfie and his assistant experience their school days via the opportunities for presence, movement and bodily touch on the carpet with other class members, as well as the corporeal marginalisation and privilege of their specialist work site in the class storeroom. These examples amplify Butler's notion of reiteration in performativity, highlighting how performances of embodied life may not only be regularly enacted, but will involve multiple practices and relations in any one time-space.

. . . corporeal realities and reiterations

The reiteration and reinvention of performative acts bears further consideration. Reiteration lies at the heart of embodied identities and relations, and chapters 13–16 illustrate both the speech acts and fleshy corporeality of these conditions. Such findings echo diversity surrounding performances involving alcohol consumption and/or gender relations (e.g. Dunkley 2004).

In younger age groups, Horton and Kraftl extend issues of performance as both reiteration and reinvention. They show how younger people like Rose and Simon may participate in the nightly reiterations of family bedtime routines, but can also physically work their bodies (Rose: 'closing my eyes really, really tight'; Simon: getting out of bed and sitting on top of the bed) to navigate and reinvent expectations of them as children of parents who have enacted and expected particular bedtime routines and behaviours. These examples convey the room to move that occurs during reiterated performances of embodied childhood. Rose and

Simon show some engagement with the parent-encouraged, bedtime scripts and acts. But they also convey the enthusiasm or assertion for creating variations and alternatives for their night-time bodies/selves.

In older age groups, O'Brien and Beale demonstrate Butler's (1990: 272) contention that 'gender is an act' that survives individual actors but also becomes 'actualized and reproduced as a reality' by individual performances. As with other modes of reiterated identity, the young women and men in these chapters articulate a reproduction of existing local and wider cultural scripts (e.g. of 'Geordie' masculinity, or working-class femininity) while individually embodying and manoeuvring within the recognised standards of macho, sturdy, physically assertive or risk-taking demonstrations of masculinity, and cool, hard, immaculate femininity.

Finally, these chapters caution us to appreciate how reiterations of performance will not necessarily sustain a steady or constant bodily experience. Beale shows the challenges and risks young women face when performing a 'cool' (smoking-based) femininity while also consciously facing the impact that smoking produced on their bodies. Likewise van Blerk's research emphasises the parallel corporeal risks and changes that sex workers encounter if their work results in sexually transmitted disease or AIDS. This complements Bell's (2007), Robinson's et al. (2004) and Thomas's (2004) accounts of the risks (of censure, STDs and pregnancy) surrounding Ugandan, US and English young people's sexual bodies and lives. These works also point to the power relations threaded throughout bodily performances.

...navigations of power, agency and marginalisation

Power is a third theme working through these chapters – a theme more understated, but all the same important to the lives of children and young people (Punch et al. 2007). While individual authors have framed manifestations of power in terms of institutional, peer, parental or client relations and expectations, we are nevertheless reading of power – and of young people's experience, recirculation or resistance of/to that power.

The marginalisation and management of young people's bodies and worlds has been widely critiqued. Consequently, while chapters here also highlight the instances where different young people are physically, socially or emotionally marginalised, attention to young people's performativity shows a much more undulating web of power relations, subjective acts and deviations.

Power relations and agency can be observed through the practical examples of contested or acquiescent bedtime, classroom, peer and sex-labour relations. And we could highlight the compliance, subjugation, stigma and othering that occur in the contrasting situations reported here. But these chapters also effectively focus on power via a consideration of mediations and opportunities. These are associated with bodily performance and are apparent at both inter- and intra-generational levels. Holt, and Horton and Kraftl demonstrate how adult (teacher and parent) power relations physically, emotionally and socially influence the bodies and ideas of their pupils and offspring. Sharon, for instance, can articulate her alternate exasperation or acceptance of her teacher's views of her physical differences, while David and Simon explain how they make temporary subversions and variations to their parents' bedtime routines. Across such examples (and similar to findings in Matthews et al. 2000, Panelli et al. 2002, Punch 2002) we see how young people can perform both compliance and resistance in varying narrative, symbolic and/or physical forms.

Intra-generational mediations and agency are also significant. Beale and O'Brien show how young people explore their experiences and form views of themselves, their social positions, their health, pleasure and gender. In these cases we are reminded of the significance of peer power relations as young people like Steve, Chris, Louise and Shannon (ch. 14) shape their own actions and sense of their bodies' gender, physicality or attractiveness in relation to other peers. While in O'Brien's case we see how repeated performances or variations of drug-taking enrol young people into complex circuits of power.

Performing further research on contested bodies of childhood and youth

Cumulatively, Part III demonstrates the efficacy of performative approaches in youth studies. While the bodies of young people may be enrolled in constructions and contestations of childhood and youth, these chapters emphasise that such bodies will always be dynamic; shifting and enacting performances in both regularised and opportunistic forms. In some ways, the contributors have recorded this as processes of being, becoming or belonging (depending on the scholars' interests). In other ways, they have highlighted the struggles that may be engaged in by particular children over specific expectations, discourses or material conditions. We have also noted how questions of power circulate through these performances – weaving young people's bodies and lives through wider discourses, phenomena and processes, which they may more or less reproduce or reinvent.

But these chapters go further. They inspire a range of additional considerations and implications for future research agendas. First, the shifting temporal and spatial fields that young people traverse enable us to acknowledge the constantly changing conditions and choices they face, even while reiterating embodied performances that, at times, may seem relentless or unending for individuals. Designing effective research programmes that can be sufficiently flexible and resourced to document this dynamism will be challenging, but also more potent for acknowledging the complexity of young people's lives and needs.

Second, the performance of embodied life needs further investigation if we are to unsettle assumptions about fixed or stable boundaries, behaviours, identities and abilities. Wider debates about touch, fluidity, music, technological consumption, biotechnological health (Longhurst 2001, Valentine and Holloway 2002, Saldanha 2005, Davies 2006) all indicate further lenses through which young lives may be better understood. For instance, the challenges, connections and distances surrounding touch and sound may provide further avenues for us to acknowledge and respect the significance of the otherness and unknowable-ness of childhood that Jones (2008) advocates so strongly. Equally, a better appreciation of youthful perspectives on media and biotechnology may provoke more diverse and original contributions to the debates on post-humanism and human/nonhuman geographies.

Third, the materiality of performing bodies reminds us of the multitude of non-textual, non-representational forms of youthful living. Jones (2008) has recently charted some directions for youth geographies. But these chapters flag other methodological and theoretical questions for future programmes. For example, how might we more adequately register the terrains and choices in the lives of young people with diverse mind–body–emotional differences? How might we better explore and report on the shifting rhythms, senses and tactics mobilised beyond language for young people involved in drug consumption or sex work?

These issues also inevitably raise questions about the aims, functions and power relations of our research, and thus a fourth consideration arising from this collection of chapters involves the additional ethics and practices we might explore in future studies. The examples of 'witness' and 'play' form two possibilities promoted by Jones's consideration of non-representational approaches in children's geographies. More practically, for those investing in participatory but primarily scholarly pursuits, the practices reported by researchers like Latham (2003), Mackian (2004) and Punch (2001) provide robust ways to extend young people's contributions in multiple media that can reflect their preferences and differences. For others more attentive to the power-sharing collaborations and activism that can be sustained in research, extensions of the numerous youth-focused and Participatory Action Research methodologies (Kindon et al. 2007) provide one avenue. Another is possible, following Whatmore's (2003: 102) advocacy of the 'generation of materials' that incorporate human and nonhuman contributions. Cumulatively, the politics of knowledge production that might acknowledge human and nonhuman worlds, and record and bridge youth worlds and adult researcher worlds (Whatmore 2003, Jones 2008) may herald a messier, more exciting, less colonisable 'multiverse' of childhood and youth and the performances therein.

References

Anderson, B. (2006) 'Becoming and being hopeful: towards a theory of affect', *Environment and Planning D: Society and Space* 24: 733–52.

Bell, S. (2007) ' "The child drums and the elder dances"? Girlfriends and boyfriends negotiating power relations in rural Uganda', in R. Panelli, S. Punch and E. Robson (eds) *Global Perspectives on Rural Childhood and Youth* (New York and London: Routledge), pp. 179–91.

Butler, J. (1990) 'Performative acts and gender constitution: an essay in phenomenology and feminist theory', in S-E. Case (ed.) *Performing Feminisms: Feminist Critical Theory and Theatre* (Baltimore, MD: Johns Hopkins University Press), pp. 270–82.

Butler, J. (1993) *Bodies That Matter: On the Discursive Limits of 'Sex'* (New York: Routledge).

Butler, J. (2004) *Undoing Gender* (New York and London: Routledge).

Crouch, D. (2003) 'Spacing, performativity and becoming: the tangle of the mundane', *Environment and Planning A* 23: 1945–60.

Davies, G. F. (2006) 'Patterning the geographies of organ transplantation: corporeality, generosity and justice', *Transactions of the Institute of British Geographers* 31(3): 257–71.

Dunkley, C. M. (2004) 'Risky geographies: teens, gender and rural landscape', *Gender, Place, Culture* 11(4): 559–79.

Holloway, S. and Valentine, G. (2000a) 'Children's geographies and the new social studies of childhood. Introduction', in S. L. Holloway and G. Valentine (eds) *Children's Geographies. Playing, Living, Learning* (London and New York: Routledge).

Jones, O. (2007) 'Rurality and the otherness of childhood in a British context', in R. Panelli, S. Punch and E. Robson (eds) *Young Rural Lives: Global Perspectives on Rural Childhood and Youth* (London: Routledge), pp. 193–204.

Jones, O. (2008) ' "True geography quickly forgotten, giving away to an adult-imagined universe". Approaching the otherness of childhood', *Children's Geographies* 6(2): 195–212.

Kindon, S., Pain, R. and Kesby, M. (eds) (2007) *Participatory Action Research Approaches and Methods. Connecting People, Participation and Place* (London: Routledge).

Latham, A. (2003) 'Research, performance, and doing human geography: some reflections on the diary-photograph, diary-interview method', *Environment and Planning A* 35(11): 1993–2017.

Longhurst, R. (2001) *Bodies: Exploring Fluid Boundaries* (London and New York: Routledge).

MacKian, S. (2004) 'Mapping reflexive communities: visualizing the geographies of emotion', *Social and Cultural Geography* 5: 615–31.

Matthews, H., Taylor, M., Sherwood, K., Tucker, F. and Limb, M. (2000) 'Growing up in the countryside: children and the rural idyll', *Journal of Rural Studies* 16: 141–53.

Panelli, R., Nairn, K. and McCormack, J. (2002) ' "We make our own fun": reading the politics of youth with(in) community', *Sociologia Ruralis* 42: 106–30.

Punch, S. (2000) 'Children's strategies for creating playspaces: negotiating independence in rural Bolivia', in S. Holloway and G. Valentine(eds) *Children's Geographies: Living, Playing, Learning* (London and New York: Routledge).

Punch, S. (2001) 'Multiple methods and research relations with young people in rural Bolivia', in M. Limb and C. Dwyer (eds) *Qualitative Methodologies for Geographers* (London: Arnold).

Punch, S. (2002) 'Youth transitions and interdependent adult–child relations in rural Bolivia', *Journal of Rural Studies* 18: 123–33.

Punch, S., Bell, S., Costello, L. and Panelli, R. (2007) 'Power and place for rural young people', in R. Panelli, S. Punch and E. Robson (eds) *Global Perspectives on Rural Childhood and Youth* (New York and London: Routledge), pp. 205–18.

Robinson, V., Hockey, J. and Meah, A. (2004) ' "What I used to do…on my mother's settee": spatial and emotional aspects of heterosexuality in England', *Gender, Place and Culture* 11: 417–35.

Saldanha, A. (2005) 'Trance y visibilidad al amanecer: la dinámica racial en las fiestas rave de Goa', *Social & Cultural Geography* 6(5): 707–21.

Skelton, T. and Valentine, G. (eds) (1998) *Cool Places. Geographies of Youth Cultures* (London: Routledge).

Thomas, M. (2004) 'Pleasure and propriety: teen girls and the practice of straight space', *Environment and Planning D: Society and Space* 22: 773–89.

Valentine, G. and Holloway, S. L. (2002) 'Cyberkids? Exploring children's identities and social networks in on-line and off-line worlds', *Annals, Association of American Geographers* 92: 302–19.

Whatmore, S. (2003) 'Generating materials', in M. Pryke, G. Rose and S. Whatmore (eds) *Using Social Theory: Thinking Through Research* (London: Sage and The Open University), pp. 89–104.

Index